Joi Lansing

A Body to Die For

A Love Story

by Alexis Hunter

JOI LANSING • A BODY TO DIE FOR, A Love Story
© 2015 TXu-1-585-930 by Alexis Hunter

All illustrations are copyright of their respective owners, and are also reproduced here in the spirit of publicity. Whilst we have made every effort to acknowledge specific credits whenever possible, we apologize for any omissions, and will undertake every effort to make any appropriate changes in future editions of this book if necessary.

Library of Congress Control Number: 2015943472

Published in the USA by:
BearManor Media
P O Box 71426
Albany, Georgia 31708
www.bearmanormedia.com

ISBN   978-1-59393-798-0 (paperback)
         978-1-59393-799-7 (hardcover)

Printed in the United States of America.

Book & cover design by Darlene and Dan Swanson of Van-garde Imagery, Inc.

Table of Contents

Foreword

It was a time in Southern California when orange groves were commonplace and smog had yet to paint its ugly brown brush across the southland's skies. The author and I enjoyed conversations and a friendship that included family, as well.

It was a time of meeting fascinating people in a wide variety of venues, of fabulous restaurants, exotic fare, endless film, and live theater.

The chance meeting with Joi—that eventually became the inspiration for this autobiography—was a rather bizarre encounter, but one that brought two women together in a manner so perfectly entwined that no poet or sage could have scripted this amazing connection.

I was there, marveling at the dynamics unfolding before my eyes: two beautiful women recognizing a depth of awareness that went far beyond the casual. The range of topics, the sharing and caring, the level of energy, and the exchange of similar philosophies created and sustained a most remarkable partnership.

It was indeed a privilege and a rare life's moment to be a witness to such an unforgettable, one-of-a-kind, true drama.

Victor Parker, our dear friend—August 2008

Joi Lansing
Born: April 6, 1929
Died: August 7, 1972

Dedication

This book is to honor my darling Joi, whose memory will remain in my heart forever.

To Joi's stepbrother, Larry Loveland…whom she loved dearly, and who was there for her, especially at the end.

To the wonderful nurses…"Big Red" Mary Tomassini, and Dolores Halkovich at St. John's Hospital in Santa Monica, who kept me from losing my mind during the last weeks and months of Joi's life.

To Ron DeSalvo…whose sensitivity and perception prompted him to send the only sympathy card I received after Joi died. I've never forgotten your kindness when I felt very alone.

Thank you!

Special Dedication & Eternal Thanks

This book is also dedicated to Leslie Todd (Joi's stepdaughter) for inspiring and convincing me that it was the right time to tell my story. She has been my friend and guardian angel and has supported me in all aspects of this labor of love.

Without her, none of this would have been possible. She held my hand when I didn't think I could bear to relive the emotional pain and sorrow and praised my efforts with each page I wrote.

I love you, Leslie.

Acknowledgements

So many people have been supportive of my writing this book, and I wish to thank many of them here.

First, a special thanks to my editor Barbara McClure, who took my feelings and gave them clarity. She used her impressive skills to prompt me to stay true to my "voice," and I cannot fully express my gratitude to this very talented professional whom I gratefully call my friend.

Many thanks to Ron Seymour and the Estate of Maurice Seymour for granting me the privilege of using Maurice Seymour's "classic" glamorous photos of Joi for the cover and for some of the additional photos inside the book. Thanks also to Arlette Capel of ABC4CONSULT for her excellent advice and direction.

Another special thank you goes to Tim Clark, Image Design Consultant of WDG Wright Design Group, for his sensitivity to tone and exacting "eye" when working with Joi's beautiful B&W photos. His work has successfully given them the original visual "pop" of the era.

I'd like to also thank professional photographer John Shupe (Joi's first cousin) for his help with organizing and sending me Joi's family photos. He has been a wonderful friend while encouraging me to share my story of Joi.

I am so grateful to James Acho, attorney and friend, for his encouragement and advice. I truly appreciate his sage wisdom as to whom I should and should not name. This will hopefully keep me from being put on a "hit list" by one of Joi's ill-reputed ex-paramours!

I also wish to thank Richard Koper for his encouragement and his love for Joi. Please read his books, *Fifties Blondes* and *Affectionately, Jayne Mansfield*. At

this writing, he is close to publishing his newest book about Joi and fellow actor Barbara Nichols through BearManor Media. He has become a dear friend.

Thanks, also, to C. Robert Rotter for his friendship and advice, and for
including me, along with Joi, on his website, *Glamour Girls of the Silver Screen*.
His book is about the private lives and times of some of the most glamorous
actresses and starlets of the 1940s, 1950s, and 1960s.

And, I must not forget, Aleshia Lee Brevard, my friend, who made all of
this possible by introducing me to Anthony Cardoza and Robert Slatzer, the
producer and director of *Bigfoot*, the movie. As you will see early on in my
story, Aleshia passed on her "monkey suit" to me, and this opened my world
to knowing Joi. Aleshia's book, *The Woman I Was Never Born to Be*, shows her
indomitable spirit and tenacity. Her gutsy attitude and spirit… along with her
encouragement… gave me the inspiration to tell my story. The sequel to her
book *The Woman I Was Born to Be* can be purchased through Amazon.com.

Susan Perrone was there for me when my health and hope for the future
were downright dismal. She is a true friend, and I will never forget her kindness and love.

Catherine Duncan acted as my final "eagle eye" catching, at the very last,
what could have been an embarrassing literary gaffe. Thanks, Cat. Purr-fectly
done.

Rev. Maria Riter was a wonderful cheerleader with tremendous encouragement. She gave me hope and confidence for this labor of love. We met
when my mother and her father were in the same hospital in 2003. My mom
died a few days before her dad.

I had her read the manuscript as it was being written… word by word…
chapter and verse… checking to see if it would offend the clergy. She was my
religious litmus test. Luckily for me, I passed the test!

Gloria Goetze Smith has been a dear friend. Her love of literature and
Bentleys made me want to write and to have a Bentley of my own.

Kate Porter, herself a very talented writer, has been a treasured friend and
"sounding board" whose suggestions were invaluable during the final months
of laborious rewrites. She helped tighten things up when I rambled and encouraged me to share my most personal feelings when I was at an impasse. On
a lighter note, she also protected me from telling too much about the "wise-

guys"...which will hopefully keep me alive a lot longer than if I had told all of the stories Joi had confided in me! Thanks, Kate.

I have always believed, if we are lucky, that there are people who come into our lives to give us hope, inspiration, and sometimes a powerful blast of air to help our wings take flight. The aforementioned individuals did that and more. I will always be grateful to each and every one of my wonderfully diverse friends.

Love,

Alexis (Rachel)

Prologue

I wrote this book for three reasons:

I wrote this book to show the dangers of using silicone injections so that no one else has to suffer injury or even death. If I can prevent one person from using these, I'll feel that it was worth writing.

I wrote it to show how tragic Joi's life was because of her vulnerability and fragile self-image and how it changed when she found someone who loved her for who she was—a gentle and sweet woman.

I wrote it to show the love that can exist between two human beings, regardless of sexual orientation. Joi had loved men the majority of her life. She was "straight." When we met, we connected as soul mates with a love that evolved into an all-encompassing committed relationship. This is not just a lesbian story. It is a love story.

At a time when so many young people are being bullied and are suffering
for being who they are, I want them to know that they are beautiful,
and that their love is something to be proud of…
not a reason for self-loathing and self-destruction.

Introduction

C. Robert Rotter, Glamour Girls of the Silver Screen

Once upon a time, there was a pretty girl from Salt Lake City named Joy Rae Brown, the daughter of devout Mormons. Shortly after World War II, she journeyed to Hollywood, where she was accepted at the famous MGM talent school. Very soon, the young starlet graced the silver screen in bit parts, and shortly thereafter, Joy Rae Brown became Joi Lansing, an all-American dream, the epitome of buxom pin-up sexiness in films such as *Who Was That Lady?* and in smash TV shows such as *The Bob Cummings Show.* After several unhappy marriages and a career in decline, she unfortunately vanished from the public eye until her early death in 1972.

Joi Lansing was one of the first actresses to be covered at my *Glamour Girls of the Silver Screen* website. I researched countless documents in the public domain, libraries, and newspaper gossip columns by the likes of Walter Winchell, Earl Wilson, and Harrison Carroll. This led to my being contacted by Alexis, a personable and endearing lady from Phoenix, Arizona, who was writing her memoirs, offering me an abundance of information by sharing her vivid memories of the last chapter in Joi's short life.

Week after week, Alexis sent me a chapter of her upcoming book, and more and more I became immersed in the fascinating world of swinging California in the late sixties and early seventies, with its unique sunlit way of life and popular culture—the innocent years of free love and free speech, of miniskirts and the man on the moon.

As a twenty-one-year-old aspiring actress by the name of Nancy Hunter, Alexis met Joi, an actress of renown, on the set of an exploitation movie, which in later years turned into a camp classic. Soon, they became best friends and lovers, sharing their hopes and dreams and passions. Together, they did New York, Las Vegas, Los Angeles, and the Caribbean.

Telling an enchanting story of days filled with fun and laughter, as well as sadness and tears, Alexis shares the private lives and times of two people who were lucky enough to experience, for a much-too-short period, the Hollywood dream and, more importantly, cherished love. I hope you enjoy these wonderful memories and the affectionate tribute to Joi as much as I did.

Jim Acho, friend of the author

When my dear friend Rachel called me recently and told me the book she'd written on the love of her life, Joi Lansing, was finally being published, I was elated for her. This has been a ten-year process for Rachel—longer, really, but I have known her for ten years—and I know how desperately she wanted to get this book out to the public. She wants people to know the true Joi Lansing, the story behind the buxom blonde who was the object of so many young men's desires in the 1950s and 1960s. And indeed Joi was a truly legendary beauty. According to some around Hollywood, she was the best-looking actress of her era, including the iconic Marilyn Monroe. But Joi had a side the public didn't see, and that is what Rachel will share with you. Above all, it is a love story, and a beautiful one, one that needs to be told. Like all of you, I can't wait to read this book, and I hope it receives great support and critical acclaim, but more importantly, I hope it sparks or rekindles an interest in the life of a lovely, talented actress … a life that was cut short far too soon.

John Shupe, Joi Lansing's first cousin

Hello, Rachel,

I would like for you to know how much I appreciate all the time you have spent visiting with me on the telephone these past many months. You have answered so many questions that I had about the final years of my dear first cousin, Joi Lansing.

Joi and I had a close family relationship, even though there were many years difference in our ages. Joi was in her twenties, while I was a young teen. She treated me like an adult, which I appreciated and respected. She was such a fun person, always cheerful, friendly, and caring so much about other people. I don't think I ever heard her say anything unkind about anyone. She had a wonderful way of engaging in conversations by asking questions about others. She rarely said very much about herself.

She was often recognized and approached for autographs by strangers we would meet on the street or in stores. She cheerfully visited with these folks as if each one of them were the celebrity. Joi was very worldly and knew a lot about so many topics that she often amazed. She had a truly amazing sense of humor that was clever and unexpected. It was the kind of humor that was never at the expense of others.

I love remembering the times we shared and was so shocked and saddened by the news of her death. Over the years, her absence has left an empty space in my heart. Although she obviously was known for her physical beauty, her inner self, to me, was even more beautiful.

Again, Rachel, you answered so many questions that I had. There is no one in my immediate family left to ask. I think Joi was very fortunate to have you as a friend and companion during the last few years of her life. I hope your new book about Joi answers a lot of questions others may have about her personal and professional life. Joi meant the world to me, and I still miss her.

Chapter 1

1969

Nineteen sixty-nine was an amazing year for me. It was the year of my big break in films and the year I met Joi Lansing, the love of my life.

It was the middle of the night, or so it seemed at four in the morning. I was rushing to get ready for my first big part in a Hollywood film. My friend Aleshia had the role, but told me she just couldn't stand wearing that "friggin' monkey suit" one minute longer. I didn't care about a monkey suit. I just wanted to be a star!

I was living at the Studio Club in Hollywood on Lodi Place, a residence run by the YWCA for young women interested in showbiz. All of the major studios wanted their young pre-starlets to have a safe place to live, and safe it was! There was a woman stationed at the front door twenty-four hours a day, and you couldn't get past her without signing in or out.

It was a great place to live, although the accommodations, which consisted of a tiny ten feet by eight feet room, pale pink stucco walls, and a single light bulb screwed in the ceiling, were not that wonderful. There was a twin bed, a sink, and a tiny closet, if you were lucky enough to have your own room. If you were new to the Club, you had to share a room with another girl, which still amounted to one sink and the lovely light bulb, but there were now two closets! Some of the girls had enough money to buy a lamp, so it wasn't as stark and unappealing.

What did we know at the time? We were out of the grasp of our parents and waiting for our big break in Hollywood. The Studio Club was perfect. It was $25 a week, including meals from the cafeteria. We had a safe haven from the Hollywood creeps and advice from the staff, if we needed to talk with someone. Mrs. Fortier was my favorite, a sweet white-haired lady with an amazing smile. She was kind and loving to everyone. She never criticized me, except for the time I took my old beat-up car and practiced wheelies in the parking lot at midnight. I woke up a few too many of the girls, and, of course, there were complaints. Even though I screwed up, she was still very sweet to me.

When I lived there, so did Farrah Fawcett, Sally Struthers, and Sandy Duncan. Farrah was under contract, and Sally was a sweet girl with big blonde curls. I was pretty friendly with Sally, but she told her mother she'd seen me smoke a joint, and that was when I was given my own room.

Well, that wasn't the only reason I was given a room to myself. There were rumors going around the club that I was gay. I had recently come to that realization myself and proudly announced it to some of the girls. Not smart! I had always known I was fascinated by women and had some major crushes in my life, which takes me back to the greatest crush I ever had.

I was a kid living in Ark City, Kansas, population 10,000. My dad had been in the Navy for over twenty years and decided to retire when he found out that his own dad was ill. So off we went from living in Hawaii and the Philippines to Arkansas City (the proper name).

There wasn't much to do in Kansas in the early 1960s but go to school and watch TV. Shows like *Adventures in Paradise, My Little Margie*, and *The Ann Sothern Show* were my favorites. That is, until I saw HER, Joi Lansing, in a show called *The Bob Cummings Show* or *Love that Bob*. Oh, my God! The minute I saw her, I fell madly in love. I would not miss one episode just to be able to see that face. The face of an angel.

That was how I spent my time until my parents decided to move to California in 1964. I was just going into my senior year of high school and was very sad to leave. Sad but excited, knowing I'd be near Los Angeles, so much closer to Hollywood and all of the magic I was sure it would bring to my life.

We moved to a little town called Charter Oak, a suburb of Covina, about thirty miles from Hollywood and not far from Pasadena. That was where I finished high school and started to understand a little more about myself and, surprisingly, my sexuality.

I was new to the school and in my senior year, which was a real bummer. It was hard to make friends because almost everyone was in a clique. I, of course, gravitated to the prettiest and most popular girl in school, Sandi Becker. She was lovely, with long blonde hair and brown eyes, and went on to become

Miss California in 1966. We became friendly, and I guess my attention to her became suspect and rumors started. She had a steady boyfriend whom she later married, so I was really just a puppy hanging around to do her bidding.

Sandi became Miss Charter Oak of 1965, and my greatest pleasure at the time was to have her crown me Miss Charter Oak of 1966.

I was becoming aware of my attraction to beautiful women. I knew I was different from the other girls and couldn't have cared less about dating boys. I went to the proms just so I could dance near Sandi and be part of the social scene.

After high school, I went to Mt. San Antonio College and took a few drama classes, hoping to learn enough to help me with my new desire…to be a "star."

Through my dad, I became acquainted with a young woman named Carolee; we became good friends and ended up moving to Hollywood together. Carolee worked for an entertainment lawyer on Sunset Boulevard, and I found a job working very close to her, also on Sunset, for Joe Whitman, whose son, Stu Whitman, was a fairly popular actor at the time.

It was actually Joe who introduced me to myself. I don't know how he knew; maybe it was because I drooled every time he told me stories about his encounters with Hedy Lamarr. For the life of me, I don't know if they were true or not.

Only nineteen and fresh out of Kansas, I was ill-prepared for what was in store for me. Joe was in his late sixties and had something I was sorely lacking… street smarts.

I couldn't wait to come to work to hear the stories about Hedy, and, for months, he kept promising to introduce me to her. The night finally came, and I was supposed to come to the office after hours, and she would be there. We waited. Well, I waited. Then, he said that he guessed she wasn't going to make it, but…he had a lady friend who would love to meet me. I look back now and can't believe I didn't spot the setup.

There she was. Not Hedy Lamarr, not anyone I would have hoped for, but I was so ready that it didn't matter. Though it wasn't the circumstance I had imagined, I had my first experience with a woman. I knew from that point on that the feelings I had held for so long were a part of my nature. Naive enough to think all I had to do now was be myself, I began my new life, happy that I was finally "me."

Chapter 2

Bigfoot

My friend Aleshia had decided she could no longer tolerate wearing a monkey suit and sweating for hours under the hot lights of a sound stage. That was my good fortune. I would finally have a part in a real Hollywood film.

Aleshia was a dear friend whom I'd met at a business dinner. We had each accompanied a gay male friend, pretending to be their dates. She was an exceptionally lovely woman who, of course, caught my eye. I flirted with her, and we had great fun being trophy dates for the evening.

At some point that evening, Aleshia told me her secret, and, though surprised, I didn't say a word to her about it. She was an actress and a transsexual and, most importantly, she was gorgeous. There was no way anyone would imagine she was anything but a beautiful woman, and, as far as I was concerned, this was simply a birth defect she had repaired.

One day she told me about her past life as a boy. Before her surgery, she had worked at Finocchio's in San Francisco, which had a female impersonator show. After a while, she decided she could no longer live a lie; she was a woman in the wrong body. Aleshia was desperate to be transformed to the woman she was inside. And what a transformation it was! She had gone through such tremendous physical and psychological pain that it was disturbing to her to have an attraction to a woman. That was it—we could only be friends.

We stayed good "pals" and allies in the Hollywood jungle. She was very protective of me and tried to help me in any way she could. When the opportunity arose and she could no longer tolerate wearing the hairy ape costume, she thought of me. And by doing so, she gave me the greatest gift of all—a chance at my first real movie!

Some of the casting calls I'd been on before were pretty creepy. One job I had was sitting at a bar next to a pool where everyone was wearing masks over their eyes. I was told later this was probably a pornographic film, and I was just an accessory in a bikini. I don't know what went on inside the house, but I made $50 for the gig.

I was anxiously hoping for a legitimate film, and this would be my big opportunity. Aleshia took me to meet the producer and director, Bob Slatzer, a friendly man who graciously spoke with me and asked if I'd like to be in the film. Of course, I would—was he serious? He offered me $200 and promised I would also get my name, Nancy Hunter, in the credits. I couldn't wait to sign the contract. It was official. I was going to be a star!

It was such a pleasure to meet a producer or director who didn't lock the door behind you as you walked into the room. Bob was a gentleman, and there were also two of us, both quite impressive in stature, close to six feet tall. Aleshia was the beautiful redhead, and I was the blonde. I don't think anyone would have attempted anything untoward unless they separated us. This was not going to happen. We'd both had terrible experiences with the Hollywood creeps and knew this was the safest way to go.

Bob Slatzer was charming and chatty and was happy for a new ear to listen to his story about his secret marriage to Marilyn Monroe. I listened, and, though I was caught up in what he was saying, I didn't really believe she would have been involved with someone quite like him. He was not especially good-looking. He was actually very average with a little bit of a paunch. I could tell, by looking at his face, that he enjoyed a few drinks now and then…and then. His cheeks were that rosy shade of scotch.

It didn't matter what he said or the stories he told. He was a gracious man, and he and Aleshia had given me the most thrilling opportunity of my life. They didn't know it at the time and neither did I, but I would be eternally grateful.

Bob told me where the sound stage was and made sure I understood I could not be late. I had to be there in the morning by six o'clock sharp. This was not a big budget film, to say the least. They had rented the sound stage for a certain amount of time, and that was it! No deviation. The film had to be completed (at least, the interior shots had to) in only a few days. This was something that would have taken most production companies weeks or possibly months. But I understood what he was saying, and it was not a problem for me. I would have gone there and waited for a week if I had to! Luckily, it wasn't necessary. I had just a few days until the big day.

It was four in the morning, and I'd hardly slept because I was too nervous. I was about to embark on my new career. Who cared if I played a baboon or gorilla or Bigfoot monster? I would finally be an actress in a Hollywood film!

I drove my '49 Studebaker to the address I was given and found a group of sound stages in the area of old Hollywood, not too far from Paramount Studios. It was not well-marked, but I knew by the address that I'd arrived at my destination. I didn't want anyone to see the old clunker I was driving, so I searched for a place to park that few eyes would see. I lucked out and found the perfect place to leave my embarrassment. It was still pretty dark and downright chilly. It was winter in Los Angeles, not like Chicago or New York, but nippy. I could hardly wait to get into that monkey suit to get warm.

There was only one building with a light shining over the door, so I walked in. As far as I could tell, no one else was shooting at any of the other stages. I was greeted by a security guard who told me to sit down and wait for someone in makeup to come and get me.

I sat quietly and just basked in the wonder of it all as I thought, *Holy cow! Here I am, the kid from Kansas, on a sound stage getting ready to be in a real movie.* A few more people came in, and everybody busily went in different directions. I just sat contentedly until a warm and friendly man asked if I was there for the female Bigfoot part. Calmly, but excitely, I said yes, and he took me to a room with an array of costumes, sat me in a chair, and began the process of turning me into a lovely Lady Bigfoot.

He started by gluing fake black hair on my face and spraying my face with black paint! I know it wasn't really paint, but it sure seemed like it, even the smell. He had me put on the monkey suit, which was heavy, scratchy, and thick, and I could feel absolutely no ventilation. Now I understood why Aleshia wanted no part of it!

But then, I really didn't mind. This was showbiz. I was in the trenches and couldn't have been happier. The makeup man then glued the fake hair on any areas that were exposed, and I almost couldn't believe it. But, I told myself, "My skin is very light and would have been really obvious if not glued with hair and painted black."

I was determined to stay chipper about it all.

Then, just when I thought we were done, came the best part of all…fake fangs were put in my mouth. They were cold and made of thick, rigid plastic, and were definitely much too big for this particular Lady Bigfoot.

We were finally done, and I was told to go out to the set. Slightly uncomfortable, but still thrilled at what was about to be my big break, I sighed a deep (if muffled), happy sigh. Even though I was very hot and very hairy, I was still filled with *Little Mary Sunshine* optimism as I lumbered off to the stage. On the way, I smiled—best as I could, beset with fangs and all—and confidently said to myself, "The show must go on!"

The stagehands were milling around, doing their respective jobs, and I was enthralled just watching the process. I saw a few other Bigfoot monsters and knew I needed to be where they were, so I walked over to them, practicing how I thought a Bigfoot should walk, and sat down on some logs that were props in the film.

I chatted with a little person named Jerry Maren, who was playing a baby Bigfoot. What a sweet guy he was! I was curious about who was cast in the film. I had seen a few movie stars since I'd been in Hollywood, but this was my first opportunity to be in their realm.

Bob told me that John Carradine was one of the stars, along with Ken Maynard. Robert Mitchum's son Chris and brother, John, were also in the film. Lindsay Crosby (Bing's son) was playing a biker. I wasn't really thrilled with what I was told, as they all seemed to be someone's relative, not important themselves. But then he mentioned the female star. It was Joi Lansing!

I could hardly catch my breath. My heart was pounding so hard I started to feel faint. I was dreaming…this was not possible. I'd been in love with her for half of my twenty-one years, and now I was going to be in the same building as her! My mind started to race with a million thoughts. The reality of seeing the woman of my dreams was beyond belief, and the idea of actually working with her in my first movie was absolutely overwhelming.

Still shaky and trying not to show Jerry what I was feeling, I slowly began to pull myself together. This had to be the acting job of my life. I could not make a fool of myself and had to be calm and confident. There was no room for mistakes, and I couldn't take the chance of ruining the greatest moment of my life. When Jerry looked away for a minute, I closed my eyes and took a breath. I could do it and would do it. I had to!

Chapter 3

Joi

I had always thought that working on films was fast-paced. I was so wrong. It's hurry up and wait. Most of the time, you're sitting around studying your lines—if you have any. That was not an issue for me. I only had to grunt and lumber around like a gorilla, which I think I mastered the first time I tried!

The other monsters and I sat around for hours and talked. I was trying to keep my mind occupied, knowing that Joi might appear at any moment. I noticed that the hair on my face was starting to fall off, so I guess the glue wasn't holding with the heat of the lights.

Needing a repair and reglue, I went back to makeup, and there she was… the most beautiful woman I had ever seen in my life!

Joi's face was perfect, with no lines or imperfections. Her hair was a gorgeous and full platinum blonde, not the overbleached blonde that looked tacky and fake, but a warm, soft color. Her eyes were a beautiful green, and she was tall and thin. Not too thin, just no excess fat. She wore a peach minidress that was to be her costume throughout the film. It was quite low-cut and exposed her trademark cleavage. She was magnificent!

As I tried not to stare, she caught my eye and began chatting with me. She had no idea who she was looking at, only a person with a woman's voice in a gorilla suit. Sweet and thoughtful, she asked if I was miserable in my costume, and I told her I was doing fine. She watched as they reglued the hair on my face and, after they finished with me, it was her turn for a makeup check. She'd done her own makeup and hair and was a pro. They simply put a little more powder on her face and makeup on her body, so she'd look more tan.

I knew I wouldn't have anything to do for a while, so I had the perfect excuse to just stay and chat. She put me so at ease that I didn't need to act. I didn't need to be anyone that I wasn't; she allowed me to be myself.

The time passed quickly, and both of us had to go to work. Walking side by side, we talked about this silly film we were doing. She had performed in so many A films and television shows with big stars like Frank Sinatra and Dean Martin; her resumé was filled with roles that ran the gamut between great and *Bigfoot*. This was definitely not a highlight of her career!

Quite young when she started, her first film was *Easter Parade*, and she was on the cover of *Life* magazine. Metro had her under contract and wanted her to be another blonde bombshell like Marilyn Monroe, Jayne Mansfield, and Mamie Van Doren. I personally thought she was the prettiest and most talented of the hot blondes of the day.

Now that she was close to forty, sexy bombshell roles were increasingly rare. The casting world thought she was too old to play the ingénue, and too young and voluptuous to play a mom with a bunch of kids. It just didn't work. She had to take the roles that were offered to her, and *Bigfoot*, at least, offered a starring role, even if it was a B film.

For the last five or so years, Joi had successfully developed a nightclub act as a singer, and had received glowing reviews. No one could believe that anyone so gorgeous could actually sing! She was a hit in New York at the Copacabana Club and appeared all over the country in topnotch venues. As film and TV parts lessened, she'd managed to find a niche to sustain her career.

Joi walked toward the set, and I went back to the tree stumps and my fellow monsters. I couldn't believe that I'd spent almost an hour with her and how relaxed and at peace I felt. She had not only made me feel at ease, but seemed to truly enjoy our conversation. Under my fur, I was smiling, even with a mouth full of fangs.

While we worked into the night, I only had a few moments in front of the camera. All I did was scratch and grunt and pick "cooties" or "whatever" out of the baby Bigfoot's hair. Not exactly an Academy Award performance, but I made sure I had the best and loudest grunt, scratched with flair, and picked cooties with enthusiasm!

We finished shooting very late. I went over to say goodnight to Joi and saw that someone had joined her. She introduced me to her husband and manager,

Stan Todd, and he greeted me with a smile. The first night of shooting was over, and I was in a trance. I could hardly wait for the following morning. I hoped I could spend more time with Joi, with or without Stan.

The next day started just as early as the day before, at four in the morning, and I was up and ready; only this time, I wore full makeup. I wanted to look as good as possible, hoping to see her before they turned me into a hairy monster. I must say I looked great!

I went back to the studio, back to the hidden parking place, and back to makeup, hoping to stall my transformation until Joi arrived. Just as they called me to go in, she walked in the room. Having no idea who I was, she smiled sweetly at me, and I pointed to the suit I was about to put on. She looked at me very carefully and said it was a pity that someone so beautiful had to be covered up in black hair and spray paint. I couldn't believe my ears…she thought I was beautiful!

Joi watched as they glued and sprayed me and helped me with my costume. Then it was time for her to finish her body makeup and extra powder. She looked even lovelier that morning than the day before, so it didn't take long to finish. Afterward, we walked together onto the set.

As Joi went to speak with the director, Bob Slatzer, I walked over to sit with my motley crew. I was so enthralled with her that I hadn't even noticed that the forest scene was filled with fake trees and boulders, with an occasional scrawny real rent-a-tree. This was truly a low-budget film, but Joi, the consummate professional, acted as if she were starring in a film for Universal. She kept her pride to herself, and she did her best with whatever was required of her. As the day passed, I watched her every move; it was impossible to take my eyes off her. Any time I could catch her eye, I would smile at her, and, to my amazement, she smiled back.

A few hours into the shooting, her husband, Stan, came back to keep her company. When he spotted me and asked me to join him, I jumped up quickly. I wanted to be near Joi, and, if talking with him would increase the chances, I was happy to do it.

Stan was a charming man, very tan, with an obvious comb-over. His hair was quite thin, even with his creative hairstyle. His face glistened with the Vaseline he kept applying to his forehead and cheeks. He explained he was an avid tennis player and used it to keep his skin from drying out from all the sun exposure on the courts. He was about five foot eight or so, with a strong and defined upper body, an obvious athlete. His smile was infectious, and he was filled with story after story about his friends in Hollywood—the big shots! Although he seemed a little full of himself, he was interesting, and he could bring me closer to her. That was all that mattered.

He told me his schedule was so busy he didn't have enough time to help Joi with her lines, and asked if I could help her. *You can't be serious*, I thought. I would have done anything to have a moment with her! I happily agreed, and, a few minutes later, Joi finished her scene and joined us. When Stan told her I would help her rehearse, she smiled and seemed so grateful. She picked up the script, handed it to me, and asked me to read opposite her. We did this for about an hour until she felt more comfortable about the upcoming scene. We chatted about when she appeared in *A Hole in the Head* and *Who Was That Lady?* with Frank Sinatra and Dean Martin, "the good old days."

It was time for Joi to go back on camera, and I realized this was my big scene…my fifteen minutes of fame. I was gonna be a star!

The Bigfoot brigade included Jerry, me, and another female running in the background. Joi was to be tied to a pole by the males of the species. Bob Slatzer motioned to me to come down to where Joi was, and said I was to untie her and run away with her. I about popped with excitement!

I stood nervously in the wings while the set was lit, wondering what it would be like to hold this beautiful woman in my arms. I think I was almost hyperventilating. I was finally called, and the scene began.

The Director called, "Action," and Joi started screaming her bloody head off! Since we hadn't rehearsed (no budget), I was startled and fell into a couple of fake trees as I lumbered toward her. Her screams got louder as I fumbled with her knot with my clumsy monkey paws. I swear I heard the crew in hysterics!

I was ready to chew the rope loose when it finally came untied. Then, I grabbed her hand, and we ran off the set as fast as my very hairy legs would carry me. Thank heaven I didn't blow it completely! Eventually, all went well, and "Beauty" was saved by the "Beast."

Chapter 4

Schwab's Drug Store

We finally finished shooting around midnight, and Joi asked if I'd like to go to Schwab's and have coffee with her. We had spoken quite a bit throughout the day, and I felt an amazing connection with her. It was as if I had known her my entire life. Of course, I would go. I can't imagine anything that would have stopped me from spending a moment with her. Stan had left hours before, and I would have her all to myself—along with all the people at Schwab's, of course.

Schwab's was famous for being the place where Lana Turner was discovered. Many a hopeful starlet went there, hoping a talent scout or producer would see her and offer her a part in a film. A lot of wannabe seducers/producers walked around with a script under their arms and took advantage of girls who were desperate to be in films. They'd promise a screen test or a part in their "next" film, but they'd have to read for the part at some clandestine apartment or sleazy motel.

I followed her black-topped convertible in my beat-up old clunker. She didn't say a word about what I was driving—she was too gracious. We met in the parking lot of Schwab's on the corner of Sunset and Crescent Heights, and went inside.

It wasn't that busy for a twenty-four-hour coffee shop in the middle of Hollywood. Joi was dressed quite modestly and was not recognizable as the sex goddess she was portrayed to be. We sat in a booth next to a wall, rather than in the middle of the room where our conversation could be overheard by strangers. We talked until the sun shone through the window. There was no shooting going on that day at the studio. Exterior shots were being finished in Griffith Park, and neither of us had to be there.

I can't remember all that we talked about…it was like a dream. I only know that, during those hours of conversation, we connected as if we were soul mates long ago parted. As we spoke, our eyes met and didn't wander. Each word that was said made us closer. She would reach across the table and touch my hand, and, with each touch, my heart would skip a beat.

When it was time to leave, she asked me to go next door to a little shop with her. When we walked in, I saw Dionne Warwick trying on sunglasses. I followed Joi around the store, glancing at clothes I'd never be able to afford. Joi noticed me looking at a fuzzy black coat, soft as velvet to my touch, and she suggested I try it on, which I did with hesitation. It fit perfectly, and she said I looked wonderful in it. I took it off and wandered a bit longer while she continued to shop. When she finished, everything was bagged, and we walked to our cars.

Standing by the car, I was shocked when she handed me a bag containing the coat I'd tried on. She thanked me for all my help, hugged me, and gave me her phone number. Since I didn't have a phone of my own at the Studio Club, she said she'd call, and we'd get together. She said she'd love to have dinner or go to a movie and asked if I would like that. With a dry mouth, I stammered and asked, "When?"

"After the last day of shooting," she answered, which was in a few days.

It didn't matter to me if we were just friends. Just being with her was enough. As far as I knew, she was happily married to Stan and just wanted a girl friend to run around with. I could understand why she might not have many female friends. A lot of women would be so jealous of her that they couldn't get past her external beauty to find the real beauty in her soul. Somehow, I knew I already had.

Chapter 5

Go-Go

I had told some of the girls at the Studio Club that I'd been trying to find work. One of them worked occasionally as a go-go dancer in a nightclub, but had plans one evening and wondered if I'd like to fill in for her. When I said that I didn't have a costume, she offered to let me wear hers, a hot little red bikini covered with sequins. We wore the same size, which was really fortunate for me. I already had the white cowboy boots, so my ensemble was complete. She gave me all the information I needed, and I was ready to go-go.

Joi and I had spoken daily since the last day we shot *Bigfoot*. Our conversations were light and fun and revolved around when we would next get together. The moment I found out about my dancing gig, I called and asked her if she'd like to come and keep me company. She said that she'd love to and might bring her friend, Sid Caesar.

During our conversation, Joi told me that she and Stan were legally separated, but remained the best of friends. He reminded her of the dearest man in her life—her grampy, Ray Shupe, who had helped raise her. When Ray died a few years before, it left a terrible void in her life. Stan had been a good friend, was there when she needed him, but was a terrible husband. She said she'd explain more later and left it at that.

This helped to fill in the blanks. I started to understand her better and could tell she was hurting deeply. I hoped I might be able to help by being a good friend to her.

I was so excited that Joi would be coming to my big debut as a go-go dancer. I arrived at the nightclub and spoke to the Manager, asking him to reserve a place at the base of the stage for Joi and her guest.

I was on an elevated platform in go-go style, dancing and swaying to the music when Joi walked in the room. She was dressed like a movie star, wearing her full-length blonde mink coat that matched the color of her hair. She was dazzling—and alone. She sat at my feet and watched my every move. I'll never forget, when "My Girl" by the Temptations started to play, our eyes met, and I danced for her and only her.

After the set, I sat down at her table. She looked at me with a concerned expression and said, "You don't belong here. C'mon."

She didn't have to say another word. Still in costume, I smiled and followed her back to her place.

Joi was living in a lovely high-rise on La Cienega and Fountain in West Hollywood, just down the hill from Sunset Boulevard and the Playboy Club. She lived alone on the fourth floor in a spacious and elegantly decorated one-bedroom apartment with a nice den/TV room. A fireplace with electric logs was in the center of the living room, controlled by a switch on the wall, and she turned it on as we entered the room. The flames lit up the room, and her apartment became cozy and warm. She made us coffee and a salad, and, while we sat on the sofa chatting and eating, time passed so slowly that it seemed we were in a time warp.

I had hoped for a moment like this…time alone with her in a setting exactly like this…and had fantasized many times how this might play out. I knew I would not do anything to jeopardize our friendship, nor make any moves that would ruin something so wonderful in my life. She didn't know I was attracted to women, and I had not said one word about it. I had decided I would keep my thoughts and feelings to myself because I couldn't bear to lose this magic or to have her think less of me. And since I had no way of knowing how she'd react if she knew, I would just have to love her from afar.

Chapter 6

Falling in Love

We spent the evening talking as if we'd known each other for a hundred years. The more we spoke, the closer we sat to one another. She would reach out and touch my arm or gently brush her hand against my face. Her life had been filled with many men and brief affairs, and she expressed how sad and alone she had felt for too many years.

Joi had been involved with Sid Caesar for a while, and, before him, it was Frank Sinatra. She had really liked Frank, but said he was quite troubled. The time they spent together was interrupted by his sadness at the loss of one of his friends. He would cry, and his depression destroyed any intimacy they had. That was the end of their affair.

The relationship with Sid, who was married, was a dead-end street. She knew he was a temporary suitor and realized exactly what it was about—sex for him and a momentary end to loneliness for her.

She told me about the creeps and the scum in Hollywood—the producers and directors who demanded favors for work in a film. The casting couch was alive and well, and she was one of its beautiful victims. Talking about her experiences made her start to cry. She had been holding in the pain for too many years. I held her close, and she sobbed for hours.

Time passed, and she was finally comforted. She felt safe, and, at this moment, she knew she was loved.

Finally, though no words were spoken, she took my hand, and we lay down, side by side, in front of the fire. There was silence and peace between us when she slowly raised herself and, resting on her elbow, looked down at me with those beautiful green eyes. My heart started to pound, and then, unexpectedly and with a passion I had never known, she kissed me!

Joi kissed me with an intensity that almost stopped my breath. She seemed as surprised as I was and told me she had never felt this way about a woman before. Her kisses were like lightning in a thunderstorm. She took me by the hand and led me to her room. Wanting nothing more than to make her happy, I took her in my arms. Thus began a night I had dreamed of from the first time I saw her.

The morning light awakened me, and, at first, I thought it must have all been a dream. But there, beside me, she lay. She was sleeping like an angel with our bodies just barely touching. She began to wake and, as her eyes slowly opened, she looked deeply into mine and smiled a smile that I'll never forget.

The day passed as we kissed and cuddled and made love and laughed. By the end of it, we were both spent…physically and emotionally. It had been heaven on earth, and two souls had merged into one. Looking back, I realize this was when we fell totally in love. That date, February 17, 1969, became our official anniversary.

Chapter 7

Stan

Joi did not want me to leave, and, if it hadn't been necessary, I would not have left either. For the next few weeks, we would go to the Studio Club to pick up more and more of my clothing. Although Joi didn't officially ask me to move in with her, within a month, almost everything I owned was there.

She told me how important Stan was in her life and that my presence would not do anything to hurt their relationship. He was part of the package, and that was fine with me. They were not lovers and hadn't been for a very long time … it was a father/daughter/friend symbiotic relationship. He felt important being married to a gorgeous movie star, and she felt protected by a father figure.

Unfortunately, Stan was also the source of much of Joi's unhappiness. She had wanted a child, and he wanted no part of fatherhood; when she became pregnant with their child, he insisted she abort. This killed any love Joi could have had for him as his wife.

Stan had been married before, was divorced, and had two daughters, Leslie and Wendy. He remained a virtual stranger to them until they were in their early teens when, in an attempt to ingratiate himself to them, he took them on a trip to New England. He told Leslie he would introduce her as his niece rather than his daughter because he was concerned women might find him "too old." His ego and vanity left his girls feeling unloved and unimportant in his life.

I listened to Joi's stories about him, but could still feel that he filled an important need in her life. He became her "Grampy" after Ray Shupe died.

From that point on, the three of us spent almost every evening together, and Stan would take us out to dinner after he finished work. He had visions of being a producer and Joi's manager, but, in reality, he worked in the rag business as a highly successful and dynamic salesman. He would always say,

"If it's not available, they want it," and that was how he managed to sell tens of thousands of men's and boys' clothing items.

Stan was the best at what he did, but that didn't satisfy him. He wanted to be important, and would never introduce Joi as "Joi." It was always, "This is my wife, Joi Lansing, the movie star." Her image kept his ego alive, but, while trying to manage her career, he had made serious mistakes. Joi had appeared on *I love Lucy*, and Lucille Ball had wanted to put her under contract. Stan felt this was a bad idea and killed the deal. I don't think Joi ever forgave him for that.

The most positive thing he did for her career was to encourage her to start singing and develop a nightclub act. He helped her find arrangers to create the sheet music, and worked with her to choose the right material to go with her image. As a result, she worked constantly in clubs across the country and also appeared in Puerto Rico at the same time as Judy Garland and Eddie Fisher.

Joi told me that Judy came to every one of her shows, and she felt so honored that someone of Judy's stature and talent wanted to see her perform. Still, Joi admitted, it made her a little nervous.

When I asked why, she said that many years before, when she and Marilyn Monroe were both under contract to Metro, Marilyn had invited her to go with her to Palm Springs for a little "personal" time. Joi hardly knew Marilyn and felt uneasy going out of town with her, so she declined. Recalling that incident, Joi was somewhat apprehensive the first few times Judy came to see her show, but Judy never made a pass at her and just seemed to enjoy the performance.

I asked Joi if she thought Marilyn Monroe was interested in her, and she said, "Yes." It was common at Metro for the studio to encourage same-sex activities because they had spent tremendous amounts of money on their stars and didn't want any pregnancies.

They also controlled their weight with uppers and, when they couldn't sleep, gave them downers. The uppers were Benzedrine and amphetamines, and the downers were Seconal and other barbiturates. Joi told me they introduced her to sleeping pills when she had trouble with insomnia—it was imperative that she get the sleep she needed to look as good as she could on film.

This was totally foreign to me. I had never taken any pills except antibiotics and the pain medications the doctors had given me in the hospital when my horse, Chico, clipped me under the chin with his nose. That little tap put me in the hospital for a week with a concussion. I didn't know what these pills did and had no interest in knowing about them.

One day, Joi took me to a friend's pharmacy on Melrose Avenue and introduced me to Ted, the owner/pharmacist. He worked with a doctor in the same building who would authorize a prescription for the Seconal and Tuinal that Joi needed. There must have been fifty or sixty of them in the bottle he gave her.

Driving back to the apartment, she explained that it was very difficult to get the pills, and she couldn't sleep without them. She had a big problem, and I didn't know it.

It was a strange day, and I knew something was bothering her. I didn't know what it was, but she became quite moody. She started to cry and said she missed her Grampy; it must have been the anniversary of his death. She picked up the phone and called John and Pete's Liquor and ordered a few bottles of scotch—Johnny Walker and Chivas. A young man arrived in about an hour with her order.

I remembered reading movie magazines filled with stories of Joi, the beautiful and sexy Mormon girl who didn't drink or smoke. The studios played up her healthy and non-drinking upbringing to portray something unusual in Hollywood—a sex symbol who was pure and innocent.

It was true that she didn't smoke. But Joi was not Mormon at this point in her life and, in fact, was not involved in any particular religion or church group, at least, when I was with her. Her affiliation with the Mormon religion was a product of the studios and their hype.

She worked for a few years with Bob Cummings, who was a real health guru of the 1950s and 1960s. Publicists jumped on this and portrayed her as being his protégé. There were endless articles about her health regimen and the countless vitamins she took daily.

This was actually true—she had bottles and bottles of vitamins lined up in her kitchen. Every day she would take a handful of capsules and pills of every shape and color. She was also under contract with Tiger's Milk, and they used her image to publicize their products. Joi did take care of her body by eating healthy foods and taking all those vitamins. She also exercised by working out with weights every day.

The one pill that was never mentioned was Seconal, and the drink they forgot about was scotch. Only people very close to her knew of her problem. Sadly, I was soon to discover one of her secrets. She suffered from terrible depression and would drink to ease the pain and then take a Seconal or two to go to sleep. When that didn't work, she'd wake up and take a few more pills. I tried to stop her, but she became infuriated and did as she pleased. This went on for a few days, and I didn't sleep because I was afraid for her. I watched her and kept checking her breathing. I had never been around anyone who drank before, at least, not like this.

I didn't know what to do, so I called Stan, who told me to stay with her, remain calm, and try to get the pills away from her. He said she'd done this before, and he'd come over as soon as he could.

Shaking by the time he arrived, I didn't know what to do for her or how to take care of her. She was delirious from the combination of pills and alcohol, and I tried to soothe her and keep her from taking any more pills. I dumped out the rest of the scotch and hid the capsules because I was so afraid she'd die from what she was doing to herself.

Stan came in and talked to her like a father and was able to calm her down. He tucked her into bed and let her have one more pill to go to sleep. That was all she wanted…sleep.

He came back into the living room and tried to put me at ease. I was stunned and couldn't believe what I had seen—the woman I loved had turned into a slurring, pathetic shell of herself. Stan told me she had "many demons," but that, with my help, "she could conquer them." He said she needed "constant companionship and support." I think he realized how much I truly loved her and that I would do anything for her.

What did I know? I was twenty-one and naive as Pollyanna. But after Stan's reassurance that I was "all she needed," I was determined to do everything in my power to prove to her that someone loved her unconditionally. I wanted to make up for all the hurt and sadness that had pushed her into bottles of pills and alcohol. I thought this was a battle we could fight together and that, if she felt enough love, her demons would leave her troubled mind and heart. If I had known then what difficulty lay ahead, it probably wouldn't have mattered. I loved this woman deeply, and that meant always being there for her, no matter what.

It was a long and hideous weekend. I felt like my guts had been torn out. How a sweet and good person who was almost childlike in her innocence could be so distraught and insane was something I couldn't get. How? Why? This couldn't be happening! My dream had become a nightmare.

Joi finally came out of her stupor when the Johnny Walker and Seconal wore off. She slept until it was out of her system, and, when she woke up, she didn't remember anything that happened during the hell she'd unwittingly left behind. I wasn't angry, only confused and sad. But then she was "my girl" again. At least, until next time.

Chapter 8

Back to Normal

The weekend from hell was over, and all was calm and back to the way things were supposed to be. Joi was as sweet and loving as anyone could ever want in a mate, and our life together was simple and happy. I loved being with her, and she loved me. She showed me that she loved me in so many ways; no one was more gentle and kind.

We stayed up late every night, not so much because she wanted to, but because her insomnia was a problem. We'd sleep late and get up in time for dinner, when Stan would come over, and we'd go out to Nate and Al's or to the Hungarian restaurant they both liked. Occasionally, we'd go to Frascati's on Sunset or the Luau in Beverly Hills. Sleeping and eating were a big part of our lives.

Life was very peaceful, and we were two lovebirds honeymooning. She treated me like a queen and would tell me, at least, ten times a day how much she loved me. I had found happiness with the woman of my dreams.

Time passed and the person who had been so insane and unkind had seemed to disappear. Joi had not touched alcohol since the last episode. Occasionally, I would mention to her little things about what had happened. She didn't recall any of it and was remorseful that she had put me through so much pain and confusion.

Joi rarely used four-letter words, but, once in a while, she could come up with some beauties. They were never directed at me, but toward some of the miserable people in the business. She hated the way they had treated her, and now that she was getting older, the phone rang less and less. Parts in films just weren't happening, and TV guest spots were rare. Going on the road with her nightclub act was tough, especially when she had to go alone. Stan's daughter,

Leslie, had traveled with her whenever she could, but she had kids at home to care for. Stan had to work, but now that I was with her, she wouldn't have to be by herself.

One day, the phone rang, and it was Stan Scottland, her agent with CMA. He had a gig for her in New York doing a summer theater-in-the-round production. It was a burlesque spoof, which would star Joi and Mickey Hargitay. Mickey was a very successful bodybuilder who had worked as an actor with his wife, Jayne Mansfield, prior to the terrible car accident that claimed her life.

Joi was thrilled to be working again and accepted the job. It paid $2,250 a week, which was amazing money in 1969. At least, it was to me. I was excited! I had never been to New York and had only been on a plane twice in my life. The first was when I was queen of the National Football Foundation Hall of Fame in Las Vegas. The second trip was to San Francisco, a publicity gig for American International Pictures (AIP) for a movie about Amazons! Such was the extent of my flying experience.

New York! This was going to be soooo exciting! Joi had a friend who lived at the Parc V Apartments next to the Sherry Netherland Hotel on Central Park. She called to see if we could stay with him while she was appearing on Long Island. He agreed, and we were ready to go.

Packing was one of the most fun things with Joi. She had her own special system! She'd stand by the closet and start tossing things into a suitcase that was open on top of the bed. If it landed in the suitcase, it went. If it didn't, it stayed. We laughed with every toss—everything was fun. Halfway through, she'd grab my hand and start to dance with me. We'd dance and kiss and dance until we fell on top of the clothes that were staying. Life was perfect. We were in love.

Chapter 9

This Was Burlesque!

We managed to get everything packed, and Stan took us to LAX for our flight on TWA. The producer, Sol Richman, paid for a first-class ticket for Joi, which was in her contract. She traded it in to pay for coach tickets for the two of us. I had no money to pay for my ticket, so she insisted upon traveling first-class. Smart cookie!

The flight was smooth, and she was as calm as I was nervous. There was only a moment or two of turbulence, but that was enough to make me rigid. She read me like a book, saw that I was frightened, and took my hand to calm me down. Within a few minutes, she had me laughing.

We were the only two people in our row. No one was across the aisle, and the people in front and in back were busy talking or listening to music, so Joi thought it would be fun to "play" under the blanket. Talk about taking my mind off wind turbulence! I don't think anyone knew, and, if they did, no one said a word. We had our own, slightly more creative version of the mile high club.

Joi was far more adventurous than I would have imagined. I was the cautious one, not wanting anyone to ever suspect anything about her. She had a career at stake, but this was new to her, and she was determined to have a good time. I kept telling her to be careful, and she'd just laugh and kiss me. She wasn't afraid and didn't think anyone would suspect anything of that sort about her. After all, she was God's gift to men—not women!

By this point in our relationship, Joi started to introduce me as her sister, Nancy. One day, however, she took me to meet her friend, Joey Bishop, and whispered something in his ear. His smile broadened, and he said, "Oh, I get to meet the bride!"

I was surprised, but it felt good that Joi had told someone she trusted about us.

Joey sat down with me, kissed me on the forehead, and said, "You don't look like a Nancy. From now on, your name should be Rachel."

Joi loved the name, and, from that day forward, I was Rachel Lansing, her little sister. Changing my name was no great loss—it wasn't exactly well-known. And I loved that Joi wanted me to have her last name, however we had to do it.

We looked similar enough to pass—both tall, leggy blondes, although she definitely had the cleavage in the family! Joi looked a lot younger than she was—she turned forty on April 6, 1969. I was twenty-one and thought I looked much older. Even with the age difference, the Bobbsey Twins act worked. If I was her sister, there wouldn't be any suspicion that we were lovers. I really don't know if people ever suspected; nothing was ever mentioned in the tabloids, and we were seen everywhere together.

Joi and Rachel Lansing arrived in New York in June of 1969. It was hot as hell and stifling. Joi's old friend, Herbie Palestine (probably an "admirer," but I didn't ask because I didn't want to know), had a limo pick us up at the airport and take us to his apartment at the Parc V. It was beautiful inside, massive and opulent. Herbie owned it and had it decorated in French Provincial. Everything was perfect—it looked like no one even sat on a chair!

Herbie showed us our room, and, since he wasn't staying there at the time, said his housekeeper would take care of anything we needed. He owned Arlan's Department Stores on the East Coast and was quite well off. Herbie liked Joi and was gracious to me. He even made his limo and driver available to take us to Glen Cove, where Joi would be appearing in *This Was Burlesque!*

We enjoyed the city for a few days until rehearsal started. The Producer had rented a studio in a three-story walkup in downtown Manhattan, and every day we would go there in the heat and climb the stairs. By the time we reached the third floor, we'd be sweating and miserable. It was an especially humid and disgusting summer in New York, but Joi was a trouper and never complained. While she rehearsed, I'd go downstairs and walk to an Italian deli a few doors away that had great food.

The first time I ordered coffee, it took a few times to get it right. I'd say, "I'd like some coffee," and the guy would say "Regular?" and I'd say no, that I'd like it with cream and sugar. He would then repeat, "You want regular?" and I'd say no, and again tell him I wanted it with cream and sugar. He finally stopped me in the middle of my Abbott & Costello routine and explained that "regular" meant "with cream and sugar!" I laughed, thinking how funny Joi would think this was.

I bought coffee for both of us and ordered my favorite sandwich, learning quickly that capicola is not cap-a-cola…it's gabagool. This was just the beginning of my education and a little more sophistication. Life with Joi was proving to be a constant adventure; every day, I learned a little more, and my life was enriched.

Rehearsal went on for a couple of weeks. Every day, we'd go to the walkup, an,d every night, we'd go back to Herbie's apartment, stopping on the way to have dinner in some cute, little restaurant.

There was one that I remember fondly, a small, intimate Italian restaurant. We were greeted outside by white twinkle lights on the tree branches and, as we walked in, the Owner recognized Joi and alerted the waiters. We were treated like royalty.

Joi had wonderful manners, and I watched and mimicked everything she did. I wanted her to be proud to have me with her, and never to embarrass her. She treated me as her partner and guided me with dignity. The age difference was never an issue and neither was my naiveté. She led and I followed—except when we danced!

Rehearsals were finished, and the Director was happy. It was time for the show to open, and everyone was ready for the big night. A press day was held when the local newspapers sent their reporters to interview Joi and Mickey Hargitay. It was a photo-op, and all of the guys wanted to be in a shot with Joi.

Opening night of *This Was Burlesque!* went well, without any snafus. Everyone knew their lines, and all of the lighting and sound cues worked. It was a success, and the show received good reviews.

After opening night, we went to Sardi's for a late dinner. New York is a late night town, and nothing starts until ten o'clock at the earliest. This was perfect for Joi because of her sleeping problems…we'd be up until dawn, sleep during the day, and set the alarm just in time to get ready to go to the theater. I loved our schedule, not realizing then how much it said about the turmoil inside my darling friend.

Things became a little tedious at Herbie's. When he came back, I think he expected more than a hug and a kiss on the cheek from Joi, and she just wasn't interested. We moved quickly to the Navarro Hotel, a few blocks away on Central Park South, where Joi made a deal with the Manager to let us stay for $600 a week. She'd saved some money while we stayed at Herbie's and didn't mind spending it to have a little peace of mind. The days of putting up with men who touched her when she didn't want them to were long gone. She was faithful to me and faithful to herself.

All Joi ever wanted to do was to work in the business. She had the looks and the talent, but to do what she dreamed of carried a heavy price.

She told me about the time that Burt Lancaster hired her to be in one of his films, and, when she showed up on the set, there was no script. He only wanted her to keep him company and amuse him while he portrayed the hell-fire-breathing preacher in *Elmer Gantry*. She became furious and left immediately. It was bad enough that sex was expected many times when she worked, but to be considered just a piece of meat for a pompous and ego-inflated actor was over the top.

Joi was not new to Hollywood and the casting couch games. The times when it didn't happen were a welcome respite for her. I'd had my own close calls, but not to the degree that she had. I had my fun times, as well as my not-so-fun times, just like many young girls in Hollywood. The predators were many, and the broken dreams and destroyed lives were the casualties of the sex-driven film industry of those times.

Sadly, Joi was one of these casualties—a victim of her own beauty and the parasitic power-mongers who emotionally cannibalized her. Her story parallels that of Monroe. She was a commodity to them, just a beautiful face and body, something to be used up and, when she rebelled, discarded.

Her husband knew the business and understood what "they" wanted of her. He told her it was only a "piece of skin," and that "doing what was necessary" was fine with him. Joi didn't want to hear this, as it further damaged her self-respect. Even he was willing to let her be a sacrificial lamb on the altar made of celluloid in big black and silver cans. He didn't understand the emotional tragedy that was imploding inside of her. He just didn't get it.

The beginning of the end between them was his insistence she abort what would have been their first baby. Joi was devastated. The final wound came the night that Stan drove her to Les Paul's home and dropped her off, telling her, "This guy can do a lot for your career."

That was the death knell of their marriage. Joi could no longer respect Stan because of his lack of respect for her. In her mind, they were no longer husband and wife, but, oddly, they would remain close friends for the rest of her tragically short life.

Chapter 10

Summer in New York

The show went well, but was only scheduled for a limited number of performances. Joi loved working with Mickey, and I enjoyed babysitting for Zoltan and Mariska, Mickey's little ones with Jayne Mansfield. Mariska was only five years old at the time. It's been fun watching her TV career, especially her success as one of the major stars of *Law & Order: Special Victims Unit*. Joi found her a charming little girl. I know she'd get a kick out of how famous that funny little kid with the big smile has become.

We had a great time in New York. After the three-week engagement was over, high on its success, we decided it was time for us to explore. Since we both loved to eat, we set out to find the best food in the city!

Restaurants in New York weren't cheap, but one place we especially enjoyed was Mama Leone's. We were guests of the Owner, and I think we ate enough to beach ourselves! The Manager brought over an array of different entrées, followed by an amazing tray of assorted fruits and cheeses—enough for six people. We ate as much as our expanding bellies could hold.

Joi had no problems with weight and had a very healthy attitude toward food. She usually enjoyed light meals and salads and occasionally red meat. Her weight was perfect for her body, and enjoying food was never a guilty pleasure.

We moved from the Navarro Hotel to the Buckingham, where they gave us two single beds separated by a table with a pink princess phone and a lamp. Joi and I weren't exactly thrilled with the accommodations, but we weren't going to say anything about wanting a king-size bed so that we could spread out. Always enterprising, Joi redesigned the layout. We moved the table to one side, placed the beds next to each other, and bingo, we had our nice, big, yummy bed. We kept a Do Not Disturb sign on the door, so the hotel maids wouldn't come in and discover our less-than-platonic arrangement. Joi told the Manager that she liked her privacy and didn't require maid service. He seemed somewhat dismayed but honored her request.

A few weeks later, in the middle of the night, we awoke to someone frantically banging on our door. A fire had broken out in a room above us, and we scrambled to get dressed and grab our purses. The sound of fire alarms and the smell of burning carpets and mattresses were terrifying! As we ran to the stairs, we banged on all the doors as we passed by, warning other guests of the danger.

There was a fragile, elderly lady in the room across from ours, whom we had seen frequently as we came and went. She heard our fists slamming on the door and seemed confused when she answered. She had turned her hearing aid down, so she could sleep, and she had no idea what we wanted. With no time to explain, Joi grabbed her hand, and we practically carried her down the fire escape!

We made it outside safely and stood shaking in the cold as we watched the upper floors of the building go up in flames. The firemen used their hook and ladder and hurried up the precarious rungs to save the man who had fallen asleep while smoking in bed. We were told he survived, but with serious burns. Luckily, no one else was hurt in the fire.

Things were crazy with the guests and firemen and police. The lady we rescued had called her son to join her, so Joi and I walked to a nearby deli for coffee. Still shaking, we stayed until the pandemonium ended and we could go back to our room to gather our belongings.

The management of the Buckingham had arranged with a few hotels in the neighborhood to accommodate their displaced guests. We took our things and readjusted the bed, not wanting to take a chance on rumors or raised eyebrows. As we were accomplished suitcase packers, it took us no time to be on our way to a small, older hotel nearby.

We had only spent a few nights there when Joi contacted Bill Dance, an actor she knew. He lived in an apartment on Central Park West and graciously let us stay with him for a few weeks until it was time for us to leave New York.

Chapter 11

Dr. Silicone

While we stayed with Bill in his elegant digs above Central Park, we had time to take care of some matters that needed our attention. Sadly, we would not realize the gravity of one of our concerns until it was too late.

Joi was having a problem with her right breast. It had become hard, and her nipple had become inverted. She blamed it on a fall she'd had before I met her, and, because I didn't want to make her feel self-conscious, I hadn't said much about it. I did mention that she should see a doctor, and she said she knew of a doctor in New York who was familiar with her type of problem, Dr. Benito Rish. She made an appointment with him and confided in me that she'd had multiple injections of liquid silicone in her breasts and didn't think what was going on now was any big deal.

During the late 1960s, silicone implants were just starting to become an alternative to pushup bras. It was a surgical procedure, and it was pretty expensive for the average woman seeking larger breasts. The alternative was liquid silicone.

Its usage began in Japan during World War II. American men were notoriously known for their fascination with large globular breasts, so Japanese women were having themselves injected with a silicone solvent, which had originally been used to lubricate machinery in the military. In fact, huge drums of the stuff had been disappearing from military warehouses for some time, and they only realized why when it became commonly known how it was being used. But silicone wasn't the only liquid that was used. Various liquids, including cooking oil and wax, were popular for engorging small breasts to make them more desirable to the GIs.

This use of silicone traveled to Main Street America, especially in the larger coastal cities. It was a relatively fast fix for women wanting a more prominent feminine appearance. The American Medical Association (AMA) allowed doctors to use the liquid in hand procedures and as a filler in non-vital areas where there was a depression or dip in the tissue. But they, as well as the Food and Drug Administration (FDA), forbade the usage in breast tissue because of possible unforeseen problems. This solvent had not been thoroughly tested, and they didn't know if the body would react negatively to it. This apparently didn't matter to Dr. Rish or to the other medical doctors who were making a killing (how true that was) by taking advantage of those who wanted to stay young and sexy.

Joi told me she'd done it because of the sex symbol image she portrayed. She knew a lot of people in Los Angeles who did it to get rid of wrinkles in their faces—even her friend, Frank Sinatra, had had some injections by the Doctor who had done her breasts and filled in her derriere. The studio had been critical of her boyish bottom, and she'd worn panties from Frederick's with rounded padding to fill out the look they wanted. Now she no longer needed them since the "magical" fluid had been added.

I didn't ask her how many injections she'd had or where else she'd had them. That was her business, and I respected her personal privacy. The shots achieved the look she wanted, since her persona and image were all about her curvaceous body and firm, eye-popping cleavage. This was how she saw herself and how others wanted to see her. Ultimately, it became who she was. She was the sex goddess with the "magnificent body," and she wouldn't let the years take this away.

Howard Hughes loved industrial-sized breasts, and the minute he saw Joi, he wanted to possess her. She finally agreed to a date, but her current beau, actor Larry Chance, burst in on their dinner and physically carried her from the restaurant! That ended her almost-relationship with Mr. Hughes... *and* Mr. Chance.

Joi loved breasts... her breasts, my breasts, breasts in general. Mine were almost a C-cup and virginal with small pink nipples, but I'd always kind of wondered what it might be like if they were larger. I had never really considered doing anything about it, but then I didn't know about the "wonders" of silicone... or, unfortunately, its dangers.

The afternoon of our appointment arrived in early September. We walked into a modest office with several treatment rooms, and I noticed it wasn't decorated especially well—just brown and white sheets on the exam tables. His staff had been sent home to respect the privacy of his high-profile patient. That was his choice; Joi had not requested it.

Dr. Rish was pleasant, but he was more of a salesman than what I'd ever experienced with a medical doctor. He was lauding the use of silicone and suggesting it was the cure for all the imperfections of the human body. A little shot here, a little shot there, and a lot more there and there, and everyone would be beautiful. I was the one for the "there and there," and he would make my breasts "spectacular," as he put it. I was going to walk out with "fuller breasts after just one injection in each." It sounded innocent enough. *Why not?* I thought.

Before he started my transformation, he examined Joi. He had not seen a problem like this before and believed that, if he injected her with cortisone, it would soften the tissue and the breast would go back to the way it was before. His attitude was not alarming, and he led her to believe that everything would resolve itself very quickly and that there was no need for concern. He gave her three syringes filled with corticosteroids after he numbed the breast with novocaine or xylocaine.

This was comforting to both of us. Joi was not happy with what was happening to her breast and was relieved that it would be okay. While I was sitting there, he handed me a waiver to sign, telling me it was a silly technicality and not to think twice about it.

Finished with Joi, he began on me by using an air gun filled with xylocaine to deaden the feeling in my breasts. It was the most bizarre sensation. He told me to sit absolutely still because, if I moved, the pressure of the liquid being propelled could tear the skin. I was rigid. No way was I going to move, even though it wasn't pleasant. It didn't hurt like an injection with a needle, but it still stung. He then followed up with what seemed like, at least, twenty tiny shots of xylocaine, which deadened my breasts completely.

Then he had me lie back on the exam table, and, when I looked at the tray with his supplies, I saw the syringe he was getting ready to use. It was the biggest needle I had ever seen! I'm not exaggerating when I say that it was, at least, eight inches long. Suddenly nervous, I asked if he was actually going to use that gigantic syringe and stick the needle that was as thick as a small tree branch inside my boobs. He told me to close my eyes, that it "wasn't going to be painful," and that he needed a needle that long because he had to "insert it from beneath my breast up into my pectoral muscle."

This was not what I had expected. I thought he would make tiny injections all over my breasts, just like he had with the xylocaine. NO. This is the way it had to go in—against the chest wall, from underneath my breast through to the top of my pectoral muscle.

All seemed to go well with the first one…no problems and no pain, so I was much more relaxed as he prepared a second syringe. It looked like there was enough silicone to fill a can with flat Seven Up. That was kind of how it appeared…semi-clear with no bubbles.

The second injection did not go well from the very start. I could actually feel him tearing the chest wall tissue with the needle! And the pain was excruciating. The sound made me sick to my stomach, and I knew that he had really screwed up. But he smiled and said that everything was "fine" and this was "not unusual." He told me to relax and that we were almost finished.

All I knew for sure at that moment was that it was finished and I was finished…and I would never, ever do this again. Though I was scheduled to come back a few more times to create "greater fullness," that was the last time I saw him.

Looking back, I knew at the time this was a serious and major mistake in my young life. Sadly, it played out seven years later when I developed very painful and cystic breasts, filled with atypical and cannibalistic cells which, as the doctors told me, were pre-malignant. I had to have a bilateral mastectomy because of the damage that was done, so I went from having pretty and ample breasts to having none. But I guess I was lucky to lose only my breasts…and not my life, as Joi did.

Chapter 12

Traveling New England

Though we both survived the visit to Dr. Rish, Joi's breast was sore from all the injections of cortisone, and I was in quite a bit of pain from the needle tear of my chest wall. We were both badly bruised. The total bill for my silicone injections and her treatment was $300. We thought it very reasonable at the time. The true price was to come much later.

Joi was having other problems that were starting to become difficult to manage. Her menstrual periods were excessive, and she lost a tremendous amount of blood each month. She'd been to doctors to find the source of the problem and, unfortunately, it was the same old story. They were too busy trying to date her, instead of seriously paying attention to her medical issues.

She dreaded her period each month because she knew how debilitating it would be. When she couldn't take it any longer, she made an appointment with a doctor in Manhattan who did a pelvic exam and said it was probably fibroids in her uterus. He suggested that she might want to do something about it later. Then he, too, asked her out.

At this point in my life, I was not familiar with medications and their uses. I was now, unfortunately, well-acquainted with Seconal and Tuinal — Joi's drugs of choice. She, also, had a prescription for Premarin which she took every day, explaining to me that a doctor had prescribed it for her many years ago when she asked him for something to help prevent aging.

Premarin is the hormone estrogen. Joi's body was already producing sufficient estrogen, and the additional amount she took every day without a break was—unbeknown to us at the time—like adding jet fuel to the breast and ovarian cancer fire that would eventually consume her body.

Even menopausal women who take estrogen are instructed to stop it for various times during their cycles. This doctor gave her the murderous pills that would very definitely prevent her from ever growing old. I know now this was a major contributor to her untimely death in 1972.

Looking back, I now feel that the excessive hormones raging through her body contributed to her emotional lows and triggered her almost monthly bouts of depression. Everything was like heaven on earth with her and our relationship until just prior to her period when she would sink into a deep black hole of inconsolable sadness. That was when she'd buy a bottle of scotch or vodka and start mixing large glasses of one or the other while taking her pills to escape.

After a few of these episodes, I knew how to keep her from hurting herself. I secretly bought gelatin capsules, and, when she would first pass out, I'd find her pills and do my own version of "better living through chemistry." I'd take out varying amounts of the drug from her capsules and substitute it with gelatin powder. I made sure that she got enough of the drug to let her sleep it off, but not enough to hurt her. I had no choice…something had to be done.

Joi wasn't in control. The combination of alcohol and pills had a hideous effect on her mind and body. Her depression and insomnia had the potential of being a lethal combination, and, knowing this, I learned how to take care of her. She had no understanding of this, nor any interest in getting help for her drug dependency. Because I was so young, I thought I could help her. My gut still told me something was very wrong with her other than her addictions, and I insisted, as gently as I could, that she see a good doctor when we returned to Los Angeles.

While we were still in New York, I recall a day when we were just driving around, and we passed a mortuary. A sudden chill went up my spine, and I broke into a cold sweat. The thought, "I'm going to lose her," crossed my mind. Another chill. I shook it off, refusing to acknowledge what I instinctively knew. I leaned a little closer to her, touching her shoulder with my head. This was not going to happen to her…not going to happen to us!

In time, Joi started feeling better, and one day she thought it would be fun to drive up to the Catskills and visit her friend Paul, whose family-owned Grossinger's in the Jewish Alps. It was a delightful drive. Trading the overcrowded, amped-up cacophony of city noise and lights for the splendor of the verdant mountains and trees in the Catskills made us both giddy with delight.

Grossinger's was wonderful! Paul Grossinger was expecting us and provided us with a lovely suite of rooms, complete with a large wicker basket overflowing with exotic and delicious fruits and cheeses.

I don't know for sure, but I think Paul and Joi must have dated at some point. I didn't ask. There were just some things I really didn't want to know. Her past and the men in her life were her business, not mine. If she told me about a certain man or details of an affair she wanted to share, that just added to our special bond, but she would tell me in a way that didn't create insecurity or jealousy between us that would have made me unhappy or uncomfortable. Our relationship was built on a firm foundation of love and trust, and we both wanted to keep it that way.

Staying at this kosher hotel was an educational experience for me. A difficult thing for me to grasp was why, if I ate meat at a meal, could I not also have butter with my bread or cream with my coffee. Joi kept explaining this was the custom and tradition of the Jewish people who kept a kosher kitchen. Though still a bit of a mystery for me, I finally got it right and learned to order without raising eyebrows.

In the public eye since she was a young girl, Joi had filed away each experience and knew exactly how to act in any circumstance. She had the ability to be with a king or queen or a street urchin and treat them all equally.

While we were at Grossinger's, Joi received a call from her agent, Stan Scottland, who knew we were traveling through New England and was trying to find gigs for her while we were there. He was able to book her appearance on Dave Garroway's TV show in Boston and, while we were in town, Ray Heatherton's radio show.

The drive to Boston was beautiful. It was the beginning of autumn, and the leaves were changing from deep green to crimson, touched with bright orange and yellow. The scenery was a candy store for the eyes. I had never seen such a brilliant array of hues and couldn't stop looking at the amazing sights as we drove, top down, beneath the color-kissed leaves.

We arrived in Boston and drove through the narrow streets surrounded by brownstone buildings. While New York was awe-inspiring with its skyscrapers, Boston was comfortable with its architecture and old-world charm. The Charles River wound through the city and was like a king-sized moat separating the city from Harvard University. Our hotel was only a few blocks from the river, and we made it a point to walk along the banks at night before dusk.

The hotel was quite old and filled with marble and crystal chandeliers. In an alcove near the grand staircase was an alabaster statue of the Three Graces, standing as a focal point, overlooking the lobby. They were the grand ladies of the house, silently watching each guest passing by. I felt they approved of us.

Dave Garroway was one of the original hosts of the *Today* show in the 1950s and early 1960s. I remember watching him on that show when I was a teenager in Kansas. He was a superstar of television when it was in its infancy, and now he was the host of his own show in Boston.

When we arrived to tape the show, Joi looked spectacular. She had recently bought a full length maxi-coat in faux fur from Best & Co. in New York. She loved animals and was delighted when faux fur fashions became available. The coat had a realistic-looking, wide fox tail fur collar and a matching faux fur hem that touched the floor. The varying shades of browns and hints of silver made the color of her hair and skin look like sweet cream and peaches.

Dave spent, at least, fifteen minutes interviewing her and talking about her summer theater performance on Long Island. She'd brought a tape of one of her songs, "The One I Love Belongs to Somebody Else", as it was common to have a singer lip sync the song while the tape played in the background. Most small shows didn't have the money or the space to have a singer and a band or orchestra, so they did the next best thing—they faked it!

Joi knew her material and had a true performer's expert timing. When it was time for her to sing the lyrics, she was right on the beat. No one would ever suspect she was singing to a tape.

We left Boston after one more stroll by the Charles River, and then stopped at Anthony's Pier 52 for a three-pound lobster and their wonderful sourdough bread. Anthony had his photo taken with Joi to place on the gallery wall beside the photos of other famous stars who'd enjoyed a fabulous feast at his restaurant. Not only was the food delicious, but the meal was comped by the owner. What a life!

Chapter 13

Cape Cod Misadventure

After our delectable lunch, Joi said she wanted me to see Cape Cod, too, and I loved the idea! Since it was still early afternoon, we drove to the ferry and were shuttled to the island. The ferry had set hours when you could come and go, and the last returning shuttle was at five o'clock. We planned to spend the rest of the day looking through the quaint little shops and return on the last ferry.

Everything went as scheduled until we got involved in a cute little dress shop where Joi wanted to try on a few outfits. Time slipped by without our noticing, and we missed the last shuttle. I was concerned, but Joi seemed game for this adventure. If plans changed, she didn't mind, and things like this didn't upset her. So, making the best of the situation, we decided to spend the night in romantic "old Cape Cod."

We drove around the island and finally found a place that had a vacancy sign. It had a somewhat eerie appeal—kind of like the Bates Motel in *Psycho*. The young man who seemed to be the manager kept staring a hole through Joi's clothes, and she was not even dressed seductively. In fact, she had on a thick jacket covering her slacks and long-sleeved sweater. There was something definitely weird about him. He showed us a room and said there were no phones except in the office, so, if we needed to make a call, we were to knock on his door.

He kept insisting we should have two rooms, and that he would discount the second room if we agreed. We both "got" that he was trying to get her alone. Joi spoke up and told him that one room was exactly what we wanted, that her "sister" was afraid of the dark, and not to be concerned that we had only one bed to sleep in. None of the rooms had two beds, and the idea of us sleeping together seemed to unsettle him.

We got ready for bed earlier than usual because we wanted to take the first ferry out in the morning at eight o'clock. Just as we were drifting off, we were startled by someone banging on the door. "Norman" (right out of the movie) was shouting for us to, "Open up!"

Joi left the chain lock in place as she peeked out. He was drunk out of his mind and insisted they go for a ride. I don't know if he recognized who Joi was since she had used a phony name when we checked in, but it didn't matter if he did or not—he was obsessed with her.

Joi was very brave (and perhaps a little foolhardy) when she agreed to go outside to talk with him. She was concerned he'd become violent if she didn't calm him down. I asked her not to go. I was afraid he might hurt her, but Joi had a mind of her own and was going to do what she thought best.

She got dressed and put a pocket knife in her jacket. *A lot of good that will do with this raving wacko*, I thought. She went outside and talked with him for a good twenty minutes, as I stood by the door trying to listen to their conversation. I was able to peek at him through a split in the curtain. My eyes zeroed in on him, and I was ready to jump out and do what I had to do to keep him from putting his slimy hands on her.

He kept inching toward her, and his voice was getting louder. I was ready for anything. She then said something to him that I couldn't hear, and he seemed to settle down. He began crying and begging her to go with him or spend the night with him in one of the other rooms. She told me later she'd explained to him she was a married woman and I was her younger sister who was having some problems, and that I could not be left alone because of my mental condition. (Little did she know that by then I definitely *had* a "mental condition!")

Cleverly, Joi had known exactly what to say to this "Norman" knockoff. It seemed like forever to me, but finally he walked her to the door and said goodnight. Then he staggered over to his truck, almost falling as he climbed into the cab, hit the gas with an angry foot, and sped off into the darkness.

Flushed, Joi quickly came back in the room and told me to hurry and get our things. We stuffed everything in our bags and ran to the car. She roared onto the highway and floored it fast enough to leave our shadows behind!

That night in the car, racing away from the nightmare scene we'd barely escaped, I sat close, holding her arm, grateful to feel her warmth and smell her scent, reassured that we were still "we." I think I heard her heart pounding. Or maybe it was mine. At that moment, we were one.

As we drove back into the village, we found an all-night diner and took refuge in hot cups of coffee and bacon and eggs. Joi was amazed that they actually got her order right —eggs basted in oil and not butter! I had to laugh. Considering what she'd just been through, that was just one more delightful example of her basic innocence. What a gal!

We stayed in the seaside eatery until the sun peeked over the ocean. The first ferry of the morning was soon to sail and, thrilled to have escaped from the local lunatic, we walked happily out of the diner arm-in-arm ("sisters" do that), just a bit ragged from lack of sleep.

Joi saw a pile of local newspapers that had just been placed in a coin machine. She saw the headline before I did, and I heard her gasp. Slowly turning to me, she read, "Police Still Looking for Cape Cod Murderer." I think we both got chills. I know I did.

We read the article as we got in the car, and hoped we'd never have to place our feet on the soil of this place again. We drove up to the line waiting for the ferry and didn't have to wait long to drive onto our escape boat to freedom, and back to safety.

We stayed in our car while the ferry hummed us home and, at one point— I don't remember who said what—we began to laugh and then couldn't stop! We were laughing so hard I was actually crying, and Joi kept saying, "Stop, stop, or I'll pee!"

Still giggling, we noticed the boys from the crew smile our way as we drove off the ferry onto the solid, safe soil of Boston Harbor. The laughter felt good. We'd survived *Psycho,* had another adventure to share, and it was a beautiful day. I sighed. It just couldn't get much better than this.

Chapter 14

Home Again

After our Cape Cod escapade, we drove back to New York and stayed at the Buckingham Hotel one more time. Joi called her agent and asked if there was anything happening. He said he'd been trying to reach her to see if she'd do a play in Las Vegas during the Christmas and 1970 New Year's holidays.

The play was Neil Simon's *Come Blow Your Horn*, and rehearsals would be in Los Angeles. Joi would star along with Jackie Coogan and the raspy-voiced comedienne, Selma Diamond, who would be playing the parents. A well-known soap opera star, Bill Hayes, and actor Ron DeSalvo were cast to play the brothers. They wanted Joi to play the "hot little honey" love interest.

She looked at me with a big grin and said, "Let's go to Vegas, okay?"

"Of course!" I replied. This would be fun!

Joi discussed money and accommodation details with her agent and agreed to a salary of $2,750 a week, plus a suite of rooms and all meals. We were both excited about going to Las Vegas and seeing the shows. Rehearsal was due to start in about a month, and we were anxious to go back to Los Angeles to get ready for our next adventure.

Everything was great, and we were due to leave for Los Angeles on a Wednesday. On the Friday before, Joi ran out of her pills and dreaded being unable to sleep. Through a friend of a friend who was a doctor, she was able to obtain a prescription for a new drug called Placidyl. We found out the hard way that Placidyl was a hypnotic, not a regular sleeping pill.

The prescription was for thirty large capsules, which were sealed and filled with liquid, not powder. I was worried. There was absolutely no way I could do my apothecary magic with these things. I could only hope that everything would go well, that she'd take just one capsule and go to sleep.

That was not the case. She slept for a few hours and woke up in a stupor that made her appear very drunk. Although she'd only consumed a small amount of alcohol earlier in the evening, her eyes didn't focus and she was slurring. She got up to look for her bottle of pills, which I had hidden. I kept only one capsule to give her in case she woke up. Agitated, she demanded the bottle. Finally, I was able to calm her down and give her the Placidyl with some water, which she took and went back to bed.

Because I could no longer "adjust" the contents of Joi's pills, I had to find a new place to hide them. I found an area near the corner of the room, away from foot traffic, and cut a slice in the green shag carpeting. I stuffed them in some Kleenex and shoved them under the padding where she'd never find them.

This nightmare lasted for two days. Joi slept for three or four hours, then cried and begged for another pill, so she could get the sleep she desperately needed. I was able to keep the majority of the pills hidden and doled out just enough to keep her from getting angry. This seemed to silence the demons that were torturing her mind.

Finally, the Placidyl wore off, and my Joi girl was back. Like before, she didn't recall anything that had happened. I told her about this new drug, that it was like poison to her, and she started to cry and tell me how sorry she was. I begged her never to take them again, and she agreed—again. I knew it was just too dangerous having pills that I couldn't "doctor" with my little gelatin kit.

We flew out of JFK and into LAX. Stan met us at the airport. He was standing at the gate with his great big smile and big thick cigar hanging from his mouth. He was never without a cigar or pipe. Often he agreed to smoke the pipe because cigar smoke gave me migraines, and he liked a brand called Borkum Riff. The particular blend he liked left a heavy but pleasant aroma. I was used to my own cigarettes, but the overpowering waft of cigar smoke just about choked me. Joi never complained—I guess she was used to it after almost ten years.

When Joi told Stan about the gig in Las Vegas, he was absolutely thrilled! He looked forward to coming on weekends or whenever he could leave his job at Regal Apparel. Since he was their top salesman, he could pretty much write his own ticket. He was the best at what he did, and he knew it.

Joi was happy to see "Hubby," as we both called him, and I think he enjoyed having an imaginary mini-harem, never objecting to being in our company. Going to Las Vegas was going to be a blast, and it gave him bragging rights with all his cronies. I can remember him saying, "My wife, Joi Lansing, is starring in a show in Las Vegas."

Back in our apartment, we had a few weeks before rehearsals began. Joi's mood was good, and her scary alter-ego was hidden in some sad and lonely place in her mind. We enjoyed being home, and our lives were back on track.

Joi loved to go to a park off La Cienega, a little north of Olympic. We'd go there often and have a picnic. She wore little makeup and had her hair up in a bun, so no one would recognize her. We'd sit on a blanket and talk for hours. I'd write prose to her while she lay with her head on my lap, watching the birds flying from tree to tree. She loved birds, and Stan and I both called her "the Birdie." She was like a little bird with a broken wing no one could see.

We needed to get ready for our big trip, and the first thing that concerned Joi was being in Las Vegas without enough pills. It was time to see Ted, the pharmacist, and she promised she just needed something for sleep. Her fear of insomnia controlled her, so back on Melrose to the pharmacy we went.

It was a very small pharmacy that relied on two doctors who had offices in his building. They would call him with prescriptions whenever a patient needed medications, and they worked together as a team. I don't know whose back was scratched, but I think it was the doctor duet.

Joi asked him for her new favorite sleep medication, the red and blue capsule, Tuinal. Ted called one of the doctors who authorized ninety capsules, a three-month supply. She also needed her Premarin prescription refilled. Ted kept renewing the script for her estrogen, even though the initial prescription was written many years ago. She had occasional episodes of asthma, too, so he gave her Pyribenzamine to control it.

She told him about the doctor she saw in New York who said she probably had fibroids. She was losing a lot of blood every month, and now it was giving her diarrhea. Ted suggested that Lomotil would help with this problem, and advised her to see a doctor as soon as she could.

Rehearsals for the play were being held in a one-story walkup on Wilshire near the Carnation ice cream factory. I knew exactly where it was, just a little past Lou Ehler's Cadillac. We'd driven in this area many times.

As we drove by the Caddy dealership, Joi zeroed in on a white 1969 Eldorado with a black convertible top. She had never dreamed she could own a beautiful luxury car like this one, and no one could ever call Joi "high maintenance." She didn't even like shopping and rarely bought anything for herself, except costumes and accessories for her nightclub act. She was one of the very few glamorous Hollywood stars who didn't indulge herself.

One afternoon, after rehearsal, I encouraged her to go by the dealership and take a look at the car. She was nervous about it, but thought it would be fun to test drive a new car, so we drove her Chevy Malibu convertible onto the lot and asked to drive "that car." The Manager recognized her and just gave her the keys, letting us drive it without a salesman to ruin our fun.

She grabbed the keys, and we jumped in and took off, staying off Wilshire and taking the side streets. She'd gun the engine and floor the gas pedal; we'd take off like a rocket for about a block, and then she'd slam on the brakes. I think if she could have popped a wheelie, she would have! I had never seen her have so much fun.

This was it! She had to have her own Cadillac. She could afford it; that wasn't a problem. We drove back to the lot, and she told the Manager she was trading in her car and to get the paperwork ready. It took very little time, and we were set. She drove all through Hollywood, taking Sunset Boulevard most of the way, a cruisy type of street where everyone looks at each other at stoplights. She was struttin' her stuff and having a great time doing it!

Buying the Cadillac was one of the best things Joi could have done for herself. She was finally beginning to feel deserving of love and kindness... and a shiny new car.

Chapter 15

Come Blow Your Horn

Rehearsals ended, and it was time to get ready to go. Joi decided to fly to Las Vegas, instead of driving her new car. She knew it would be safe in the parking garage of our apartment. We would probably be spending most of our time at the Thunderbird Hotel, and, if we wanted to go to any of the other hotels, a cab was a fast and cheap way to get there. If Stan came to visit, she could always rent a car. We were scheduled to be there for almost two months. This was going to be the trip we would never forget.

Joi had appeared at the Fremont Hotel a few years before, but it wasn't one of the A-list hotels on the Strip. She was hoping that, by getting more exposure in a play, other stage opportunities would evolve. One of her great dreams was to appear on Broadway, and this might be the vehicle to get her there. When she was working at the Fremont, she was doing her nightclub act and singing two and three shows a night.

The great part about being in this play was that she had time to rest in between some of the scenes, and we could have dinner in between shows. There was a two-hour break between performances, which made this an easy gig.

Hubby Stan took us to the airport in Joi's car and dropped us off in front of the terminal. He hugged us both, and, as he was driving away, we could see him drop the top to the convertible. All he had to do was push a button, and it folded into an area behind the backseat. Joi knew he was on his way to have some fun. Stan had his own convertible (a metallic gold 1967 Buick Electra with a manual top that took more than a few minutes to lower), but it wasn't nearly as nice as hers.

Stan was probably going to pick up one of his girlfriends and show her the town. He occasionally dated, but never seriously, and being married to Joi was to his advantage. He didn't want to remarry, and this was the perfect foil. If they divorced, that would also end the bragging rights that he had enjoyed for all these years.

Joi didn't want a divorce, either. Although our relationship was secure, marriage was not an option for us, and Joi's marriage deflected any rumors that might ensue. "She's a married woman—there's no way she could possibly be gay!" It worked for all of us.

When we arrived at the Las Vegas airport, it seemed so much larger than I remembered from the two times I'd been there in the past. It had only been a few years, but the city had grown, and there were new high-rise hotels that changed the skyline. The new Hilton International Hotel was the biggest and the best in 1969. There were a lot of big stars appearing while we were there, and one of the biggest stars in the world was playing at the International—Elvis Presley, the King.

I noticed the names of the headliners as we drove down the Strip in the limo sent by our hotel—James Brown: The Godfather of Soul, Ike and Tina Turner, Liberace, Vic Damone, Lainie Kazan, Totie Fields, Steve and Eydie Gormé, Anthony Newley, and many others. I had been in Herbie Palestine's limo, but it wasn't as fancy nor did it light up inside with twinkle lights like this big black stretch Lincoln. It was like Mardi Gras inside the car. We were in Las Vegas, the town of excess, and we were loving it!

As we drove closer to the Thunderbird, I saw Joi's name up in lights, and I tapped her on the arm and pointed, so she would see it. She jumped up and down in her seat like a schoolgirl at her first prom! The only thing missing was a carnation corsage!

The driver swung our monstrous vehicle as wide as he could into the portico to avoid wiping out the milling pedestrians at the entrance to the driveway. Then, he pulled up to the massive front swinging glass doors and motioned for the Bell Captain. Four bellmen removed our bags, and security surrounded us as we walked into the lobby. We were escorted to the front desk where Joi was handed a large manila envelope that held our two room keys and a stack of neatly typed papers with everything she needed to know about her first rehearsal on their stage.

We had a few days until opening night and had every intention of enjoying ourselves to the max. We planned to see a few shows and dazzle the city. Joi had brought some of her hottest dresses and, as luck would have it, they fit me, too. She thought the most fun would be to see Elvis, and I agreed. We rested for a few hours and then got ready for our night on the town.

I helped her get dressed and put electric rollers in her twenty-four-inch long human hair fall. Her own hair had been thinning and was not long enough for the effect she wanted. She didn't know why she was losing some of her hair and decided to see a doctor about it when we returned to Los Angeles. The hairpiece fit just behind her Veronica Lake dip in the front, was very full, and matched her color perfectly, even down to the Tempting Taffy rinse she used on her own hair.

Working on the fall reminded me of an evening out that Joi and I had shared soon after we met. I still lived at the Studio Club, and one of the girls had given me a fall which matched pretty well. I pinned it securely to my own hair, or so I thought, as we went with friends to the Factory, which was THE hot spot for celebrities and wannabes. I thought I was pretty hot stuff as I danced to the frenzied disco beat, swinging my head to the left and right, whipping my hair to the thrum of the music.

Suddenly, as I swung around in a particularly enthusiastic twirl, I felt my fall disconnect and saw it fly about eight feet—right in the face of Peter Lawford! His expression was total shock, and then he started laughing hysterically, as did all those around him. I kept dancing, but far and fast in the other direction! I managed to make my getaway with a lot less of my long blonde tresses, leaving the evidence on the floor in front of this gracious, humorous star. I'll always remember how delighted Joi was with this colorful gaffe, and how hard she laughed as we hurried through the A-list crowd and out the swinging doors!

Joi called the Maître d' at the International Hilton and made reservations for the dinner show in the main room where Elvis was appearing. I finished curling her hairpiece, and she put on her most spectacular evening dress, filling out every inch of fabric. She let me wear one of her other beautiful dresses, and we both looked marvelous!

The only way out of the hotel was through the casino, so we strutted like beautiful peacocks past the slot machines, clanging with lights flashing. As we walked by the one-armed bandits, we noticed that Joi's co-star, Selma Diamond, was seated with a glazed look in her eyes while she pulled the lever. Her ashtray was filled with butts, a cigarette was hanging from her mouth, and it looked like she'd been there for hours. Her voice was raspy and gravelly for a reason—she was a chain smoker.

When Joi said hello, Selma looked up momentarily, nodded, and went right back to her passionate one-armed lover. The casino was filled with people and so much smoke that it started to make us cough. I smoked at the time, but even this was too much for me. Joi had never smoked, and this heavy cloud of dingy gray cigarette entrails was affecting her asthma. We left before she had an attack, breathed the cool winter air of the Nevada desert, and cleared our lungs.

There were, at least, thirty cabs lined up, waiting for high rollers to hire them for the night. We just wanted to go a few blocks to the Hilton. The Cabbie that we chose didn't seem to mind that the fare would be the minimum, so Joi gave him an extra ten dollars for his time. He was very appreciative, making sure that he dropped us as close to the front entrance as possible. He gave her his card and asked that we call him again if we needed a ride. She handed it to me, and we kept it for our next adventure.

 The International Hilton was an amazing edifice, the biggest and grandest hotel I had ever seen. I'd been in the Plaza Hotel in New York with Joi, and it was amazing in its grandeur, but this was Las Vegas elegance. The ceilings were as high as cathedrals and had mirrors reflecting on the gambling tables. Joi explained that there were security people looking through these one-way mirrors, watching every movement of every hand on these tables. There was a tremendous amount of money passing from dealer to gambler, and the house wanted to make sure it got all it deserved.

As we followed a line of people entering the main showroom, a plain-clothes security guard approached and escorted us to the front of the line. The Maître d' smiled as he put his hand out, waiting for a tip. Joi quickly grabbed $20 from her evening purse and slipped it into his hand. Still smiling, he took us to a banquette overlooking the stage, one level up from the main floor, which gave us a better vantage point because the stage was elevated a good ten feet from the floor.

We enjoyed a lovely meal with all of the forks and knives possible on a dining table. As I was never schooled in the art of fine dining, I carefully watched as Joi took each piece of silver in hand. I knew how to eat properly with my mouth closed, but didn't have the faintest idea which fork was for which part of the meal. I managed to be just one beat behind her as she picked up the appropriate instrument. We finished the meal and not one utensil was left. Miss Manners would have been proud.

Suddenly the lights dimmed, and it was show time. I couldn't believe the audience when Elvis appeared on stage. The roar that went up almost shook our table!

Elvis was "on" and, ohhhh my, was he HOT! His white fringed outfit fit like a second skin. He was tall and muscular, dynamic, charming, and had a grin and confidence that melted me. He was amazing. Joi was as taken as I was, I think, but she'd been around so many famous people that she seemed to take that part a little in stride, but we had great fun and the show was terrific.

Chapter 16

On the Town

After the show, almost everyone left the room. Joi had sent a note backstage to Elvis, letting him know she was there and, soon, a security guard came to our table and asked us to follow him to the dressing rooms.

It seemed like we were walking forever as we snaked our way through the catacomb-like halls to the back of the stage. We finally arrived. The ornate, beautifully furnished room was buzzing with people, some sitting, most standing. It seemed the King was holding court. There must have been, at least, twenty worshippers basking in his presence.

Elvis was the closest thing to a god on this planet. He was still fairly young, and no longer had a belly of overindulgence. His involvement with karate had earned him a black belt and a flatter stomach. His act consisted of a choreographed routine of his famous pelvic thrusts along with his newfound karate moves. Women and a few brave or foolhardy men had swooned at his every move.

His hair was a deep brownish-black, and he had lots of it. His trademark sideburns were amazingly perfect on each side of his face. He must have had his own stylist on staff to make sure that every hair was in place—on his head, on his face, and even the hair on his well-defined chest. He was a great male specimen, tall and in perfect proportion.

I looked around the room to see if I recognized anyone, and there, seated on a loveseat in the center of the room was his wife, Priscilla, and next to her, Della Reese. As Joi and I walked in, Elvis immediately walked forward and greeted us, smiling with that famous upturned lip. He was the capital C in the word "charming." Joi quietly said a few words to him and introduced me as her baby sister, Rachel.

Elvis asked us to follow him and then introduced us to Priscilla and Della. I don't know if the two ladies were insecure in Joi's presence or if they were just pre-occupied in conversation, but the effect was the same. The way we were ignored seemed obvious to me, but Joi stayed as gracious as the lady she always was.

We didn't stay long since this was not a meeting of long-lost friends, but just a quick hello from a fellow performer. When it was time to leave, Elvis kissed us both good-bye. I can think of a million women who would have given a body part to be in our place as he kissed us with his soft crooner's lips, and I won't say it wasn't nice having a living Adonis show such sweet affection. He may have noticed how we'd been ignored and wanted to make a point. His kiss was a gentle lightning bolt to me, and one that probably sent a message to Della and Priscilla. They couldn't have been happy with it.

Security took us out the way we came in, then escorted us to the front door where our little cabbie, Jimmy, was waiting. Joi had asked him to come back and pick us up at midnight. He took us back to the Thunderbird, where we coughed all the way through the casino on the way to our room. Obviously just fine with the smoke, Selma was still sitting at the same machine, automatically feeding it quarters as she puffed away on her cigarette. She seemed hypnotized! Pull, puff... pull, puff... pull, puff. Joi didn't bother to say hello as we passed. She knew she wouldn't be heard.

We got to our room and fell on the bed, laughing in delight at all we'd done on our first night in town. It was now our time to be together with no one watching. We could be two women in love without others sitting in judgment. I felt like we were two little girls who'd been lost and had now found one another and would never let go.

Throughout the night and into the late morning, we stayed wrapped in each other's arms. The hours were filled with all the love and passion we felt for each other, and we fell asleep spooning. When the soft light of day filtered through the thick hotel drapes, we woke with sleepy eyes and a glow that true love leaves only for the fortunate few.

We slowly rolled out of bed. It was time to start our day, and we shared one last kiss to start it off right. Caffeine was our drug of choice, and we needed a serious infusion of it. Joi called in our order, and we sat talking in our big fluffy terry cloth robes while waiting for our food to arrive.

I loved room service. Our breakfast was served as usual on a shiny rolling cart with a crisp white tablecloth and a single rose in a clear crystal vase. We ate very slowly, savoring each blueberry, dipping it in fresh cream and light sugar. We were hungry, but didn't want a lot of food—just a dish of fresh berries and croissants and, of course, two pots of coffee. Yum!

After breakfast, Joi began to read the volumes of paper in the manila envelope she'd received when we checked in the day before. According to her schedule, she had a late rehearsal, and, after a few hours, we would again be free for more Las Vegas fun.

Today would be a full dress rehearsal where Joi's microphone would be checked and attached to her costume. The Wardrobe Mistress had come the day before to pick up her costumes and to make sure everything was pressed and in perfect condition. That was one less thing we had to deal with. It was such a pleasure to be part of a professionally managed stage production. I didn't have to carry a sewing kit, just in case Joi's chest spilled over the edge of her low-cut mini-dress. (Gravity and sheer pressure sometimes had a way of creating a costume emergency!)

Rehearsal went exactly as scheduled, with the sound and lighting crews at the top of their game. They were the best in the business, and everyone felt secure that the production would go off without a hitch. Joi knew all her lines, as did everyone in the cast. We'd been practicing a few hours a day since she'd received her script. In fact, I amused to myself; I knew everyone's lines so well that I could have been an understudy!

Joi had brought a change of clothes and, after rehearsal, was out of costume and into her evening wear in record time. It usually didn't take her long to get ready, not like some women who seem to take forever to dress. Looking glamorous was her career, and she had it down to a science. She could get dressed with full makeup and hair in less than a half-hour.

We were both ready to paint the town red when she asked me who I wanted to see. I'd always enjoyed James Brown, the Godfather of Soul, so I suggested his show. Joi agreed, and we were on our way. She'd already called our cabbie, who was waiting patiently by the front door. Jimmy jumped out of the car, opened the back door of his freshly-washed yellow cab, and we were down the drive before you could blink.

James Brown's show at the International Hilton was not far from the T-

Bird, and we arrived in less than ten minutes. Jimmy pulled up to the main entrance, and our door was opened by a young man in a bright red jacket with golden epaulets and white starched pants. We walked through the entrance of yet another massive casino, with the obligatory chandeliers, huge and glistening, hanging precariously from the gilded and mirrored ceiling. The extra-thick plush carpeting was dark cherry red with a golden pathway winding its way past the many blackjack and crap tables. Surrounding the serious gamblers were hundreds of red, white, and blue Triple Seven slot machines. In a quiet corner, the "heavies" were playing baccarat with glowering security guards standing by. I wondered why, and Joi told me that some of these games had a million dollars at stake!

We found the showroom where James Brown was about to perform. The Maître d' had his hand out in exactly the same manner as his counterpart the previous evening. Subtle they were not! Joi placed $20 in his palm, and he graciously showed us to our table. This was an early evening show and only cocktails were served. I was so grateful when Joi ordered a cup of coffee right after I did. Life was going so well, and I knew that any alcohol could ruin the evening, if not the entire trip.

The crowd was ready for a good time, and James Brown's performance was so high energy that I got tired just watching him. His feet didn't stop moving for the entire hour he was on stage, and we found ourselves moving in our seats to the sultry beat of the drums. His face and powder blue suit were drenched with sweat from the hot lights and constant movement of his muscular body. By the time the show was over, the audience was exhausted from the fever pitch of his performance, but "a good time was definitely had by all!"

Like the evening before, Joi told the security people to let Mr. Brown know we were there and would like to say hello. Joi had never met him but wanted me to experience Las Vegas to the max. This was not a big deal for her, but she knew it was very exciting for me. Security came and led us back to the star and his minions.

James was standing in a hip-length red and black brocade smoking jacket over a silky pair of black pants. Huge pieces of gold and diamond jewelry donned both hands and hung around his shiny damp neck. He had a towel across his shoulders to soak up the perspiration, and his assistant kept wiping his face and brow. When he saw us, he smiled and introduced himself to Joi and and asked if we enjoyed the show. Joi said she thought he was amazing and couldn't believe the energy he had. She wanted to know how a human being could keep up that frenetic pace for over two hours a night. He looked her in the eye with a bad boy grin, winked, and said, "It ain't no nickel bag."

Although we laughed with him, neither of us really understood what he was talking about. We were totally "blonde" and clueless. Now, looking back, of course he was experiencing "better living through chemistry" and having one whale of a time doing it!

We stayed for only a few minutes, and then Joi told me her friend Louie Prima was appearing nearby. After we got a bite to eat, she took me to see the show and, afterward, meet him and Keely Smith, his wife and musical partner.

By this time, we were ravenous, and the Sands was known for its delectable Chinese food buffet. The food was copious and as good as we'd heard. Finally, satiated, we headed for our late evening with Louie Prima.

Louie was delighted to see Joi and announced her presence as she walked into the lounge. Everyone applauded and made her feel welcome, treating us like visiting royalty. Louie was a master on his horn. While he played, he watched Joi, and I could tell he was playing just for her. His music filled the casino and made the noisy, clanging room seem romantic and sexy. Lots of percussion and rhythm kept the pulse going, and Keely's smooth voice was the perfect complement to the show. I could hear and see why they were so popular with the LasVegas audiences.

After a few sets, Joi whispered that it was late and she was ready to go. Her show was opening the following evening, and she needed to get some rest. We left to another round of applause, and most of the men stood up and cheered! This does wonders for the ego. We both felt appreciated, even if only for the way we looked.

Tomorrow was going to be a big day. There were always critics and reporters at the opening night of a new show, and everything had to be right on the money. Joi knew the importance of good press and had a great rapport with reporters and photographers. They loved her and gave her great reviews. I think they were surprised that she actually had talent!

Because she was a "blonde bombshell," most people assumed she couldn't have any real ability, but Joi was different. She was a talented comedienne with an uncanny sense of timing, a lovely singing voice, and a commanding stage presence. Walter Winchell, the well-known syndicated columnist and radio commentator, often praised Joi in his column. Since he was never known as effusive, Winchell's kudos meant a lot to Joi's career, and she was always grateful.

Back at our hotel safe and sound, we were escorted to our room by the on-duty security guard. On our way to the elevator, we saw Selma at her "home away from home," the quarter slots. It was déjà vu…yet again. The only thing different were the clothes she wore. The cigarette hanging from the side of her mouth was just where it was the last time we saw her.

Minutes later, we were in bed, Joi's Tuinal kicking in right on schedule. Relaxed, she sighed and snuggled next to me, sleeping like an angel in my arms. We were both grateful for a good night's rest.

The show started exactly on time the following night. (They must have pried Ms. Diamond from her Lucky Sevens in time for her entrance!) I stayed in Joi's dressing room while she was on stage, ready to help with her hair and three costume changes when she rushed in between scenes. The play lasted about an hour and a half, including a short intermission, and the audience absolutely loved it! *Come Blow Your Horn* was a smashing success!

Congratulatory telegrams to Joi came from all over the country. Her mother, Virginia, even sent a telegram addressed to both of us. I had met her a few times when we were in Los Angeles when she'd come to visit Joi at her apartment. Even then, though rather cool with Joi, she was very gracious to me. I don't think she ever suspected the depth of our relationship, but was happy that Joi had a friend to keep her company.

Joi had a hard time being on the road and had called her mother a few times when she was depressed and under the influence of barbiturates. Virginia seemed to feel a sense of relief that Joi was not alone, and that she could perhaps relinquish some of her parental responsibility now that I was in the picture.

Even though they had little in common except the same gene pool, Joi loved her mother very much. That she'd bothered to send a telegram meant a lot to her daughter, and I was glad she'd taken the time to do it.

Come Blow Your Horn went like clockwork every evening, two shows a night. We had the routine down and could do it by rote. The reviews were consistently good. Joi was twice on the cover of the entertainment magazine section of the *Las Vegas Sun* newspaper, uncommon in this town where good publicity is pure gold.

The *Sun* had used several of the photos Maurice Seymour took of her while we were in New York. They chose two of these photos for their covers and another much more seductive shot for an inside ad. The third one caused quite a stir—a side view of Joi holding her black see-through blouse that barely covered the fullness of her breasts. Being almost nude from the waist up was apparently shocking, even in Las Vegas, which had its own special sense of morality and propriety. Shocking or not, it was one of the most popular pictures the paper had ever used. Joi's career, at least, in this land of sand, sex, and stars, was definitely booming!

Before the show's run was over, Joi's mother and brother Larry came to visit. Then, my parents decided they'd come, too. What a dance that was for us! My parents had no idea about our true relationship, at least, consciously. They seemed hopeful that Joi would be my mentor and help me break into the business, which I couldn't have cared less about at that point. I was happily wearing Joi's ring and carrying her name, the closest to marital bliss we were allowed by law.

Considering how far attitudes have evolved, it's odd to look back at those times and realize how much stress was added to our lives because of how things were. At the beginning of the 1970s, being gay or living in a homosexual relationship was far from acceptable. If known, it would have instantly ruined Joi's career, and that just couldn't happen. I wasn't about to tell my parents because they were very "old school" in their attitudes. The truth would only have been hurtful for everyone. They thought our relationship was mutually beneficial and treated Joi like a daughter. I do sometimes wonder, though. They must have felt the love we had for each other, but nothing was ever said or discussed.

Joi's handsome brother Larry was young, just a few years older than I was. He was going through an ugly divorce at the time and having a rough time dealing with his situation. Joi wanted to help him relax and have some fun, so she invited him to visit, then totally shocked me when she told him about our relationship! I didn't think she would ever tell anyone in her family. Larry was very sweet about it, and he then became like a brother to me. As a result, I felt even more secure in my love for this beautiful, special woman.

The only person who hadn't come to visit yet was Stan. He'd been so busy at work that he hadn't been able to get away. It was now almost New Year's Eve, and no one was working, so this was his opportunity to catch a flight and spend a few days of R&R. We rented a car and drove to the airport to pick him up.

Having the Hubby there made Joi happy. Stan held a certain spot in her heart that gave her a sense of security. One of the main reasons our relationship worked was because I understood her need for him in her life and wasn't jealous or intimidated. Loving Joi as I did, I didn't want to take away anything or anyone from her life—only to add to it, never to diminish.

We all wanted to see Tina Turner. Stan loved her music and phenomenal energy, as did Joi and I. We decided to see Tina's early performance and then catch Liberace's second show, a perfect combination. Tina would get us all amped up, and Lee would put us to sleep!

The next night, we went to see Totie Fields, an old friend of Joi's. Seeing Joi walk in, Totie immediately introduced her, and the applause was enthusiastic. A very funny lady, Totie had the audience turning purple from laughter.

Totie's impression of Joi was hysterically funny, as she strutted around the stage with her back arched and her chest protruding. Joi especially appreciated her wit and delivery. Always a good sport, she laughed at the portrayal and clapped and cheered right along with the rest of the audience.

Chapter 17

Fears & Cheers

After *Come Blow Your Horn* closed, we decided to stay on another couple of weeks to continue our good times. Unfortunately, Joi came down with "Vegas throat," a common ailment for singers and entertainers because of the dry desert air. She developed a terrible case of laryngitis, and the house doctor was called in to see her. It wasn't just a vocal problem, but blossomed into a raging infection in her sinuses and throat. He put her on antibiotics, and she was suite-bound for almost a week.

This put a damper on our "star-mingling" pursuits, but the Manager of the Thunderbird was sympathetic and extended our stay for another week. He even comped our room while she was ill. The Doctor thought there might be something else going on with her, though, and suggested she see her personal physician when she returned home.

Joi was experiencing a lot of pain in her right breast. She had hoped the cortisone Dr. Rish had injected would soften the breast and ease her discomfort. So far, it hadn't done much of anything on either count. She asked the Hotel Doctor if he knew anyone in town who did silicone injections, and he gave her the name and phone number of the local "pumping" doctor who injected many of the showgirls and exotic dancers.

One day, the pain was making her so miserable that she called and made an appointment for later that afternoon. Joi didn't want anyone to know she was seeing a doctor who was well-known in town for creating big breasts. She didn't want snide comments or rumors flying around about her. No one, so far, had questioned whether her boobs were real or fake, and she wanted to keep it that way.

We took a cab from a different company, not wanting Jimmy to find out about our trip to "Dr. Hooters." Las Vegas was a small town in the early 1970s, and a juicy story about Joi would have traveled fast. It's not that she didn't trust Jimmy, just concerned he might accidentally slip while hanging out with his buddies.

We made it to the medical office right on time. There were no nurses or other office workers, only two doctors waiting to see her. One was middle-aged with a thick head of salt and pepper hair; the other was a considerably younger man who wore thick wire glasses and appeared to be doing his plastic surgery residency. Both were very professional in attitude, having obviously seen many a lovely who brought their breasts to that office.

The younger man had a clipboard and took voluminous notes while the "silicone expert" poked and prodded Joi's breasts. She told him about the cortisone injections, and the younger doctor shook his head while questioning the reason for them. I could tell he found this disturbing. He mentioned that more and more women were electing to have silicone breast implants, rather than injections, and asked if she had considered having this surgery.

I could see Joi was becoming uneasy, and I saw her shrink at the thought of what he might be suggesting. He said he was a little concerned by the way her nipple was retracting and inverting under the areola.

To Joi, her breasts defined who she was professionally. They were her image in Hollywood and in the business in general. She could not conceive of being without her trademark cleavage. Just the hint that there might be a problem and that she could possibly need surgery was unfathomable to her. She skirted his concern and suggestion and changed her focus to the older Doctor.

He was the silicone man, the doc with the platinum needle. Puffing out his chest, he bragged about all of the exquisitely large breasts he had created. He was proud of his work and the new and better formula he had blended to prevent future hardening of the tissue. He examined her carefully and dismissed his minion before the young man could muck things up any more than he already had.

After the resident left the room, the Doctor told her there was "absolutely nothing to be concerned about." He said that her breast would soften with a little more cortisone injected and the use of a topical cream he would blend for her. He assured her that it would "eventually go back to its normal shape." Those were the words Joi wanted desperately to hear. She didn't want to hear about implants and surgery and an inverted nipple or anything negative about her breasts. Her entire life and career revolved around her sex appeal to men, and they loved her voluptuous figure. After all, she was Joi Lansing, the sex symbol.

After numbing the area with xylocaine, the Doctor injected cortisone throughout her breast. He then applied a thin, whitish cream he'd blended with what appeared to be estrogen and progesterone. He filled a plastic jar with his concoction and told her to apply it twice daily and then apply a hot pack to help it absorb into the skin. This magic potion, he assured her, would take care of the problem.

We left with a heavy pall hanging over our heads. Neither of us spoke. The young Doctor had struck a nerve, and Joi didn't like what she'd heard. This was the one thing that she *would* never, *could* never face emotionally. Those shots better work…they had to work! There was no other option in her mind. She would do everything he told her to do, and do it religiously. She would apply the cream and put on a hot pack. She would be a "good girl" and do as she was told. Sure, she'd do what she was told, as long as what she was told was what she wanted…and needed…to hear.

On our ride back to the hotel, I began some small talk to try to diffuse the unsaid words that haunted us both. Where would we eat tonight? Chinese again? Maybe Italian or that new buffet Joi had heard about? The ride went on forever, and I was almost sick to my stomach with fear…fear that I would never be able to express to anyone. Especially not to my Joi.

When we got to our room, we noticed the little red light on the phone was flashing. Joi wasn't expecting any calls. She called Stan in the evenings; he rarely called her. Joi said it might have been the other Stan, her agent. *Please, please let this be good news*, I remember thinking.

She was right. It was Stan Scottland from New York. He had just received a call from the Booking Agent at the Sahara Hotel, saying that Lainie Kazan had Vegas throat and couldn't go on as scheduled the following evening. They knew Joi was still in town and asked if she'd be able to fill in for Lainie. It would only be for two performances and a rehearsal with the house orchestra that afternoon. They would pay her a thousand dollars for the gig, and assured her that Ms. Kazan and the hotel would be eternally grateful.

When she got off the phone and told me what he said, we both jumped around like the little girls we were inside at that moment. Gone was the weight of the afternoon, and up, up and away we were going! Dinner tonight would be a real celebration, not the wake I was so afraid it might have been. I had never felt such gratitude in my life. Things were going to be good again.

Filling in for Lainie would not be difficult. It was the last-minute request that Joi knew could be complicated. All of her musical arrangements were in Los Angeles. Even if she had them, they were for a small band, not a full orchestra. She needed to get them there immediately, so the Conductor, at least, would have something to work with. I could see her wheels working.

Professional to the core, she quickly called Stan at work and asked him to get her expandable leather music bag from her apartment and put it on a plane. He'd done this for her in the past and knew the drill. He told her he'd take care of it and would let her know when and where to have it picked up.

Then, I guess he thought about it for a minute and decided to surprise her and bring it himself! He'd never seen her sing with a full orchestra and thought it would be a wonderful experience. He left work, went straight to the apartment, found the bag, and then jammed in rush-hour traffic to his ranch-style home in Woodland Hills. Stan was living the good life, and he could now add that his "wife was performing at the Sahara in Vegas." The Thunderbird was a good hotel, but didn't have the status of the Sahara. This was hot stuff, and he couldn't wait to pack his bag and go to the airport.

Stan and Joi's music bag were in Las Vegas within five hours after Joi made her call. He grabbed a cab and went straight to our hotel. There was a knock on the door, and, when I answered it, there he was with her music in tow and a beaming grin. She saw him and yelled, "Hubby, Hubby!"

He hugged her and said, "The Birdie is going to be a big star at the Sahara!"

She laughed and did her little Birdie dance, jumping up and down in place like a happy child. Joi had been a little apprehensive about singing with a full orchestra without really having sufficient prep time, but she was a trouper and had to try. Though she was confident in her ability as a singer and performer, it would be a challenge without the tools of her trade. She really needed arrangements for a lot more pieces, but that wasn't going to happen.

We went to the rehearsal and brought the arrangements for ten of her songs. She had an opening medley of tunes that was peppy and would get things moving. Joi liked to start with upbeat arrangements and then work up to the ballads. She'd sung these songs hundreds of times before and knew her act by rote. Two of her favorite standbys were "The One I Love Belongs to Somebody Else" and "The Web of Love."

Joi had recorded three of her songs for a company named Scopitone, which started the first music videos that played on a special type of jukebox. Joi was one of the first singers contracted to perform on this new type of media, an audio/video machine. It became pretty popular, and a lot of well-known musical artists soon jumped on the bandwagon.

On that night, however, Joi was not doing a lounge act or a Scopitone. She was appearing in the main showroom of one of the hottest hotels on the Las Vegas Strip, and this was going to be the highlight of her career as a singer.

The Conductor of the orchestra seemed delighted with her. She was easy to work with and had no temper tantrums or diva delusions. She was thrilled to be working with him, and he was appreciative of her trust in his ability to make it work. He told her not to worry—that once the guys rehearsed her music, they would be able to work without sheet music.

Her arrangements were like the scaffolding that supported Michelangelo as he painted the Sistine Chapel. The Conductor just needed the basic melody, and from that he could create beautiful music with the masterful support of his musicians. He handed out the five-piece arrangements to the vital instruments. She had sheet music for piano, bass, drums, and a few horns. Never in her wildest dreams did she imagine that she would need music for ten violins, a viola, and a triangle!

Joi had brought one of her nightclub costumes, a strapless, floor-length black gown with striking, almost luminous black beads that had been sewn on individually. It looked as if it had been painted on her body as it molded itself to every voluptuous curve. She was breathtaking!

It was time for the show, and we were backstage in Lainie's dressing room preparing for Joi's debut. I put the electric rollers in her fall as she did the finishing touches to her makeup. She could step into her gown, so she didn't have to worry about smearing her lipstick or staining the fabric. She was as beautiful as I had ever seen her, radiant with the excitement of what she was about to do. Mike, the stage manager, rapped on the door saying, "Two minutes, Miss Lansing."

Joi turned to me and winked. "Show time, baby. Let's go."

The lights had dimmed as we stepped into the wings. I stayed back a bit, knowing that Joi needed the seconds before she walked out on stage completely to herself. Suddenly the "God voice" of the announcer boomed, telling the audience that Lainie Kazan was ill, but that Miss Joi Lansing had kindly agreed to perform in her place. The audience hesitated just for a moment and then applauded warmly. I could hear their response and was relieved.

I'll never forget that night. Joi walked on to that stage and owned it immediately. The support and sound of the violins and the other string instruments lifted her voice as no music ever had. It had wings, and she sang as she had never sung before! Her performance was flawless, and the audience rewarded her with the kind of acceptance, enthusiasm, and applause she had only dreamed of.

The next day, Joi received rave reviews from the press and a personal "thank you" with gorgeous flowers from Lainie. The night had been one of the happiest of her life, everything she had ever wanted from her career.

I'll always be grateful that I was there with her that night. The magic of those moments with the woman I loved so deeply, watching her face so filled with life and excitement, and hearing her voice become the voice of an angel. I'll never forget it. Or her... my dear, dear Birdie.

Chapter 18

Men at Sea

After Joi's stellar success filling in for Lainie, we stayed a few more days to savor our time in Sin City without sinning! We saw a few more shows, and I learned how to play blackjack with the help of a pit boss at the Thunderbird. Joi had no interest in playing, but stood behind me as I was dealt the cards.

The Pit Boss came over and picked up my cards, looking first at my hand and then the Dealer's. Then, he took chips from the Dealer and bet them for me. It wasn't a lot of money, maybe $20, but I was so excited that I won. It was obviously rigged, but so what? He was smart. Twenty men stood waiting their turn to sit next to Joi and me!

I played a little longer while Joi patiently watched, and then we walked around the casino to try different games. Spotting a roulette table, I put a dollar on black 17. It hit, and I won almost $60! That was the end of my gambling luck, though, as I gave it all back to the house. In the end, I decided I'd much rather be lucky in love than at the tables.

The next morning, it was time to leave and go home. After spit-shining his cab and giving each of us a long-stemmed red rose, Jimmy took us to the airport and hugged us good-bye. We promised we'd definitely call him when we came back. Our time in the Entertainment Capital of the World was put to bed as we winged our way back to Los Angeles.

We had an amazing time in LasVegas, but were ready to recuperate and come back to reality. Joi returned to her health regimen, taking her handfuls of daily vitamins and resuming her workout with ten- and twenty-pound dumbbells that toned her upper body muscles. Much more dedicated to exercise than me, Joi was great at sticking with a program and doing it religiously.

This was also true of the way she cared for her skin. With no imperfections or blemishes, her skin had the smooth appearance of vanilla ice cream. Keeping her beauty intact cost her very little money, as she cleansed and moisturized her face with only Oil of Olay. Joi would look at me and the numerous freckles scattered across the top of my cheeks and nose, and tell me I'd better start taking care of my skin or it would dry up by the time I was forty. Unfortunately, though her crystal ball was off by a few years, she was right.

Life was good, and we were both happy. Joi wasn't drinking, and I naively thought it was because she felt more secure in my love. Her bouts of depression seemed to diminish as well.

Joi didn't like being idle and wanted to work. After being at home for a month without a job call, she began to think no one wanted her anymore. She was now forty, and there weren't many "sex goddess" roles being offered.

Just when she started to get really nervous, Stan Scottland called with a guest-starring role for her on a sitcom called *The Governor and J.J.*, with Dan Dailey and Julie Sommars. Joi had worked with Dan before, so this would be like old home week. She jumped at the opportunity and told him to send the contract.

The show was being shot at CBS on Beverly Boulevard, just around the corner from where we lived. She could fall out of bed, roll down the hill, and be there in ten minutes. This was great! She didn't have to fly anywhere, and she didn't have to pack. It was a one-day gig, but it would give her a few bucks, and she'd feel better about her fading career.

The studio sent a script along with the contract which gave us plenty of time to rehearse her lines. She had a great memory, so it wasn't much of an issue. I enjoyed playing opposite her character—acting was always something I loved to do.

The day of the shoot was here before we knew it. She was allowed to wear her own wardrobe, so she wore a white knit mini-dress with a wide red patent leather belt. It was long-sleeved with matching oval red patches on the elbows. Her spike-heeled red patent leather boots were the icing on the cake. She knocked 'em out when she went on the set. Dan loved her outfit and could not take his eyes off her.

Later in life, I had the opportunity to see Dan again. I was working as the day bartender at a women's bar called the Palms on Santa Monica Boulevard. Business during my shift was usually pretty slow as this was a night spot. Since I was the newest kid on the block, I naturally got the crummy shift.

I'd just unlocked the front door at ten o'clock sharp, and was doing prep work for later in the day when the door opened slowly. I was startled because I usually didn't see anyone until around noon.

The bar was quite dark inside, so I could only see a very tall woman in a dress and heels framed by the outside light. As my eyes adjusted to the brightness—and to my great surprise—*Miss* Dan Dailey was walking toward me in full drag! He was wearing a bright red and white polyester shirtwaist dress with a bold floral pattern. The seams on his nylons were unevenly aligned, and his white pumps had a fat heel, much needed to support his two-hundred-plus pound, not-so-girlish figure. A long strand of white plastic pop beads wound twice around his neck and draped across his padded, stuffed bosom. A vision of bad fashion sense, Dan Dailey was dressed to the nines! After adjusting his dress and straightening his nylons, he sat down at my bar.

Dan and I chatted for about an hour over a cup of coffee, and he made no pretense as to who he was. I said I'd met him many years before with Joi, and, though he was gracious, I doubt he remembered me as he said he did. He had a great sense of humor about his little diversion and didn't take himself seriously in the least. He just loved dressing up, and acknowledged he could use a little help with his wardrobe.

He finished his coffee and left a perfect lipstick mark on the rim of his cup as well as a nice tip. That lady was a true gentleman!

Joi's taping went well with only a few retakes, and it was wrapped up in half the time expected. The Director was pleased with her, and the crew was obviously pleased with her dress! Joi was delighted with their attention.

She was always on a natural high when she felt wanted by her chosen profession. This rush would last for a few months until the merry-go-round started again. I watched as she kept trying to grab the brass ring, and comforted her as it continued to elude her.

We were back into our normal, everyday lives after a whirlwind year of excitement. Joi dreaded going to a doctor for help with her terrible periods, and I kept trying to encourage her without nagging. I knew just how far I could push before it would send her into a tailspin, but she finally agreed and made an appointment to see a gynecologist. He did a pelvic exam and suspected endometriosis and possible fibroids, so he took a pap smear and told her he'd notify her if anything unusual came back.

I had agreed to do my turn in the stirrups that day if Joi would do the same. I undressed and put on a gown that didn't close—never understanding what the point was in wearing these stupid things! I was lying on my back, trying to cover strategic areas, when the Doctor walked into the exam room. He moved the gown, exposing one breast at a time, first palpating the left breast. As he moved the gown over the right breast, his face turned beet red! I didn't know what had embarrassed him until I looked down and saw a perfectly placed set of lips embossed around my nipple! I almost laughed out loud. Joi and I had played around a little as we were getting dressed for our appointment, but I hadn't realized she'd left such playful evidence behind!

I was lost for an explanation. At this point, what could I say? So I just smiled. The Doctor finished the exam without a word, and I could see he had a twinkle in his eye and what I was sure was a slight, but approving grin.

Before leaving the office, I showed Joi her lipstick mark, and she started to laugh so hard she almost cried. When she finally regained her composure, she whispered to me she was sure that the Doctor would never forget either of us. I think she was right!

On the way home, I asked how her exam went. She told me about the pelvic exam, and, when I asked what he thought about her breast, she said she didn't have him check it. I got a chill. Joi had not let him examine her breasts because she was afraid he might say something she didn't want to hear. She told him she had recently been checked and, "Everything was just fine."

The truth was that the cortisone injections had done nothing to soften the tissue. Her nipple was becoming more inverted and the symmetry of her breast had started to change. She didn't want to think about it, so she didn't. She said she'd find someone in town who was familiar with silicone to do more cortisone injections, and would "find someone soon," she promised me.

Though a week passed without hearing from the Doctor's office, we weren't really that concerned. We'd been told it could take up to ten days to get pap smear results. I was feeling fine, and Joi had been dealing with these wretched periods for a long time. She'd seen doctors, at least, twice a year, and no one had found anything wrong. The last few she saw were more interested in going out with her, and were too busy putting the moves on her, to take her complaints seriously. Ultimately, she was a victim of her own beauty.

One slow afternoon, Joi called her agent, Stan, and asked if there was anything happening. We were in luck. He'd just received a call from the meeting planner for a large corporation about a three-day cruise out of Miami to Nassau, in the Bahamas. It would be a conference for their top producers, and they wanted to have someone spectacular for their entertainment. Stan Scottland had the perfect client for this soirée. Joi was definitely spectacular, and most importantly, available at the right price—and very excited about doing it!

It was high season in Miami. All the snowbirds had flocked from the Northeast to escape the winter months of shoveling snow and rock salt on the sidewalks. Stan always made sure Joi's contract provided for a first-class plane ticket. He knew I'd be coming along, and she'd turn it in and get two tickets in coach. This way, it didn't cost her anything extra to bring along her "little sister."

Joi thought it would be fun to fly into town a few days early, so I could see Miami Beach. She had old friends living in the Florida Keys and wanted me to meet them. Larry Matthews and his wife lived in New York most of the year and had a winter home in the Keys. We had missed them while we were in New York.

The Larry Matthews Salon was a wonderful blend of all flavors of humanity. You would see Broadway stars and junkies and exotic dancers and drag queens. The salon was a destination that only New Yorkers knew about, which Joi discovered years ago when she appeared in her nightclub act at the Copacabana. With her insomnia and habit of sleeping late during the day, she had to find a place that was open at night. We went there a few times late at night to have Joi's roots colored, since her hair was a natural light brown and peroxide was a monthly necessity. She had met Larry and his wife at the salon, and they had remained friends all these years.

It was time for us to pack. Joi opened the suitcases, lay them on the bed, and started tossing skirts and blouses, slacks and dresses. In keeping with our usual custom, whatever landed in the suitcases went with us, and what didn't, stayed! We'd pack a bag until it was stuffed. My responsibility in this production was to sit on it while she snapped the locks. I weighed more than she did, so my butt got the job!

Being with Joi was like being a little kid with her best friend. At times, we'd laugh and dance around like six-year-olds. Sometimes, it was just for fun, but other times, it was like we were holding on to the innocence of our love. Things could get scary in the life Joi lived, and her fear of time passing so quickly had begun to bother me, too.

I remember one day when I woke up before her. Smiling down at her beautiful sleeping face, I slowly became aware of feeling a terrible, nameless fear. Panicky, I pulled her into my arms, waking her gently. She smiled, eyes still closed. Then, driven by the need to still the shuddering of my frightened heart, I lost myself in our passion as we made sweet morning love.

Joi called Larry and told him we'd be in town for a few days and would be staying at the Fontainebleau Hotel. He said he'd pick us up at the airport, and we could all have dinner that night. Stan took us to the TWA terminal at LAX, and we were on our way!

The skies were friendly for us that day, with only one white knuckle bump. Joi was a seasoned flier, and nothing seemed to rattle her. As for me, the slightest suggestion of bouncing stiffened my spine and made my eyes bug! Joi would take my hand and hold it until the rocking stopped. Luckily, this was an easy flight, and I retained my composure, though dry-mouthed for the entire five hours it took to arrive at our exciting destination.

Larry was waiting at the gate with his pretty, friendly wife at his side. They seemed like a lovely couple, and I could see how Joi would consider them friends. They took us to the hotel by the scenic route through the city. Everything was beautiful, especially the reflection of the white high-rises on the blue of the ocean. Miami Beach looked like a glossy picture postcard, pristine and opulent, with endless rows of yachts moored and bobbing in their slips near the hotels.

The evening was fun and going well...that is, until the "lovely" Mr. and Mrs. Matthews started drinking and tossing verbal digs at each other. Joi and

I had no idea what was going on with the two lovebirds, just that things were starting to get ugly. Wifey ran out of the dining room, but not before she threw her mink coat at me! She shrieked a few words of profanity at her husband, and told him she didn't want that "fucking coat" and to let his "girlfriends have it." Unbeknown to us (at least before this moment), we were not just their guests, but nicely dressed, glamorous bones of contention as well!

Unquestionably, Larry's wife was not pleased with him. He was visibly embarrassed, and apologized for her tantrum while hastily excusing himself to run after her.

All eyes were on us as we were left holding a raven black, full-length mink coat in the middle of a dining room filled with crisp white tablecloths, crystal glasses, and sterling silver flatware—and several dozen elegant guests to enjoy it all. This was a quintessential case of "being left holding the bag."

Heads high, we walked out of the restaurant like the ladies that we were. I carried the coat draped over my shoulders as if it were mine. It was a fun and short-lived fantasy of having a coat similar to Joi's. Hers was a blonde color that matched her hair, and this one looked especially nice on me....

Larry called the following morning and said he'd be right over to pick up the coat. (Oh, well! Easy come, easy go!) As if the debacle of the night before had never occurred, he said nothing about the outburst as Joi handed over the mink— just that he hoped we'd "all get together again after the cruise." (Yeah, right!)

Later that morning, we arrived at the ship with our bags and suitcases. Oddly, we realized we were awash in a sea of men. Just men. No one had told us we'd be the only females on the cruise! There were hundreds of corporate types in knee-length walking shorts and short-sleeved polo shirts. The officers and crew were in starched white uniforms and spit-shined shoes, with nary a waitress or cabin girl among them!

We were taken to our cabin, which was the size of a jail cell. It had a tiny porthole and two beds on opposite walls that were even smaller than twin beds. We could tell this was not exactly the honeymoon suite, but the cruise was only for three days. Because we were good sports, we thought we could tolerate staying in a room that was barely one step up from a brig.

The first officer, Mr. Everett, came to our room to welcome us. He apologized for the bare-bones accommodations and hoped it wouldn't be intolerable. The corporation that booked the ship needed all the rooms, and the only sleeping room available was in steerage with the rest of the crew! We weren't aware of ship-to-shore communication, so we had no way to reach Joi's agent and, besides, with an earth (or sea) shaking groan, the ship was leaving port. Little did we know what an unforgettable three days lay ahead!

Joi was hired to do two performances—one on the first night and the next on the second. We were on our way to Nassau and would be able to leave the ship for half a day when we arrived. (The thought of jumping ship had occurred to us, but we thought better of it.) After all, we kept telling each other, it was "only three days."

The first night's performance went well, and the audience was respectful and appreciative. They'd been in seminars all day from practically the moment we left Miami that morning to dinner time that evening. They were starting to relax and seemed to be enjoying themselves. The evening was pleasant.

We arrived in Nassau the following morning after a somewhat sickening night. We'd felt every wave sloshing loudly against the hull and, though we valiantly fought the urge to vomit, we were not very successful.

Pulling into the dock, the welcome call from *terra firma* was like a siren's song. Joi and I put on matching Bermuda shorts and modest tops to go ashore. The smell of testosterone was starting to overpower the ship, so we tried to be as nondescript as possible—very little makeup and sunglasses to cover our eyes, but it was not easy to go unnoticed when we were both blonde and female!

We enjoyed each step on the quaint streets of this colorful island. Joi spotted a cigar shop and bought a box of Havana stogies for the Hubby. He liked the shorter, fat cigars, and she knew he'd be thrilled with them.

Next, we found a few little Bahamian souvenirs and a couple of navy blue T-shirts with "Nassau" written in white on the front. There was nothing else we really wanted to buy, and, besides, we didn't have a lot of time to shop. We stopped at a small sidewalk café for a snack and listened to local reggae musicians with their amazing steel drums. We could have stayed for hours enjoying the music, but time was passing, our abbreviated cultural experience was over, and we had to get back to the ship.

Not wanting to walk shoulder to shoulder with a bunch of partygoers, we hurried back before the throngs of men reboarded. Since there were no more obligatory meetings or educational seminars, this was their first taste of freedom. It was their turn to have some fun now, and they were obviously going to make the best of their vacation.

That evening, Joi went on stage at seven o'clock to perform her second and last show of the cruise. The band started playing her intro music as she walked on singing, but the seated male audience began whooping and hollering as soon as she stepped on stage. Their raucous hoots drowned out the music. It seems they'd been drinking in the local bars all afternoon while they were on land, and to say they were drunk would be a colossal understatement.

Joi tried to sing above their screaming and whistling, but they muffled every musical note with their mindless ribaldry. Seeing this as an exercise in futility, Joi walked off the stage.

Never in her entire career had Joi prematurely ended a performance, but this disgusting, unruly crowd made it impossible to continue. Mr. Everett, the first officer, had seen what was happening and rushed back to walk us to our tiny cabin. He didn't like the change in mood that pulsed through the noisy room and was concerned for our safety. He told us not to leave our room until he came to escort us off the ship the following morning. The ship was due back in Miami around eleven o'clock, and we were scheduled to disembark soon after.

The crew was on alert and had been told to stop serving alcohol, but apparently many of the passengers had bought bottles of Jamaican rum and brought them on board. Now, they had their own booze and continued drinking far into the night.

For hours, crashing and banging and shouted obscenities kept us from sleeping. We wedged our suitcases under the door knob, hoping to keep the raging beasts away from us. Holding hands, we nervously watched out of our porthole at what seemed like hundreds of objects being thrown overboard. We were barely able to make out another ship way off in the distance, but thought we could see a red cross on the port side.

Dawn was not that far off, and we were almost beginning to get used to the thuds and slams and yells, when suddenly the force of fists banging and bodies slamming against our tiny cabin door sent us into one another's arms. We fell to the floor and huddled against the wall opposite the entrance to what had now become our fortress.

Again and again, the men hit the door with their fists, yelling Joi's name the whole time. We were terrified and crying, but kept as quiet as we could, not wanting them to know we were inside. There was no doubt what would happen to us if these maniacs got in the room. How strong could the door be? This was just a closet!

I honestly can't remember exactly when the noise stopped. Eventually, I guess, the drunks got tired and went someplace else to pass out. I only know we spent the rest of the night holding on to one another for dear life.

The light of day could not have come any sooner for us after our night of hell on the high seas. Mr. Everett knocked on our door, but we were too afraid to open it. Kindly, he assured us again and again that it was safe to unlock the door. I unwedged the luggage and slowly opened the door in case I needed to slam it shut again. But he'd spoken the truth and was standing there, ragged and obviously exhausted. It was finally safe, and we could come out.

Apparently, by staying quiet, we had perhaps saved our own lives. Mr. Everett told us the gang had gone from door to door looking for Joi and her "little sister." We were lucky they didn't know which room we were actually in.

The crazed mob had then tried to commandeer our ship to take them to the hospital ship we had seen out of our porthole. They knew there were nurses on board, and, in a drunken rage at not being able to get to them, they had cruelly raped a cabin boy. The crew finally contained them and locked some of the more violent cretins in their rooms. No question, we were truly lucky to have survived the "lovely Bahamian cruise" unscathed and alive to talk about it.

We heard that many corporate heads had rolled because of the lack of security and planning, but, in the end, there was never any press about the violent, terrifying weekend. Joi and I never spoke to anyone about it. We didn't want to relive this nightmare, and those were the days when celebrities were expected to keep their mouths shut. Everyone was kept in the main meeting room while we left the ship. The crew detained them while the Miami Police Department came on board.

Exhausted, we took a limo that was waiting for us to the Eden Roc Hotel where we'd decided to stay for a few more days. We were sick from lack of sleep and just wanted time to forget. Joi had offered a deal to the Manager to exchange one performance for three days of accommodations and meals, and he was more than happy to oblige.

We slept for the first day and night and were feeling better by the following morning. Joi woke with a smile and pulled me close. She had never held me so tightly, and I saw her eyes begin to tear. She said she'd been so afraid something was going to happen to me. Soon, we were both sobbing in relief, holding and rocking one another.

Looking back, I realized we had escaped the wacko in Cape Cod and now the corporate marauders of the high seas. Our guardian angel had scooped us up and carried us away from both—just in the nick of time.

As promised to the Manager, Joi appeared in the hotel showroom with a five-piece combo. The audience was filled with little old ladies and gentlemen from New York and New Jersey, retirees who were there for the winter. She sang to them with an open heart and gave them all she had to give. The "oldies but goodies" couldn't show enough appreciation, and the night was great fun. The music and warm feelings were like cool water on a hot day, and we both just soaked it up.

We took it easy for a few more days and were then ready to go back to Los Angeles. The stress and terror we'd endured on the ship had taken its toll on Joi, and she began to have a terrible pain in her belly. It wasn't a dull ache, which she was used to with her period, but a piercing pain that made her gasp. The pain didn't last very long, but was sharp enough for her to want to see her doctor.

She called Hubby from the hotel and asked him to pick us up the following day. After taking an early morning flight, we arrived around one in the afternoon, California time. Stan's smile, when he met us at the gate, was a welcome sight.

Joi had taken one of the Cuban cigars out of its wooden box and stashed it in her purse. After hugging Stan, she handed him the cigar with a big grin, knowing this rolled-up leaf of tobacco would delight him. She'd also bought him a cigar cutter, which he used to snip off the tip. Then, savoring the moment, he slowly lit the cigar with one of the stick matches he carried in his gentleman's leather shoulder bag. Hubby was indeed a happy man, and this pleased Joi very much.

We left the airport and got into Joi's pretty new car. Stan had driven it more than Joi, and now it was her turn. She made him sit in the back while he puffed away, and, winking at me beside her, she started the car and dropped the top.

Her smile was bigger than I'd seen in a long time. It said, "Hang on, Hollywood! Here I come!" A laughing "Lady Andretti" peeled out of the airport parking lot! Whoooooooeeee, what a ride! The airport was usually a little over forty-five minutes from our apartment, but this time we made it home in under thirty.

Watching Joi as she talked excitedly to Stan while carrying her makeup case into our home, I found myself smiling and thinking, *Good times are back.*

You cannot know how deeply I wish this had been true....

Chapter 19

Paradise Lost

We were glad to be back in our apartment and started to unpack our luggage. Joi had the hottest pink suitcases I'd ever seen. She didn't especially like the color, but she never had to worry about confusing them with somebody else's bag at the airport. We could spot them thirty feet away from the carousel! Now they would be put away in the closet until our next trip out of town.

Joi had stacks and stacks of unopened mail waiting for her on the dining room table. Along with the usual bills, the studios forwarded fan mail to her whenever they received it. Though she had a publicist who handled a lot of her correspondence, her fan mail was bundled and sent to her on a regular basis. I took care of answering the mail and sending out her autographed 8 x 10 glossy photos.

A few fan letters were mixed in with the other white envelopes, but rather hidden in the stack was a postcard from the Doctor she had recently seen. Something was printed on the back. I picked it up and looked at it quickly while Joi was in the kitchen making lunch for us. It said her pap smear had shown some "abnormalities," and requested she come in for retesting.

Nervous, I knew too well how she would react if she saw this. She could go into one of her depressions and start drinking again, along with taking pills. I also knew she wouldn't go back to the Doctor if she saw what was written on the card. I had to make sure she followed up on the pap smear results, but had to give her a reason she could handle. I slipped the note into my pocket just as Joi came back into the room.

She asked if there was anything from the Doctor, and I knew better than to say "yes." I lied and said I hadn't seen anything, but I felt we should go back since she had that awful pain in her belly. She thought about it for a few minutes and then agreed. If there was a serious problem, we would deal with it after we knew for sure. But, for now, since her mind would have gone to the worst case scenario, I had to make certain she didn't suspect anything. As long as she agreed to go to the Doctor, that was all that mattered to me.

When I called, the receptionist said the next available appointment was almost two weeks away. I couldn't make a big deal about it because Joi was standing right next to me, so I made the appointment and asked that Joi's name also be put on a waiting list for a cancellation. Joi didn't mind the delay, but I was nervous.

One evening, Joi decided she wanted to take a long, relaxing bath. I ran the water for her, put in bath oil and bubble bath just the way she liked it, and made sure the water was just the right temperature. She loved having me keep her company, so I sat on the floor next to the tub while she soaked. She stayed in the water for, at least, a half hour.

When she'd had enough, I got her towel and began to gently wrap it around her shoulders. That was when we both noticed some strange, slightly elongated bumps on her body. There were quite a few below her breasts and underneath her arms. Then we found more of these pecan-sized, pinkish lumps in her groin area. Neither of us had ever seen anything like it.

Joi nervously raised her hand to her head, then almost as if she was talking to herself, she whispered, "Rachel, they're here, too."

My mouth went dry, and I suddenly felt sweaty. She couldn't wait two weeks to see a doctor. This "whatever it was" couldn't wait for two weeks!

Perhaps slipping yet again into denial, Joi decided she wanted to see a dermatologist instead of going back to the Doctor she had just seen. She was more concerned about the bumps on her head than the ones on her body. I wasn't happy with her decision, but, at least, she was willing to go to a doctor, even if it wasn't the one I thought she should see. Although I only knew basic anatomy, I was pretty sure the swellings were where her lymph nodes should be. I didn't say anything, but had a terrible feeling in the pit of my stomach.

A friend gave her the name of a dermatologist, and Joi called for an appointment the following day. She was able to get an appointment for that same afternoon. Oddly, the lumps seemed to disappear overnight, and we both felt relieved. She still wanted to see the dermatologist, though, because she'd noticed a tiny sore on the tip of her nose that morning which bled for no apparent reason. Joi hadn't picked at the little red scab, or even rubbed it with her hand, but it had bled profusely for almost fifteen minutes, a long time for such a little spot. She put an ice cube on her nose, and it finally stopped.

To Joi, this blemish on her face was almost more upsetting than the mysterious swellings. Though it was minute and hardly noticeable, she knew it was there. Always insecure about the way she looked, she had to be perfect when she left home, her hair beautifully styled and her makeup impeccable.

Lately, I'd noticed she spent far more time getting ready to go out. Her hair was getting thinner, and she frequently wore her fall, which she used to wear only on stage. She also had to draw on her eyebrows. She'd plucked them for years and then they'd stopped growing back. After finding a plastic stencil at a beauty supply store on Melrose, she used it to create a shape she liked.

I watched as she finished her makeup and got ready to go. Before we left, she stuck a little round flesh-colored Band-Aid bandage on the tip of her nose. She thought it would be less obvious than if she had a dark red scab showing, however small.

Joi drove to the doctor's office in Beverly Hills on Wilshire Boulevard near the intersection of Canon Drive, in the heart of the hamlet. A-list shoppers strolled their way toward Rodeo Drive and their favorite stores. The sun, in fine Los Angeles fashion, bled predictably through the city smog. I watched it all. Numb.

We knew the area well because it was not far from Ye Little Club, where we often went to see the many popular performers who appeared there. It was a quaint little nightclub with a bar and maybe twenty small tables. I busied my mind thinking about the last time we were there.

Joan Rivers was appearing at that time, doing her hysterical comedy routine. In public with Joi, I always tried to be reserved and proper, so no one would suspect anything scandalous, but Joi would have no part of that. We sat at a little round table in the middle of the room, and Joi immediately took my hand and held it throughout the show. She said she loved me and didn't care what people thought or said. Joan Rivers had to have noticed, but didn't make any of her pointed remarks toward us. In fact, she was very gracious as she introduced Joi, and I think that she, too, had an unspoken respect for Joi and her reputation.

When I came back to reality, I saw that we'd arrived at the doctor's office. We parked and walked into the elevator. My mind was crystal-clear for some reason, like I was on some kind of speed. The light seemed brighter than usual, and I noticed every detail of the gilded wrought-iron outer gate of the elevator. I took Joi's arm to help her over the small rise as we stepped out of the elevator, onto the shiny chrome floor.

A few doors down, the Doctor had a small but efficient office. We were greeted by a receptionist and given the obligatory forms to fill out with insurance and health-related information. We sat down while Joi wrote down the information from the insurance card that Hubby had given her. Stan had kept her on his health insurance even though they were separated.

The form asked questions about her health in general and the reason she was seeing the Doctor today. She mentioned her heavy period and the sharp pain she'd been experiencing recently. Her primary concern was the bumps that had appeared on her head and body and the sore on her nose that seemed to come out of nowhere.

A few minutes later, the Doctor took us into his exam room. He was kind and took time to listen to her concerns, then examined her head and looked at her nose with what appeared to be a tiny microscope attached to his glasses. He took a biopsy of both areas and then asked her to wait for a minute while he made a quick call. The "quick call" worried me because he seemed slightly uncomfortable.

When he came back to the office, he told Joi he wanted her to see his friend, an internist whose office was just down the hall. He said Dr. Axelrod had agreed to see her right away. Joi was reluctant until he said that Dr. Axelrod was an expert on "bumps" like the ones she described on her body and could also help with the sore on her nose. Those seemed to be the magic words. If this guy could help, why not?

We walked next door and were met by Dr. Axelrod as we opened the door. He was standing in the waiting room and immediately took her into his exam room. I was asked to wait, not something I did well because I was used to being there for my girl, no matter what. Time passed, and I started to get a little uneasy; she'd been in there for over an hour.

At last, Dr. Axelrod came out and asked me who I was, in relation to Joi. I told him I was her sister, and he invited me to sit down with him.

He looked me straight in the eye and said he had examined her thoroughly. He found she had cancer that had spread throughout her body. He had felt "a massive tumor on her ovary, and those bumps were lymph glands that were filled with malignant cells." My heart began to pound, and I wanted to run. He took my hand as he told me he didn't think she had very much time.

His words didn't make sense to me. I felt as though I was in a long, empty tunnel…his words coming slowly, one at a time, echoing off the walls. I tried hard to hear what he was saying over the roaring in my ears and the cries of "No! No! No!" that ripped through me. My breath was coming in short bursts. His hand tightened.

Then, I heard him say, "You must listen, Rachel. You have to know the truth…the exact truth…so you can protect your girl, your Joi."

It was as if a bright light had turned on in a very dark room. *Of course*, I thought. I felt something inside me begin to firm up. I had stopped melting and became determined to focus on what he was saying. So that I could be there for her…be her strength when she needed me.

Dr. Axelrod continued softly. He said he didn't know for sure if it had started in her breasts or in her ovaries, but it had spread, and there was nothing that could be done to help her. I could hardly speak. His words were slowly tearing my heart out of my chest.

I found my voice and asked if there was anyone else who might be able to help her. He gave me the card of a Dr. Donald Rochlin in Santa Monica. When he asked what the family would want him to say to her, I said to tell her he'd found a growth on her ovary and that it needed to come out. He nodded and then held me gently for a few moments as I broke down and sobbed.

How was I going to pull myself together? I couldn't let Joi see me like this. I needed to call Stan and tell him what was happening, so I asked the Doctor to keep her inside while I made the call. He agreed and wished us well. His face was sad as he expressed how sorry he was that he couldn't do anything more for her, but hoped that Dr. Rochlin and his partners could.

There were only a few minutes to call Stan before Joi came out of the exam room. I called his office, and he answered the phone. Stuttering, I rushed to explain what had happened and that we needed to get her in to see the doctors in Santa Monica. He was dumbstruck by my words and choked up as he started to cry. He assured me he'd be over right after work and would help me keep her calm. He, too, knew what might happen if she became upset.

I gave him Dr. Rochlin's name, and he promised to take care of making an appointment. He begged me to try to be strong for Joi's sake. He was right, and I knew it. I couldn't let my sorrow and breaking heart affect the way I acted toward her. Her life depended on it.

Finding a box of Kleenex, I wiped my eyes and blew my nose. Joi had a little hand mirror in her purse which she'd left with me. I took it out and looked at my face. My eyes were red and glassy, but I could blame it on allergies. She would believe me because I had a lot of allergies to trees and grass. As we walked into the office, the wind had been blowing, and it carried a lot of pollen with it. When a gust hit us in the face, I had even said that I hoped it wouldn't trigger an episode of hay fever and make my nose run. Mercifully, it was a breezy day, and I had made that comment to her completely out of the blue.

As she came out of the exam room, Joi said this was the most thorough examination she had ever had, that Dr. Axelrod had spent all of this time with her, checking every inch of her body. When I asked what he thought was happening, she said he felt something on her ovary and she really needed to see someone about it. She showed me the card he'd given her with the names of Drs. Rochlin, Wagner, and Wilson. They were oncologists and hematologists with a specialty in surgery.

Joi didn't know what oncology was, but assumed it was something to do with abdominal growths. The thought of surgery didn't seem to enter her mind. She would do what Dr. Axelrod suggested because she had formed a great respect for his ability as a physician. She told me she wished all doctors were as conscientious as he was, and as thorough.

She looked at my eyes and could see that my nose had been running. At the same instant, we both said, "Pollen!" She pulled a bottle of Visine from a zippered pocket in her bag, opened the top, and put a few drops in each of my eyes. Then she kissed me on the forehead and promised that my eyes would clear up in just a few minutes.

I'll never forget the feel of that kiss, slowly washing over me like warm oil. Just for a moment, I believed everything would be all right. Just for a brief moment.

As we started to open the exit door, Dr. Axelrod came into the waiting room and shook our hands. He said he hoped he'd "see us again if we ever needed a doctor."

If we ever needed a doctor? I thought. She needed a doctor a long time ago! Oh, why hadn't she found him before it was so damn late? I thought bitterly of the many self-serving, uncaring doctors she had seen. Not one had even hinted at a tumor, let alone found it growing maliciously, hidden deep beneath her smooth, sweet skin.

Dr. Axelrod went on talking to Joi as she was smiling and responding to his warmth. I watched her…so alive, so beautiful and charming. They continued to talk.

She couldn't be dying…this couldn't happen to her. It couldn't be happening to us. We were so happy; we were in love. She had stopped drinking and was controlling the pills. Her depression had lessened, and she finally felt loved and secure. There had to be a way to save her!

Maybe Dr. Axelrod was wrong, and the tumor could be removed, and there'd be some sort of treatment to stop what was taking over her body. I wasn't going to give up—no one would take her away from me! No one had ever loved me with a whole heart and soul until Joi came into my life. At that moment, I knew, if I could give my life to save hers, I would.

The drive home from Beverly Hills was like a slow motion film for me, but Joi seemed relieved knowing there was something happening to her body, that she was not "just imagining things," as so many other doctors had insinuated through the years. Her pain was real, and the excessive bleeding was real. And now, since the problem had been found, maybe they could find the answer. Dr. Axelrod had assured her that Dr. Rochlin was the best in the city and that he'd be able to help her. He said the growth on her ovary had to come out, and her life would be much better without it. With his very soothing manner, he had calmed her anxiety.

The day was warm. and the breeze felt good against our faces as we drove easily back to the apartment. My girl was upbeat, believing it was just a matter of time before she'd feel like herself again. I tried to match her positive words with some of mine. They felt like sand in my mouth, but she seemed to believe them and smiled. I knew right then this would be the performance of my life.

Stan was waiting for us in the apartment. He had taken off work and rushed to beat us home. Knowing that things might be getting difficult for me, he was there to lend moral support. I gave him a hug, and the smell of brandy hit me. Stan wasn't much of a drinker, but I think he needed a little confidence from a bottle this time.

He had spoken with his daughter, Leslie, who was a registered nurse, and told her what happened. She wanted to find out more about what the Doctor had said and invited us to dinner. Joi really cared for Leslie and had great respect for her ability.

It was a forty-five minute drive to Leslie's home in Northridge with all the rush-hour traffic. Joi wanted to drive, so I rode shotgun, with Hubby in the back, grinding his Cuban cigar and taking little nips of brandy when he thought no one was looking. Joi cranked up the music, and we all sang along. We were too uptight to talk about what was really on our minds.

Leslie was waiting for us and asked if we were ready to eat, but Stan and I had lost our appetites. Joi was the only one who didn't know how bad things were. Stan and I both agreed, when we spoke on the phone earlier, to keep the ugly facts to ourselves. He'd been honest with Leslie, though, so she knew the awful truth. She also understood that Joi needed to be spared until there was no longer false hope to protect her.

With her medical background, Leslie knew the right questions to ask. Joi answered by filling her in on all the details, doctor visit by doctor visit. When Joi told her about the Premarin, Leslie knew the estrogen had created the tumor on her ovary. She understood that prescribing estrogen for a woman who was not menopausal just poured gasoline onto a raging inferno.

The evening moved on with Leslie assuring Joi that seeing the oncologist was the best thing she could do. Stan told Joi that he would make the appointment the next day and not to worry. She was calm and listened to every word they said. I hoped this calm was not just the eye of the hurricane, one that would explode into full chaos at any minute.

We drove back to the apartment, where Stan decided to spend the night. Driving to Woodland Hills would have been too much, especially after downing half the flask of Christian Brothers he'd had in his bag.

The following morning he placed a call to Dr. Rochlin's office. Joi and I were still asleep with our door closed, and he took the phone, with its twenty-five-foot cord, into the kitchen where he could talk privately. Stan spoke personally with Dr. Rochlin, who had already conversed with Dr. Axelrod after Joi's appointment the previous day. Checking his schedule, he found a time slot later that afternoon long enough for blood work, X-rays, and a thorough exam.

In talking with Dr. Rochlin, Stan stressed his concern that the Doctor provide Joi with some hope, and not hand down a death sentence to her. He responded that, while he would respect the family's wishes, he also didn't want to lie to his patient.

Santa Monica was not far from West Hollywood where we lived. The oncology group had offices across the street from St. John's Hospital. Of all the hospitals in the greater Los Angeles area, UCLA and St. John's had the best reputation for excellent patient care. Stan and I sat in the waiting room while the Doctor examined Joi and ran a battery of tests. She must have been with him for close to two hours.

Stan and I cried off and on while we waited, and he would take a sip from his flask whenever his emotions started to sabotage his stoic image. He didn't like showing his feelings, but the sorrow was uncontrollable. We promised each other we'd be strong, that we had to protect the Birdie, no matter what. I kept putting Visine in my eyes, so she wouldn't realize I'd been crying.

The Doctor came out and sat next to us in a quiet part of the room. He affirmed Dr. Axelrod's diagnosis. Joi had a malignant tumor the size of a football on her right ovary, and her lymph nodes and other organs were involved. He didn't think there was any real point in doing surgery, but felt it might give her a little more time if the tumor was removed.

We told him to do anything he could to give her extra time. It didn't matter if it was just six months … a month, a week, a few days … anything! He couldn't guarantee how long she'd have, but said he would do everything in his power to extend her life.

Dr. Rochlin had told Joi that she had a large growth on her ovary, which was the reason for the pain and excessive bleeding. He said the only way to take care of the problem was to remove it. Apparently he was able to instill confidence in her, as she readily agreed to the surgery. He wanted to do it as quickly as possible and arranged for her to be admitted to St. John's the following day. He told Joi to "go home and take it easy."

Joi wasn't as nervous or apprehensive as I thought she'd be, though she had never faced major surgery, especially where she would end up with a scar. I think she knew there were no other options, and this was the only way to stop the pain. She admitted to me the pain had come back and was like an ice pick stabbing her gut. Not wanting to upset me, she had hidden the truth about it. She now felt relieved, thinking the growth would soon be gone and, with it, the excruciating misery.

The Doctor had prescribed some pain pills to make her life more tolerable. I had never heard of methadone, but the pharmacist at the Rexall Drug Store on La Cienega and Beverly warned us it was very strong and to be sure not to take more than the Doctor prescribed.

We got back to the apartment, and Stan went to pick up some Chinese food, so we wouldn't have to go out. Joi was in the bedroom getting her little hospital bag ready when the doorbell rang. I opened the door and saw Stan's attorney, Milt Golden, standing in front of me with an envelope filled with papers. I had a weird feeling about the timing of his arrival and asked him why he was there. He said that Stan wanted Joi to update her will, so there would be no problem if anything were to happen.

I couldn't believe what I was hearing! I looked at him and told him to "get the hell out of there and to leave her alone." Not ready for my reaction, he awkwardly excused himself and said to tell Stan he'd call him in the morning.

Joi was still busy, so I had a moment to myself. I stood shaking against the door jamb, breathing deeply, trying to calm down. So far, she had no idea that the operation might be life-threatening, and, as far as I was concerned, she never would.

Stan came back with my barbecued pork fried rice and char siu pork slices, with some moo goo gai pan and vegetables for himself and Joi. Because she had to stop eating at midnight, she delighted in eating everything in sight. Stan offered to stay with us and help when she came back from the hospital. Leslie also said she'd come over whenever she could, even though she had kids and a plate that was overflowing.

After dinner, Stan lay down on the couch in front of the TV and lit up one of his cigars. It wasn't long before he dozed off, and I took the cigar from the ashtray, put it out, and covered him with a blanket. He'd sleep through the night now. We were used to his snores.

Joi and I got ready and climbed into bed. I knew she was nervous about the surgery, so we cuddled, and I reassured her. I told her that this was just another one of our adventures, but, this time, no cuckoo motel keeper would pound on our door! That made us both laugh, and she began to relax. Soon, she was soft in my arms and breathing deeply.

As Joi slept that night, I held her close, trying to feel every part of her against me. I couldn't sleep…I didn't want to. I just stayed awake, looking at her peaceful, beautiful face.

How many nights had we done this…had I done this? Would this be the last night I'd feel her next to me, hear her breathe, watch her sleep? Silently, my tears fell, wetting the pillow beneath my cheeks. That night, my darling girl slept the sleep of the angels…while I sensed the beginning of hell.

Chapter 20

Surgery

The night before surgery, the methadone had stopped the pain, and Joi slept peacefully. We needed to check into the hospital by noon for final tests and prep for surgery later in the day.

We got up around nine o'clock, and Joi took a warm shower. I'm not sure if it was the medication she was taking, or if she was just resigned to what she had to do, but I was relieved she was quiet and relaxed.

When we got to the hospital, Joi insisted I be allowed to stay with her in her room. St. John's had fold-up cots which could be used by family members when a patient was upset or quite ill. Dr. Rochlin knew how important it was for us to be together, so he ordered a private room with a cot for me.

Joi was in a special area on the third floor with private suites where VIPs and celebrities would stay. Betty Grable, the bathing suit pinup girl during World War II, was very ill in a room just a few doors down. This floor, it seemed, was for cancer patients who were having surgery or were seriously ill from their disease.

Stan and I were taken to Joi's room where nurses were bustling about taking her blood pressure and temperature. She'd already had blood work, full body X-rays, and an EKG to be sure her heart was strong enough to withstand anesthesia.

When they finally finished poking and prodding, Joi was able to rest for a little while before surgery. No one else was in the room when she asked me to lie next to her. We wrapped our arms around each other, not speaking, but holding on as if it were our last time.

Surprisingly, Joi wasn't as frightened as I was, but she must have seen the fear in my eyes. Pulling me closer, she kissed my cheek and told me how much she loved me. She said she'd "never leave me," and would see me "in a few hours." Not to worry, she assured me, because she was the Birdie and was tough! Sweet baby, she couldn't begin to know how tough she'd need to be to fight this terrible, powerful enemy.

I stood up just as a surgical nurse came in to start her IV and give her medication to help her relax. The gurney was wheeled in shortly after that. She was so thin that she was easily moved onto it. She looked over at me with a gentle, nervous smile as she was taken from the room. I followed her for a bit as she was wheeled down the hall to the operating room. Then, as they turned a corner, I lost sight of her. I felt sick to my stomach.

Stan was pacing the hall. He'd added some brandy to the cup of coffee he'd bought at the next-door coffee shop. I knew he was trying to stay calm. When he noticed I was trembling, he put his arm around me as we sat down together. We talked about wanting to have more time to spend with her, praying the tumor could be removed and they would put her on chemotherapy. The Doctor said it might be a possibility if the tumor was not attached to a vital organ, and if they could remove it without doing too much damage, but we had no guarantee of what would happen in surgery, and that truth hung over our conversation like a cloud, although neither of us voiced the words we were thinking.

Time crawled by. Joi had been in surgery over three hours, and Stan could not sit and stare at the clock a moment longer. He said he'd like to take a walk outside and have a cigar. I told him to go ahead … I'd stay and wait.

I kept looking toward the door where the doctors came in to talk to the family after surgery. I closed my eyes and saw Joi's sweet face as she assured me she'd be fine. Then, I heard the door open and looked up to see the Doctor coming toward me. I didn't like his expression.

Holding my breath, I got up and walked toward him. Then he said the words I'll never forget as long as I live. Placing his hand on my arm, he said, "Rachel, there was nothing we could do. We removed the ovarian tumor and closed her back up … I'm so very sorry."

With a roar in my head, I started to drop. I grabbed a doctor or male nurse who was standing next to me, and fell into his arms. As he caught me, I began sobbing. This could not be true. I was devastated, inconsolable, my feelings quickly flashing back and forth from grief to rage, rage to grief.

"How *dare* they?" I screamed inside. Joi had been seeing doctors because of pain in her belly for years. If even one of them had been more interested in what was destroying her body rather than dating her, this terrible, terrible thing would not be happening. My darling was dying, and there was nothing I could do to help her. I wanted to die with her.

The Doctor and the man who had caught me took me, still sobbing, to a room where I could be alone to make phone calls or pray. Dr. Rochlin asked if I had someone who could come to be with me. I think I said that her husband was there some place. He gently patted my shoulder and left the room.

I sat alone, stunned. *This couldn't be real*, I thought. Like in the movies, I was hoping a doctor would come back and tell me it all had been a mistake, that everything really had gone beautifully and Joi would live a long and healthy life.

My fantasy was short-lived as Stan came through the door. He'd been looking for me desperately and found me with the help of a candy-striper. We both broke down crying. I didn't have to say the words; he knew. We cried until there were no more tears, then sat silently together, but alone.

When I was finally able to speak, I told him what the Doctor said, that they couldn't predict how long she had, but didn't think more than a few months, or even weeks. Determined to get all the answers, Stan called Dr. Rochlin, pleading with him to try something more for Joi.

The Doctor said the cancer had spread throughout her body and was attacking her vital organs. He was willing to give her chemotherapy, but didn't feel it would extend her life by more than a month, at the most. He told Stan it had "been growing for a very long time," and it "was amazing she had not been hospitalized a lot sooner." He couldn't believe anyone could bear the kind of pain she must have endured for so long. *That's my tough little Birdie*, I thought.

Stan and I took turns asking questions, but there was nothing more to say, only to ask him to please try *anything* to keep her here a little longer. He told us he would start chemotherapy while she was still in the hospital recovering from surgery.

When I called Joi's mother, she said she'd ask Christian Science practitioners to start praying for her, and she would come to see Joi the following day. She and Stan had a mutual dislike for each other. They couldn't tolerate one another for more than a few hours, but knew they had to establish a truce for Joi's sake.

I called Joi's brother, Larry, and told him how terrible things were. Joi had left home when Larry was still a young boy, and they had become more of a family as he grew up. They were close now and loved each other very much. Larry was shocked, but did his best to be strong. He was her little brother, but now it was time to reverse their roles.

Eventually, a nurse came into the "crying room," as it was called, and told us Joi was out of recovery and being taken to her room. She said we could meet her there in about ten minutes. She, also, said that Joi had tolerated the surgery fairly well and was doing a little better than expected.

I went to the closest bathroom, splashed cold water on my face, and washed off the caked mascara and eyeliner that made black streaks down my cheeks. The water soothed my red, tear-soaked eyes. While brushing my hair, I tried to pull myself together. I had to act as if everything was great and the surgery had been successful. I wouldn't be lying when I told her they'd removed the tumor; it was true. To give her hope, I would also find a way to tell her about the chemotherapy. It was important that she thought she had a chance. Her attitude could affect the way her body responded to the chemicals they'd be pumping into her. Stan and I agreed to keep things light and positive ... at least, we'd do our best.

When we got to her room, she was still sleeping off the anesthetic. Stan and I sat quietly on either side of her bed, waiting for her eyes to open. It seemed like hours, but it was only forty-five minutes until the Birdie came back from her dream world. Her eyes opened very slowly, and it took her a few minutes to focus. She looked at me and said softly, "My Rachel."

My heart jumped. I took her weak little hand and held it gently, so that I wouldn't disturb her IV. Then I told her to look to her right, and she saw Hubby sitting there with his great, big grin. With a slow, sleepy smile, she said, "Hubby, Hubby, you're here."

Stan stood up, leaned over, and kissed her forehead.

Dr. Rochlin had put Joi on a morphine drip that kept her out of pain and caused her to slip in and out of consciousness that night and most of the following day. I had been with her the whole time and, at one point, he and his partner, Dr. Wilson, the hematologist, came by. Dr. Wilson would manage her chemotherapy and would alternate with Dr. Rochlin in seeing Joi. He would begin her treatment with a nitrogen mustard drug called Cytoxan. It was originally developed as a chemical warfare agent, and then it was discovered that it could destroy malignant cells. The doctors would see if it could slow down the malignant firestorm raging through her body. It had been successful with other patients who had a similar diagnosis, so I felt cautiously hopeful.

Joi stirred and began to wake as they slowed down the morphine dosage. She was tolerating the pain well. They wanted her to start eating and drinking on her own as soon as possible to regain the strength she'd need to handle the chemotherapy.

As the days passed, Joi stayed awake more and more, and we talked when we could. Stan had to work and would come to the hospital at the end of the day, but we had the rest of the time together. The doctors predicted she would be in the hospital for about two weeks, which they felt was ample time to see if the chemotherapy worked.

After the first few treatments, she began to respond well to the drug, and her strength came back twice as fast as everyone hoped. She had a voracious appetite and even enjoyed the hospital food! I could have had a tray if I wanted, but Stan brought me my fried rice almost every day. I ate a quart of it, and that was enough to sustain me. Because I was burning nervous energy from all the stress, I was losing weight, dropping, at least, a size or two. My stomach was in knots, and my mind constantly raced. I asked Stan to pick up a few pairs of corduroy pants for me that he had in his inventory. Joi noticed and liked the way the pants molded to my "curvaceous caboose." She winked, and I laughed when she told me.

Joi slowly mastered holding on to her IV pole with one hand and holding onto my arm with the other, as she walked up and down the hall. I would walk behind her and hold her waist to give her a little more stability.

I could feel her getting stronger, and every day was a precious gift I treasured.

As Joi's strength increased, our walks became longer and steadier. The Cytoxan was working, and my little angel was feeling better! Dr. Wilson was amazed to see that her blood work was showing some improvement. There were fewer cancer cells than before, and the doctors didn't know why Joi was gaining weight since she'd lost about ten pounds just before surgery.

There were no answers to these questions, but the "why" didn't really matter. The only thing that did matter was that she might be able to go home soon, something unthinkable that day after surgery when the prognosis had been so terribly bleak.

Though secretly excited about Joi's amazing progress, I feared hoping for too much. Still, the vaguest thought of having more time with her was so wonderful! I decided to embrace the thrilling possibility that we could actually be "us" again, even if the other thought lingered harshly in the shadows … waiting.

Joi's skin began to take on a soft pink tone, instead of the ominous yellow hue that had so cruelly heralded the passing of her life. Her beautiful green eyes were clear, and the sparkle of life began to reappear.

Dr. Rochlin was obviously surprised by this turn of events and watched in amazement as Joi improved a little more each day. She would walk out to the patio, craving the sun's warmth, and lie on a lounge chair in the soft pink nightgown I'd bought for her at the hospital gift shop. With a soft smile on her resting face, her eyes would gently close. I loved those moments. She was so at peace and, for that moment, so was I.

After Joi had been in the hospital for almost two weeks, Dr. Wilson and Dr. Rochlin agreed she'd improved enough to go home. She would have to come to the doctors' office every week to have her blood monitored and to check on how the chemotherapy was working. It was important to make sure it was not doing damage to her liver or another vital organ.

When Dr. Rochlin came in early one morning to see her, his normal unsmiling face was beaming with delight. He came over to her bed, gently took her hand in his, and asked if she would like to go home. Her eyes lit up like a child's at Christmas, and she asked, "When?"

He told her she could go home that afternoon, if she'd like to. She turned and looked at me with a grin and said happily, "Call Hubby, so he can pick us up!"

The Doctor explained that, although she was doing exceptionally well, she would still need to be monitored every week. Since Stan and I had asked that he keep her condition "hopeful" when he spoke with her, he also said she was "responding well to the chemo and could have some quality time ahead." He seemed to understand how important it was for this still beautiful but now fragile woman to feel hopeful, and I was grateful for his kindness. As he left,

I called Stan at work and gave him the wonderful news. Happily, he said he'd leave immediately to pick us up.

Joi didn't have anything appropriate to wear for the ride home and for her convalescence. Luckily, I found a full-length opaque gown and matching robe in the same lobby gift shop. The fact that she was interested in looking her best was a wonderful sign. The Birdie was coming back, at least, for a while.

She was still in quite a lot of pain. Her incision site, closed with staples, started just below the sternum and reached to her lower abdomen. The long, angry, red, zigzag line jaggedly crossed what was once her smooth belly. I had expected her to be upset about the large scar, but she wasn't. She was so happy and grateful to have the growth removed, and said she now realized how it had drained her energy for so many years. She could hardly wait to go out and do things, and promised we would now "be able to enjoy our life together and live it to the fullest." All I could do was smile and agree. My tears would have to be silent… and alone.

A few minutes before Stan arrived, Dr. Rochlin removed Joi's staples and put on a new dressing. He showed me how to care for the wound and gave me some antiseptic ointment to protect her from infection. The Nurse filled a large plastic bag with gauze and dressings, along with written instructions and prescriptions for antibiotics and pain medication. The Doctor gave her a one-week supply of the Cytoxan pills.

As we walked to the car, our arms were filled with her clothes, dressings, and flowers sent by her mother, stepfather, and brother Larry. We were relieved that no one seemed to notice us leaving. Joi didn't want any publicity about her going in the hospital, so had purposely not mentioned it to anyone.

Hollywood was funny, and not in a good way. It wanted to know all about the lives of celebrities—their prey. It wanted to know the heartbreaks, illnesses, weaknesses, addictions, affairs, peccadilloes, and transgressions, each filled with the painful and possibly ugly details. That aspect of the press survived on the spilled blood from the wounds of these fragile souls. No one was left unscathed. The lucky ones only had flesh wounds, but, sadly, the most vulnerable were often mortally wounded. My Birdie was vulnerable.

With my brave girl lying on the backseat, Stan drove us home in Joi's car. I was in the front, twisted around, so I could watch how she was doing. Stan drove with uncustomary care, knowing that Joi's belly was very sore, and that any bumps or fast turns could cause her unnecessary pain. We made it home without any major jostling and with Joi sleeping peacefully.

Stan pulled the car into the garage and parked it temporarily next to the elevator. A pushcart was conveniently placed near the parking space, and we loaded it with what we'd brought from the hospital. Stan wheeled it into the elevator as I held onto Joi to steady her for the ride up to the apartment. Getting off the elevator at the fourth floor, I realized just how comforting it was to be home with my honey girl. Stan was planning to stay and help, which would be greatly appreciated. I could take care of Joi, but couldn't leave her to shop for food or pick up prescriptions and medical supplies. It would be nice to have him there.

Joi's friend, Jack, was the manager of our apartment building. Stan saw him in the lobby and mentioned that Joi had just returned from the hospital, so Jack said he'd come up a little later to say hello. I knew Joi wouldn't mind because she liked him very much. Stan had casually asked him if he had a larger apartment available, and Jack said he would check his inventory and let him know when he came to visit later that day.

In the afternoon, after we'd settled in and Joi was resting, Jack rang the doorbell. He came in with a gigantic bouquet of freshly cut pink roses surrounded by baby's breath in a lovely cut glass vase. It was so huge and magnificent that it was hard to see his face as he walked into the room; the flowers obscured his body from his waist to above his head! We were only able to recognize him by his dapper wardrobe and wonderful taste in shoes! Jack was a snappy, impeccable dresser, and Joi loved his taste in clothes. He was actually the only "out" gay man we were friendly with.

Joi delighted in the flowers, and Jack was sensitive enough not to ask why she'd been in the hospital. As he left a few minutes later, he touched her shoulder gently and said, "Hey, pretty lady, get well, and we'll all do the town…on me!"

I had a feeling he knew more than he showed, as his eyes connected with mine just a few seconds longer than usual as he left the room.

Chapter 21

The Penthouse

As Jack was leaving the apartment, Stan asked if he'd checked on what they had spoken about earlier. I was standing near the doorway when I heard them talking and was curious. Jack said the only two-bedroom apartment available was one of the penthouses—Penthouse 6, which also had a den and a wonderful view of the Hollywood Hills and the Playboy building.

I recalled working for Jerry Porter at *Playboy* in 1967. We could see these penthouses from our office, and I always wondered who lived there. Someone told me Anne Heywood lived in the one on the far left. I was intrigued after I saw her appear with Sandy Dennis in *The Fox*, one of the few A films about female lovers. Hollywood had to keep the censors happy, so there were no happy endings for homosexuals at that time. Too often, the ending was suicide! In this one, Anne's character went off with her male lover, while Sandy Dennis was hammered like a nail in the ground by a felled tree. I guess the idea was that even God was angry at "gays!"

When Stan asked about the rent with a year's lease, Jack offered to let Joi have it for $620 a month. She'd been paying $450 for her one-bedroom place, and this sounded so much nicer and larger. Stan was staying with us often, and had mentioned selling the "ranch" because he was tired of the freeway drive to his office every day. He also understood things were going to get tough and wanted to be here to help us.

Perhaps feeling guilty, he offered to pay the rent, something he'd never done before, even when he and Joi were living together as husband and wife. This would really help since Joi couldn't work at this point, and no one knew if she'd ever be able to again.

Actually, Joi was pretty well fixed for those days. She had quite a few savings bonds in a safe deposit box, as well as a small life insurance policy she could cash in, if necessary. She didn't trust the stock market because she'd heard too many horror stories from friends. Her "Grampy Ray" had taught her to be careful with money, so she religiously bought the bonds every time she received a paycheck, holding them to maturity.

Joi was elated when she heard that Stan was willing to pay the rent on the penthouse. Since she'd always paid her own way in their relationship, in her mind, this would be "justice." Stan would finally be doing the right thing, and she could save more money in case she ever needed it.

Jack had actually shown us the penthouse apartments before we left for Las Vegas in December. They'd been recarpeted and freshly painted after the last tenants moved out. We liked Penthouse 6 and had watched for a few minutes while they put in the white plush carpeting which blended so beautifully with the snow-white walls and towering cathedral ceiling.

The master suite was spacious, with floor-to-ceiling windows looking out on the Hollywood Hills, and a walk-in closet that was larger than my whole room at the Studio Club! The mirrored doors on the closet provided extra depth and made the room seem even larger.

The living room and dining area had floor-to-ceiling sliding glass doors leading out to a balcony, with space enough for a bistro set and lounge chair. I'm petrified of heights and would no doubt stay far away from this hanging terrace, but I knew Joi would probably enjoy lying out in the sun, and I knew Stan would for sure.

Jack asked if we wanted to see the penthouse again, and, although Joi wasn't up to it, she said she remembered it very well and liked it. Jack just happened to have the lease with him, so both Stan and Joi signed the agreement. Then, Stan wrote the check, covering the first month's rent and security deposit. *Voila*! It was a done deal, and we would move into our gorgeous penthouse apartment the following day.

Stan followed Jack up to the penthouse, and, if Joi could have jumped up and down, she would have! She was deliriously happy knowing we'd now have a wonderful new home overlooking the city. I hugged her cautiously and suggested she lie down for a bit.

Joi was still in a lot of pain from the surgery, but the Methadone was definitely helping. Her belly was back to its normal size now that the tumor was gone, and she could wear her clothes again. The chemotherapy was working without a lot of side effects, but Dr. Wilson had said she might lose some or all of her hair. That didn't seem to bother Joi very much, since she'd been troubled with thinning hair for several years. Besides, she could only deal with one thing at a time, and right now she was giving her all to getting stronger, so she could get back to her career.

My Birdie desperately wanted to work again and go back to her normal way of life. She realized she could never wear a bikini on film or TV again because of her long, angry-looking incision, which was not at all what she'd want others to see. Still, she didn't want to think about any of these things now. Joi wanted to think about the good things in her life, not the negative. In fact, she wanted to start moving right away, and not wait until the following day!

Jack had given us three keys, one for each of us. When Stan came back from seeing our new digs, he had a new little skip in his walk as he grinned his way into the room. He loved the penthouse and could not have been happier. He said he'd get some food for dinner and a few urgent supplies for the apartment. Knowing how much we adored the industrial-size sandwiches at Greenblatt's, he offered to pick up whatever we wanted. Joi and I both loved the rare roast beef with raw onion slices and blue cheese dressing on sourdough bread. Stan's favorite was the corned beef on rye with Swiss cheese and a little dark mustard. Three inches thick, the sandwiches were enough for two meals. Joi had eaten very little in the hospital, but now she was salivating at the thought of having one of these culinary delights. As we made out our list, it felt so good to be back to our life again…back to normal. At least, for a little while.

After Stan left, Joi got off the couch and said she wanted to go alone with me to see "our new home." I liked that. (More "normal." Nice.) We walked down the hall to the elevator and only had to wait a minute until it arrived. In we went, Joi pushed PH, and, with one quick swoosh, we were there. Penthouse 6 was halfway down the long, thickly-carpeted hall. I noticed it was quiet, the rugs and wall hangings acting like insulation to keep the usual noises of apartment living at bay.

We walked up to our new front door. Joi unlocked it and slowly pushed it open. Then, turning, she surprised me by slipping her arms up and around my neck and asking me to carry her over the threshold! I was in heaven. I carefully lifted her in my arms and stepped into our new home. More than a little bit flushed with the romance of the moment, I gently put her down.

She looked at me with a soft smile, and her amazing green eyes seemed to see right into my heart. For just a minute, I wondered if she knew more than I thought, but then, breaking her gaze, she pulled me close. And there we stood, holding one another like we were the last two women in the world… eyes closed… hearts open. Standing there high above the noisy city streets, in our beautiful new home, I felt safe and loved and hopeful. It was wonderful!

Then, like an excited child, Joi took my hand and led me from room to room, picturing in her mind where everything would be placed. She knew Stan would bring a few pieces of furniture from the ranch for his room, and she had an adjustable twin bed she'd left in Woodland Hills that would be perfect for him. Stan's room wasn't large, but it had two huge doors that opened into the spacious living area with cathedral ceilings. All of the ceilings in the apartment were close to twenty feet tall, which gave the distinct feeling of floating on a cloud above the city. This was the closest thing to living in the Taj Mahal I could ever imagine!

Joi worked her entire adult life and had always been successful, but she had never allowed herself to live in what she'd considered opulence. She didn't pinch pennies, but was frugal in her lifestyle. I, however, knew this was not the time to deny herself anything she wanted. She deserved as much comfort and happiness as was financially possible, and Stan's paying the rent on the apartment was a great help. Joi had always been afraid of running out of money and didn't want to touch her rainy day funds. That rainy day was definitely here, even though she didn't know it, but I understood it all too well. I was determined to do everything I could to make sure the rest of her life would be filled with enough happiness to make up for the forty or so years she would never see.

We walked through every inch of the penthouse, making mental and written notes as to how Joi envisioned the place to be. We made another list of items for Stan to pick up from the Mayfair Market, down the street on Santa Monica Boulevard.

Returning to the apartment, Joi couldn't wait to start moving things and was so excited she couldn't sit still. I asked her to rest on the sofa and just tell me what she wanted me to move. Her belly was still very tender, and the staples had just been removed only a few days ago. I told her she couldn't overdo, or she'd end up back at St. John's. Joi finally listened to my reasoning and agreed to let me do the schlepping.

There were supermarket baskets conveniently left near the elevator that would be invaluable in the move. I could take small items from the bathroom and the kitchen and fill the carts. I made a few trips that night, so she'd feel the reality of this happy time…that her dream was really coming true.

By the time I finished, Stan had returned with our dinner, and saw that most of the kitchen had been stripped, with only three dinner plates, three glasses, and enough utensils for this one meal left. He couldn't believe the move had already begun, but wasn't inclined to lift anything because of his "bad back" (although he was able to lift his tennis racquet and play three grueling sets with men half his age)! He never carried groceries and would either use a basket or have me carry them if I was around. Joi and I both knew about his "ailment" and played along. I didn't mind doing a little lifting. I was young and strong, and he was being very helpful to Joi and me, so it wasn't any big deal.

Stan handed me the bag of sandwiches, and I put them out for us on the table. We all ate way too much, without guilt, thoroughly enjoying every single bite!

It was still early enough to take a few more things up to our new "heaven." Joi walked beside me as I pushed the clothes rack, hung with her beautiful gowns, down the hall. I wanted her to rest, but she didn't want me to go alone. Stan did what he always did after he ate—he fell asleep in front of the TV.

We took our time going up to the new apartment, and she watched as I unloaded each hanger and placed it in our new and larger closet. Our bedroom was like a large white canvas, one we'd fill with exciting splashes of color and design. Joi had a wonderful sense of aesthetics and would turn this empty space into something stunning. I was delighted with the possibilities.

It was almost midnight by the time we had moved almost everything that weighed less than ten pounds into Penthouse 6. The "muscle" would move the heavy pieces of furniture in the morning, so we went back downstairs to get some sleep.

The next morning, two burly guys showed up, over six feet two and around 200 pounds each. Joi showed them where she wanted everything placed and had them bring the sofa up first, so we could sit and supervise.

We had no doubt they could do the job, and they finished in less than two hours. Joi gave them a little extra in appreciation of their hard work and the gentle way they treated our things. Everything was finished by noon, and we could enjoy almost a full day in our "dream cottage without the white picket fence."

Stan went to Woodland Hills to pick up a few pieces of furniture he'd need for his room, and he had the guys follow him in their truck, so they could do the actual lifting and moving. Joi had urged Stan not to bring his recliner because it was a hideous, dirty-looking goldish-brown color, accented by more than a few badly worn spots on the cushions—definitely not a designer's asset. But Stan's mind was set on having his favorite chair, and was immovable on the subject. Disappointed, Joi convinced him to, at least, keep it in his own room, so she wouldn't have to look at it.

Our home was almost complete, except for a few new pieces of furniture and throw pillows she wanted for the living room. She also wanted some artwork for the walls, but this could be taken care of in a week or so when she had more strength.

Now it was time for her to take it easy and recuperate, in a place that, for the first time in her life, actually felt like home. She had battled her demons with alcohol and won. She had controlled her addiction to barbiturates and won. She had found someone she really loved, who also loved her unconditionally. Joi was now home…in the truest sense of the word.

We watched as the burly movers brought Stan's things inside. Joi wanted to make sure they didn't accidentally leave his recliner in the living room. They started to, but she quickly pointed to the open wide doors and said sweetly, "Oh, I think Stan would like that in his room."

I had to laugh but didn't, since Stan was watching with a definite pout on his face.

As the boys left, Stan suggested we celebrate "if the Birdie felt up to it." He wanted to take us to Cyrano's Restaurant, which was only up the hill and around the corner from our building. It was a great little restaurant, not only known for its great steaks, seafood, and amazing salad dressing, but also for its very unusual acoustics. The main room was circular with a domed ceiling, and the tables were placed all around in a circle. The interesting thing was that you could hear every word of conversation of the people seated exactly opposite your table … on the other side of the room! For those in the know, it provided a little wicked fun, but you really had to watch what you said, or it might come back to bite you!

Joi loved Cyrano's and told Stan she was feeling "quite well after my nap." I smiled and called ahead for reservations. When we arrived, we were seated at a table directly facing the entrance. We could hear who was coming in and their conversations, but we were very careful not to discuss anything we might not want repeated.

We had a lovely meal celebrating this new plateau in our lives. Keeping our secret was, for the moment at least, not keeping Stan or me from enjoying our time with Joi that night. We all had a delicious dinner and good (if careful) conversations.

My favorite meal at Cyrano's was their London broil with a twice-baked potato. Joi had broiled halibut with béarnaise sauce and rice pilaf, while Stan had a rare New York steak with asparagus and baked potato. Joi and I ate like we'd been doing all the lifting and hauling, instead of delighting in our hedonistic afternoon. I was relaxed for the first time in weeks. It felt like old times, and I was taking in every sweet moment.

We had a final cup of coffee and left the restaurant. The parking for the restaurant was alongside the building and behind a strip of little boutique businesses. Stan had driven Joi's car and, as we got in and were ready to leave, Joi spotted her dear friend, Marjorie Meade, parking right next to us. Delighted, Joi called out the window and caught Marjorie's attention.

Well, it was like old home week! Marjorie ran over to Joi, laughing, and slipped into the backseat with her. They hugged and started talking a mile a minute. Marjorie had not seen Joi in well over a year, before Joi and I had met. Neither one could believe it had been so long.

When they finally stopped talking for a moment, Marjorie greeted Stan, and then Joi introduced her to me. She seemed pleased to meet me and couldn't have been friendlier.

Joi and Stan and Marjorie and her then-husband, Fred, had been good friends for a long time and had often gone out together. After the introduction, Marjorie announced that she and Fred were getting a divorce, but assured us that "everything was, at least, pleasant."

Then Joi told her about being in St. John's Hospital and having surgery to remove a growth on her ovary. Marjorie looked horror-stricken until Joi calmed her and said they had removed it and were "giving her a medication that was controlling the problem."

Marjorie was a smart lady, and I think she picked up on our silence. She didn't delve any deeper into the subject, but said she'd love to get together and spend time with Joi. They made a date for Marjorie to come and see the new penthouse.

She kissed Joi on the cheek and said good-bye to us. Marjorie had been on her way to one of the small shops in the area that was open late. We waited to see her in safely before we drove away.

It had been a good visit. Joi was happy to see her dear friend, and I was happy to see her smile. She told me they had known each other "forever," that she and Marjorie, as well as their good friend, Eartha Kitt, had spent many an evening going to fun places together through the years.

The drive home from the parking lot at Cyrano's took less than five minutes. As soon as we pulled into our new parking space, we heard the ding of the elevator right next to us. The door opened immediately, almost like it was waiting for us. What a perfect end to a magnificent day!

Stan put on the TV in the living room as Joi and I sat together on the sofa. We watched the tube for about ten minutes as Stan fell sound asleep in the chair. He was totally predictable! It was a sure bet, and it didn't matter if there was company or not. There he'd sit with his mouth open, a cigar hanging halfway out, the ash barely hanging on. He'd let out a gigantic snort and wake himself up, then realize the cigar was resting on his chin. Grabbing the soggy end, he'd put it in the ashtray, then mumble something, grin, and go back to sleep. This was Stan, without deviation.

I liked how predictable he was, especially at night. Joi and I got up and, hand and hand, went into our new bedroom. I sat up in bed while she had her turn at the bathroom sink, thinking about what a great day we'd had. Tonight we would cuddle, something we'd always done and seemed to like almost as much as our more rambunctious times. Joi was "my girl," and we were in love. That would never change.

The thought moved me, and I had to fight to hold back my tears.

"But this was the way it had to be," I said to myself.

The time we had left was too precious and fleeting to be ruined by my sadness, my fears. *And, besides,* I thought, *I'd have the rest of my life to cry. Tonight? I'd love instead.*

Chapter 22

Palm Springs

Joi was responding very well to the chemotherapy. She had blood drawn every week to see if the Cytoxan was destroying too many red blood cells, and if the dosage or medication needed to be changed. Her blood was consistently good with a high hemoglobin rate. Dr. Wilson would examine her, checking for swollen lymph nodes. He'd smile and tell her she was doing great and "to keep up the good work."

Cytoxan worked like a miracle drug for Joi. She said she felt better than she had in years, and, luckily, she kept most of her hair. In fact, after a few months of treatment, some of the thinning hair she'd been self-conscious about actually began to grow back. Dr. Wilson said that her nails, which hadn't grown for a long time, would also begin to grow as she continued her treatment.

I finally had to tell Joi about her condition. Though I explained to her the growth was cancerous, I emphasized that the new medication she'd been taking could control and even stop the malignancy. She took the information better than I had thought. Her attitude was good because she was feeling great. She had energy and wanted to do things and go places, and didn't want to sleep all day. The doctors hadn't expected her to last three weeks, but the chemotherapy and her tremendous will to live seemed to make the difference. So, here she was, feeling good and the happiest she'd been in many, many years. Everyone was amazed.

Stan was so thrilled she wanted to do something other than stay in the apartment that he suggested we go to Palm Springs for a few days. Both Joi and I loved the desert and hadn't been there in years. Delighted with the idea, we began packing our suitcases that same evening, so we could leave the following morning.

Joi was down to one sleeping pill at night in addition to her Methadone four times a day. I'd heard it was quite a strong pain pill, but it didn't seem to make her drowsy during the day. I guessed her metabolism had changed with what was going on inside her little body. She was no longer troubled with insomnia and fell asleep almost immediately after she snuggled in and put her head on my chest. I would watch her sleep for a little while before I, too, nodded off. I loved seeing how peaceful she looked, often with a slight smile on her face. I hoped I was, at least, partly responsible for that smile.

In the mornings, Joi always got up a few minutes before I did to make coffee and rye toast for us. She'd bring it to me while I was still in bed and often woke me with a kiss. What a lovely alarm clock she was! That morning, we had our coffee and toast and finished preparations for our trip to Palm Springs.

It was fall and a little nippy in Los Angeles. The nights in the desert were also cool, so we needed some warm clothes to feel cozy. That day, we all dressed for comfort, not glamour.

Joi wanted to drive, at least, part of the way to Palm Springs. It was a clear, crisp day, and she was elated to be at the wheel, blasting the music while singing joyfully along with the songs she knew. She liked a lot of the same music I did. Barbra Streisand, as well as Tina Turner, Tony Bennett, and the Beatles were her favorites. When we stopped for coffee, Stan insisted on driving the rest of the way, while Joi slept on my lap in the back seat.

The ride from our apartment to Palm Springs was a little over two hours. It would have been a lot nicer without Stan's cigar smoke eating up the oxygen in the car. I hacked and choked every so often, but he didn't take the hint and wasn't about to give up his precious cigars.

With relief, I began to notice the desert mountains that heralded our arrival in Palm Springs. We passed the Palm Springs Aerial Tramway and drove past regal palm trees as we entered the town.

There is an ethereal feeling that takes over when you enter Palm Springs village. It's a peace and tranquility I've never experienced anywhere but here, it feels as if the weight of the world has been removed from your shoulders. All is serene, and a quiet fills your mind and heart. I loved it then—and I love it now—especially with all the sweet memories Joi and I made there.

When we arrived in town, it was early afternoon, with plenty of daylight left to enjoy. Stan had heard of a relatively new club for tennis lovers. He'd been to Charlie Farrell's Racquet Club many times over the years, but this was the new "members only" Palm Springs Tennis Club. Stan found it easily. We parked, walked up to the entrance, and Stan told security that "Miss Lansing" was there to have lunch and was also very interested in learning about membership in the club.

The door opened immediately, and we were escorted by one of the membership personnel up to the restaurant overlooking the tennis courts. Introducing himself as Bud, he gave Joi a brochure and invited us to take a tour of the club after our lunch.

Our meal was exquisite. The Monte Cristo sandwich Joi and I both had was phenomenal. I'd never had one before, but when Joi described the French toast with turkey and Swiss cheese and raspberry jam—deep fried with powdered sugar sprinkled on top—I knew I had to have it! Remember, eating was one of our favorite things!

Being more health-conscious than either of us (except for smoking like a chimney), Stan ordered his usual assorted greens and a small, skinless chicken breast with a little oil and vinegar. My girl and I were into instant gratification, though, and we both managed to thoroughly enjoy and finish our monstrous sandwiches, while Stan just picked at his fare. I think he secretly envied our choice.

The tour guide returned just as the check was placed on the table. He picked it up and scrawled "comp" across it, and, with her signature smile, Joi thanked him graciously. He shyly smiled back and said it was their pleasure to have someone as lovely as Joi show an interest in joining the club. He then took us on a most pleasant tour of the grounds.

The club was pretty and had quite a relaxed atmosphere, not at all snobbish as I imagined it might be. Everyone was cordial, and the bar was friendly with a warm, inviting ambience.

Stan was in heaven. They invited him to come back a little later to play with one of the pros on staff. That was all they had to say…nothing could have stopped him from returning! He said he'd call ahead to let them know when to book the court, and we left the club with Stan floating on Tennis Nirvana.

With most of the afternoon still ahead of us, Stan suggested we look at some houses. Joi, still feeling good, was all for it. We stopped in the first real estate office we came to and asked what they had available. The Agent knew good prospects when he saw them, so he quickly locked the door and asked us to follow him in our car. We drove around awhile and saw a few interesting houses, but Stan thought the prices were a little high.

As we drove down a narrow, brick-lined road past charming little houses with a definite European look, Joi glanced up the hill and saw a "for sale" sign on the back of a house on a parallel street. She told Stan she wanted to see it, so after alerting the realtor and navigating a few tricky turns, we pulled up in front of 2460 East Tuscan Road. Later we learned the community was called Little Tuscany, a name that suited the area beautifully.

After finding a lockbox on the water pipe, our agent entered the combination and out popped the key. We were surrounded by four-foot evergreens as we walked up the path and onto the front porch. When the Agent opened the door, I watched Joi's face as she stepped inside. Her eyes opened as wide as I had ever seen them. The place was beautiful!

The Agent started walking toward the kitchen, but Joi went the opposite direction, into the master bedroom. I followed her as she walked into a lovely, large square room with a walk-in closet. The room was more than big enough for a queen-size bed and had windows all across one wall, making it light and airy. Stan gravitated to the second bedroom that was half the size of the master. There was plush wall-to-wall carpeting throughout that looked brand new. It was beige and white and had probably been installed when the owners decided to sell the property.

The house was lovely, but it was the view that really captivated us. As we walked onto the plant-filled brick patio in the back of the house, the city of Palm Springs sprawled colorfully below as far as our eyes could see.

"The lights must be spectacular at night," Joi said quietly to Stan, showing an interest he picked up on right away.

Stan casually questioned the realtor about the asking price, and, when he was told $60,000, we couldn't believe our ears! How could it be so reasonable? He looked over at Joi and asked (as if he didn't know what she was going to say), "Well, what do you think? Do you want it?"

Laughing, Joi jumped up and hugged him.

"Of course!" she said excitedly. "Rachel and I can stay here during the winter, and you can come up on weekends." I felt a rush. She continued, "We can spend half the time up here and half the time at the penthouse."

I couldn't believe it. I was going to be alone for weeks at a time with my angel. Nothing would be more wonderful, especially at this time in our lives. I was thrilled!

Stan and Joi signed the contract that very afternoon. He knew he wouldn't have any trouble qualifying because the price was so low, and, when the Agent called the Owner, the deal was accepted. Stan then called the Tennis Club and told them he'd be back in about an hour and to reserve a court with one of the pros. I thought he'd pop with pride and excitement!

Right after his call to the club, Stan went shopping and decked himself out head-to-toe in fashionable (and obligatory) white garb. Joi drove back to the club and parked while Stan went inside. Since this was the first time we'd been alone, she found a place away from the other cars where we couldn't be seen. Always braver than I when it came to our relationship, she leaned over and kissed me. I melted. She said she'd been waiting all day to do it and tell me how much she loved me.

I loved her sense of adventure, and we carried on like two teenagers, "necking" for a good ten minutes until I started to get nervous, hoping no one would start looking for us. Reluctantly, she pulled away and then asked if I liked our new house, adding that she wanted it for us, to have a quiet place to get away. I told her how much I loved the house and her, and how ecstatic I'd be with her in our new winter home.

Finally, after giggling a bit at how disheveled we must have appeared, we took a few minutes to become presentable and then drove back to the restaurant. Stan saw us as we walked in and waved. He looked very happy. Why not? He was in his element—a private club in a ritzy area, playing tennis with the local pro. He was buying a house and seriously thinking about joining the Tennis Club. And he was cementing his social position by having Joi Lansing as his "wife"! Stan was in the catbird seat, and he knew it.

Joi and I had coffee at a table near the courts. When Stan finished his game (that the pro had graciously lost), he came over and asked Joi if she'd like to join the club.

"If you can afford it," she said, "I'd love to!"

Business had been good for Stan, and he was owed commissions and bonuses that were a lot of money in 1970. He had more than enough for the down payment on the Tuscan Road house, as well as a family membership at the Tennis Club. He'd even have extra money to invest if he wanted.

Stan and Joi discussed the possibility of eventually leaving the penthouse and staying in Palm Springs for most of the year. When Joi asked how I felt about leaving Los Angeles and living in the desert, I told her I loved the idea, and I loved Palm Springs, and I loved her! Wherever she wanted to go was just fine with me. I was ready for the ride wherever it took us, and I couldn't have been happier.

Joi and I were excited at the prospect of having our desert paradise to ourselves. There was almost no smog or pollution in the air, and it would be a healthier lifestyle for both of us. We would be living in a perfect climate for walking, and Joi could play tennis when she felt like it with the upper echelon of desert society. Staying as active as possible would be great for Joi. The Doctor suggested walking and light tennis as long as she wasn't in pain, and, so far, the Methadone had kept her discomfort manageable.

An impressive number of the wealthy and famous lived in this beautiful retirement mecca. Private golf courses were profuse, surrounded by the elegant homes of their members, drawing celebrities and elite golfers to their annual tournaments. Our social life, when we wanted it, would definitely be fun.

We decided to have dinner at the Tennis Club before spending the night at the Palm Springs Spa Hotel. The restaurant, much more beautiful at night than during the day, was built into the side of a mountain, with heavy framed glass separating the main dining room from the boulders. Lit from the bottom and on all sides, the natural rich gray wall was breathtaking in its majesty.

The best tables in the house were the ones closest to the tennis courts or next to the mountain. We'd had our lunch overlooking the courts, manicured lawns, and the multi-colored pansies and poppies in full bloom. Tonight, we'd sit facing the natural beauty of the mountain.

As new members, coupled with Joi's celebrity, we were given the royal treatment by everyone at the restaurant. We were seated immediately at a table of our choosing; the waitstaff was attentive but not overbearing. The club was managed with a professional touch, and every detail was addressed.

We hesitated to order seafood in the desert, but took a chance after our server assured us that all their seafood was flown in daily. Feeling reassured, and because the lobster sounded wonderful, we decided to have it. Each lobster weighed over two pounds and was cooked to perfection. Our server made the major cracks in the shell, making it simple to remove the white scrumptious delicacy. There was more than enough drawn butter to soak each morsel as it dripped onto the fresh green beans on its way to our mouths. We finished every bite and sat for a while until we could move again.

The dessert tray was filled with fruit tarts and cheesecake, crème brûlée and eclairs, each an ambrosia to the eyes. We were filled to capacity, and these luscious desserts seemed out of the question. Joi had really wanted the cheesecake, so, refusing to say "uncle," she asked that a slice for her and an eclair for me be boxed to take home. (Ahh, midnight would be fun!)

The bill arrived, but, since we were now members, no cash was needed. Stan handed the check to Joi and asked if she wanted to be the first to sign as a member of the club. She was delighted to sign her name, especially since the bill would be going to Stan!

Joi wasn't working and needed time to recuperate, so Stan had made it clear he would take care of most of the bills. She would pay for her cosmetics and clothing, and he would pay for housing and food.

Chapter 23

Back to Hollywood

We left the restaurant happily filled to the brim and already looking forward to the next dinner we'd have there. Joi drove while Stan stretched out in the back seat and lit up his Antonio y Cleopatra cigar. How we hated that smell, but, unfortunately for us, it went along with Stan. Joi, in some odd way, actually loved the man. Me? I was grateful and needed him to be in her life at this point.

When we arrived at the hotel, Stan checked in as we waited in the car. We knew he had booked a beautiful suite for us all. Happy, Joi and I couldn't wait to end our wonderful day together in our king-size bed, behind closed doors… finally alone.

The evening went by quickly. A lot had happened that day, including buying a new house and joining a private club. Joi was already sleeping soundly as I slipped in beside her. Waking just enough to know I was there, she rolled over and put her head on my chest, pulling her knees up to rest them across my body. Comfortable and in our special position, we slept soundly through the night. Sweet.

My girl and I slept until nine in the morning. Realizing that Stan had gone out for his usual morning coffee and newspaper, we took advantage of his absence to enjoy a quiet and loving time together. Making love in the morning had always been special to us, but with Stan around most of the time now, we had to catch our moments when we could. That morning was a treat.

We showered and were putting on the last bits of makeup when Stan knocked on the door and asked if we were ready to check out and get some breakfast. Joi, already dressed, joined him while I finished up.

When I was ready to go, I carried our overnight bags out to the car. Stan didn't offer to help. He wasn't much on lifting, as I've mentioned, needing to "save" his back for tennis, not for carrying luggage or groceries. I didn't mind, though. I was young and strong, and it was the least I could do. After all, he never complained about my being Joi's companion or paying for my food. He didn't know I would have paid *him* to be with Joi for even one day, let alone a lifetime!

We headed out to Louise's Pantry, a tiny restaurant on Palm Canyon that was famous for its homemade food and great pancakes. The long line in front proved its popularity. When we finally sat down, we soon enjoyed big fluffy pancakes, thick bacon, and perfectly prepared eggs. Rich hot coffee topped off our sumptuous repast. Sighing with satisfaction and smiling all the way, Joi and I then waddled out to the car while Stan lagged behind, lighting his cigar. Though we were ready to head back to the big city, our time in beautiful Palm Springs had been memorable, and I couldn't wait to return.

For Joi, our few exciting days, though fun, had been physically and emotionally exhausting, and she wanted to nap during the drive home. We got into the backseat, and I cradled her in my arms. I could see Stan in the mirror, and, as usual, he was oblivious to us. I wondered how he didn't seem to know that our relationship was more than we said. Maybe he did. Maybe he just didn't care. Comforted by his ignorance, I rested my head back, too, while snuggling Joi. We both dozed during most of the two-hour drive.

I woke when I felt Joi sit up and heard her whisper nervously, "Look at the traffic."

Stan's driving always made her uncomfortable, but now we were in downtown Los Angeles where cars sped along like an angry river of steel. We were just a hair away from panic. Stan was used to driving in Los Angeles traffic, but his eyesight was far better for seeing tennis balls flying than for three-thousand-pound cars roaring past on all sides.

Joi and I closed our eyes and held hands, our grip much tighter than usual, and we hoped (as I recall, we may have prayed) for the best. We managed to make it to the Sunset Boulevard off-ramp and finally exhaled, feeling out of harm's way at last.

Sunset Boulevard wasn't crowded for a late Sunday afternoon. Joi suddenly leaned forward, so Stan could hear, and asked if we could go up to Hollywood Boulevard to check on her star. She wanted me to see it, and Stan thought it would be fun. I don't know how I'd missed seeing it before, and I was excited. After all, I'd been smitten with her ever since she was a star on *The Bob Cummings Show*!

Stan parked, and Joi couldn't wait to get out of the car. She grabbed my hand and pulled me along behind her to the Hollywood Walk of Fame. Her star was near the corner of Hollywood and Vine. I was so impressed!

The moment we arrived, she beamed from ear to ear and stood proudly next to it, looking for my reaction. I looked down at the star and then up into her smiling, beautiful face. Laughing, I threw my arms around her, and we danced around like a couple of kids. She couldn't have missed how I felt. It was a great moment for both of us.

The Hollywood Chamber of Commerce had certainly shown its appreciation for her talent and hard work in the industry. She told me she'd also been crowned Miss Hollywood many years ago and was Grand Marshal of the Hollywood Santa Claus Lane Parade. Joi was one of the few true queens of Hollywood in the 1960s. Positive proof of the affection and respect she garnered was the shining star with her name engraved on the Hollywood Walk of Fame.

Since Joi's star was embedded in the sidewalk and people walked on and around it daily, it was dusty and needed some cleaning. I decided to take an old brush and paper towels that Joi kept in the car and scrape out the dirt and debris stuck in the crevices. People watched as, on my knees, I almost spit shined her trophy! Some recognized her and asked for her autograph, which she was always happy to give. Her fans were very important to her, and she never denied a photo or an autograph. She was thrilled that people remembered her; their attention breathed life into her and made her feel loved. Joi desperately needed the adulation and felt her autograph was a way to show her gratitude.

When I finished cleaning and polishing Hollywood's homage to its beautiful queen, we stood and looked at it for a few more minutes and then walked back to the car. Stan had watched from a few feet away, observing her admirers. He would visibly "puffed up," with his chest out and belly sucked in, whenever she was recognized.

Back onto Sunset, we enjoyed seeing the billboards that lined the famous boulevard so colorfully. Passing one of our favorite restaurants, Frascati's, we decided to go there for dinner a little later that evening.

Home at last, we decided it was nap time for all of us. It had been a long and wonderful weekend, and Joi was holding up even better than I was. Her energy level was double what it was before the chemotherapy. Dr. Axelrod had told me the reaction to chemotherapy was very different from patient to patient, and some do quite well. He was right...Joi was doing great! She wanted to go places and see things and live every day to the fullest. And now, she wanted to take a nap, which was just fine with me. It gave us time to be alone in each other's arms, something we could never get enough of. Wrapped around one another, her sweet head next to my heart, we slept the sleep of lovers, happy and at peace.

Two hours was Joi's idea of a perfect nap. Waking with stretches and yawns, and nicely rested, we realized we were both getting hungry. It was almost six o'clock and a good time to get a reservation. The main dinner rush was seven-thirty or eight, and we wanted to be in and out before the onslaught of diners. It didn't take any of us long to get ready.

Stan wanted to drive this time, and I was fine just riding along as usual. Joi drove most of the time when we were together, and I didn't care about having my own car because I had no interest in going anywhere without her, especially now that every second of every minute, of every hour, of every day, was precious to me. Even if I tried not to think of it, I knew I had to live a lifetime with her, one day at a time, for whatever time she had left on this earth.

Dinner at Frascati's was always an Italian food lover's delight. Joi loved the chicken scaloppini with white wine and mushrooms, while I enjoyed the chicken piccata with lemon zest and capers. Stan's favorite dish was osso bucco, an Italian recipe of veal shanks, vegetables, herbs, and pancetta. We always knew what we wanted to order. It wasn't that we were in a rut, but we knew what was really good and what we liked. Like they say, "If it ain't broke...don't fix it!"

Dinner was delicious, as usual, and Joi seemed to enjoy herself much more than I'd seen in the past. Everything delighted her...the food, the service, the ambience...it was all good. My girl was enjoying life.

It had been a long day and, even though Joi had wonderful bursts of energy, she finally wore down. She and I slept like babies that night.

The following morning after Stan left for work, Joi decided it was a perfect day to have lunch at the commissary at Universal Studios. She believed that, if you weren't seen in films or on TV, you'd be forgotten. Universal Studios was one of the biggest players in the business at that time, and was where most of the big action was happening in films and television.

Joi was feeling great and thought she looked good. There had been those days when she didn't want anyone to see her, when the sore on the tip of her nose would start bleeding. Today her nose had healed, and there were no signs she ever had a problem. No one in the business knew she had even been ill or had surgery, as we made sure it was kept private from almost everyone.

That was one of the major drawbacks of the entertainment industry. If they thought you were ill or had a problem, you were automatically off the list when a part came up. "You're only as good as your last performance," was one of Joi's favorite lines. You could be great your entire life, but, if the last thing you did was a bomb, you'd have one hell of a time trying to get hired again. Joi knew the game and played by their rules.

She also wanted to go to Universal to see Gary Morton, who was involved in *Lady Sings the Blues* with Diana Ross. She called his office and told his secretary she was coming in to see him, was bringing her sister, and would have lunch at the commissary. Gary got on the line and told her everything would be arranged and he'd love to see her. A pass would be waiting at the black tower, and we could go into the lot from there.

This kind of reaction from a big producer like Gary Morton made Joi very happy. At one time, she'd been friendly with his now wife, Lucille Ball, and her ex-husband Desi Arnaz. They had worked with Joi on their show, *I Love Lucy*, and admired her comedic ability. Lucy thought Joi had a lot more talent than she was given credit for, and believed they could find a vehicle to make her a bigger star. Lucy even proposed a contract that would have given Joi work for a long time, but Stan didn't like the deal and killed it. Joi was devastated, but trusted him and didn't know what a mistake his decision would turn out to be. That was the end of any other work with Desilu Studios.

Joi had a red silk dress she absolutely loved, a shirtwaist sheath with round gold buttons from top to bottom. It had two false pockets with smaller gold buttons on either side of her bust. She wore a thick rope belt that wrapped around her waist twice which tied and hung by her side. It was her good luck dress that she wore any time she had an interview or wanted to impress someone. That was the era when minis were very popular, and this dress was about six inches above the knee, sexy but not trashy. It looked great on her and accentuated her tiny twenty-four-inch waist and very ample bustline. We both knew she wouldn't be ignored this time—or forgotten.

She found a pretty aqua dress in her closet that fit me perfectly. I could wear most of her clothes, except they hung on me a little differently! I was a C cup, and she was a double D, but she wanted me to look good, so she chose my wardrobe for me.

We both dressed a little faster than usual, not wanting to miss the lunch crowd at the commissary. You could usually see three or four major stars and two or three big name producers and directors sitting around chatting. It would be fun!

Joi and I were ready and "lookin' fine." She drove, as usual, particularly happy since this was the first real day we could spend without Stan. We were like a couple of kids playing hooky from school. Joi turned the radio on as I tuned it to the top 40s station. We knew most of the lyrics to the popular songs, and Joi sang along. Oh, sure, I could sing, but it was always in the wrong key! One singer in the family was sufficient. Besides, my job was to play the wind drums and air guitar, accompanying her as she sang her heart out.

We bounced in time to the music as we drove to our appointment with Gary and some great food. No two people in the world were as happy as we were on that lovely, lovely day. There were times when I could forget and, thankfully, this was one of them.

It didn't take long to drive to Universal City. It was right over the hill from her star on Hollywood Boulevard. Vine turned into Cahuenga Boulevard, and it fed right into the studio's entrance. We drove up, and Joi was recognized immediately. Before she could announce herself, the guard handed her a pass with both our names printed on it…the two Miss Lansings, Joi and Rachel.

Joi parked in a special VIP area next to the ominous black high-rise tower, the famous building where corporate bigwigs took care of business. Universal was one of the first studios more interested in the bottom line than in the actresses' bottoms! It was run more like a big corporation instead of the good old boys in pursuit of their toys. Hanky-panky still went on, but not to the extent that it did at Metro and the other big studios. The producers and directors at Universal had to answer to bean counters who had a lot of power.

These forgettable guys in their same gray suits and wimpy ties were account-able to shareholders who wouldn't approve of hiring some little who-who just because someone wanted to date her. No one could play without paying at Universal. Changes were on their way in Holly-weird.

It was eleven-thirty, and Gary Morton was expecting us. A security guard directed us to his little white stucco cottage office, with its old California style and Spanish tile roof. The office was decorated with green hanging plants, and mahogany-framed awards hung everywhere we looked. His secretary ex-plained that Mr. Morton was finishing some phone calls and would be out in a few minutes, so we sunk down in an overstuffed deep brown leather couch.

We were seated only a few moments before Gary opened his massive ma-hogany door. Out he stepped, handsome and powerful, epitomizing success as he smiled and walked toward Joi. As he gave her a big bear hug and held on to her for a few extra moments, he seemed genuinely happy to see her.

Very graciously, Gary led us into his private office. Joi and I were both surprised at how small and low-key it was. There was a large framed photo of Lucy on his hand-carved mahogany desk and photos on the wall of the two of them. *His desk is the size of a dining table*, I thought.

Gary showed us a drawing he was considering for his new production, *Lady Sings the Blues*. It had a large modified L as the outline of a woman's face, with tears falling from her one visible eye. At the top of the outline was a white gardenia, Billie Holliday's trademark. When Joi told him I was an artist, he asked if I'd like to come up with a different idea for their main billboard and newspaper ad. I explained I wasn't a graphic artist or illustrator, more of an abstract mood painter, but told him I'd try my best.

Joi was my biggest fan when it came to my artwork. She bought all my art supplies and took me to magnificent galleries filled with the work of great and off-the-wall artists. I loved the style of Leonardo Nierman and tried to grasp how he created his fluid way of putting paint on canvas. Joi took me to vari-ous artist supply houses as we searched for the key to what appeared to be a brushless application of liquid pigment. We finally found it at a marine supply store. Joi encouraged me with each piece of art I created, and told every gallery owner we met how wonderful my work was!

It came as a shock when the Owner of an elegant Beverly Hills gallery actually offered me a one-woman show after viewing my artwork. The show was a success, people seemed to appreciate my work, and one of my favorite pieces sold to a collector of modern art. Joi's faith in my ability appeared to be well-founded, and not just because she loved me.

Before we left for lunch, I told Gary Morton that I'd work on a few ideas and bring him what I came up with in a week or so. He had a luncheon appointment off the lot and excused himself with regrets for leaving so soon. After warm hugs and kisses, we thanked him again for the pass and said our good-byes.

The commissary was only a five-minute walk from Gary's cottage. It was lunch time, and people were milling about. There was just a short wait for a table, with a lot more people standing behind us, so our timing was good.

We hoped to end up with a good table where we could be seen. That was the key to commissary showmanship. You needed to be in the most visible area at a desirable table where you'd be recognized. We lucked out! The hostess took us to a large semi-circular booth where we could sit side by side. Joi sat where she could be seen from every angle in the room. The commissary was a very large open space with different levels. On that day, we were seated on the top tier, which did wonders for Joi's fragile ego.

Joi always worried she might not work again because she was now over forty, and there weren't many "sexy babe" parts in film or television she would be right for. The 1960s and 1970s marked the beginning of the sexual revolution and feminism, and Joi was the epitome of everything they fought against. Her beauty and sexuality had always been objectified in photos and in the media. Now, however, producers and the corporate money men were beginning to shy away from the sex goddess types that had been so popular in the 1940s and 1950s, when Marilyn Monroe and Jayne Mansfield were in their heyday. The gorgeous blondes who were adored for years had now become a liability because of the changing of the times. Occasionally, there would be bit parts done as more of a spoof than a real character, and they weren't taken seriously. More often, they were the butt of jokes than anything. The blonde bombshell was now a celluloid dinosaur on the cutting room floor, and Joi could feel every inch of it.

That day, however, men walked by and slowly checked us out, each trying harder than the next not to be obvious in their appreciation of Joi's physical attributes. The area where we were seated was not normally a pathway in or out of the dining area, but that afternoon there was enough traffic in front of our table to wear out the carpet and put in a toll booth!

The only people we recognized from our vantage point were John Cassavetes and Peter Falk. They were buddies of Joi's from the old days, and they had worked on a lot of projects together. John noticed Joi while he was chatting with Peter, and excused himself to come over to our table, asking if he could join us. Of course, Joi welcomed him gladly. He expressed his admiration for her work and said he hoped they'd have the opportunity to work together in the future. With an easy charm, John was gifted at putting us at ease. He thanked Joi for allowing him to sit for a moment and kissed her hand like a grand knight of the roundtable before he left. He also kindly acknowledged her "little sister" and said he had enjoyed meeting me.

When we finished our lunch and asked the Waitress for our check, she told us Mr. Morton had taken care of it. We were happily surprised at this and thrilled with the chivalrous treatment we were receiving.

Our outing at Universal Studios had been a lot of fun. Joi felt great. Having a day filled with positive energy from her peers had lifted her spirits, and, by the time we got to the car, she was soaring!

Joi had always thrived on attention and adulation from men, and, at this point in her life, she was feeling insecure about her looks. Sadly, her self-image was reflected in the eyes of those who desired her, but Joi knew that, in show business, she was a commodity, with a sell-by date stamped on her beautiful, but aging forehead. The camera had been an adoring lover throughout her career, but would soon be unforgiving and unfaithful as the years progressed. I was always relieved when she had a good experience like she did that day. It was good for both of us.

Starting to tire, Joi actually asked me to drive the fifteen minutes to our home, and I was thrilled to be behind the wheel of her sweet Caddy. The last time I'd driven a car was when I took my old clunker to a used car lot and sold it for $200, only a few dollars less than I'd paid for it when I first moved into the Studio Club. Besides, I certainly wasn't going to chauffeur her around in that, even though she once told me she'd be "as proud as the Queen of England in her Bentley," just sitting next to me in whatever I drove.

It was a classic California day and her Caddy was as smooth as silk driving down Cahuenga and onto Sunset. I glanced over at my sweetheart and noticed she was starting to nod off, so I suggested that she lie down. As she put her head in my lap, I stroked her hair and kept my right arm resting on her shoulder. She lifted her hand and put it in mine. Her touch was warm. Too warm, I worried.

As we drove through the late afternoon Hollywood traffic, I felt my throat tighten and my eyes begin to fill. I kept swallowing to keep from crying. My girl seemed to be exhausted in a way she hadn't been for months. Could the specter of her cancer be starting to raise its ugly head again? We had an appointment to see the Doctor the following day and would know more then. I was apprehensive, to say the least.

I drove into the parking garage at the same time Stan arrived from his day at work. Our spaces were side by side, and he saw Joi sleeping in my lap. He glanced at me, and our eye contact told him more than my words ever could have. He opened her door and helped her out of the car. Joi leaned weakly on him for a second, then seemed to gain strength and began to walk toward the elevator, holding his arm. I followed behind them with her purse, quickly wiping the tears from my face, determined never to show her my pain.

By the time we got to the penthouse, Joi seemed to be feeling a little better and began excitedly to tell Stan about her day at Universal. He loved hearing all the minutiae about the hot shots in the business.

Joi told him about her conversation with Gary Morton and gave him a minute-by-minute replay of the visit by John Cassavetes, including every nuance and expression on John's face. Joi knew that Stan thrived on the stories about her admirers; they made him feel even more important. They could want her, but he was still legally married to her. She had told me about the time one of the big stars in films had made advances toward her in front of him. Stan looked at him and said, "Take your best shot."

Joi was embarrassed by his comment, but she knew how he was and still loved him in spite of himself.

Their relationship was now platonic, but his help was really needed at this time in her life. Things would have been very difficult without the health insurance he carried for her as his wife. The surgery and hospitalization would have easily wiped out the savings bonds she'd been stashing for years. This was his opportunity to make up for some of the hurt and betrayal he had exposed her to for most of their marriage.

After relaxing for a while, Joi appeared to feel better, and I was relieved. We were all hungry, so Stan offered to take us to Ben Frank's Restaurant, a wonderful coffee shop that was very popular with the showbiz crowd located on Sunset. Joi and I loved it because it was open twenty-four hours and had the best roast chicken in town, a huge meal with veggies and a choice of potato. The half chicken dinner was perfect to split since Joi loved dark meat and I liked the white.

During regular hours, the restaurant attracted local residents from the hills above Sunset, but, in the wee hours of the morning, characters of every kind managed to find their way like homing pigeons to their nest. There were nights when we couldn't sleep, so we'd go to Ben's for some serious people-watching. Restaurant and bar workers stopped by after the bars closed at two o'clock, and occasionally you'd see an entertainer or two who would come in after a gig. By three in the morning, every offbeat group was represented—hookers and drag queens, hippies and college students—a regular cornucopia of humanity.

Still a little tired, Joi asked Stan to pick up three chicken dinners for us, instead of taking us out. There would be plenty of food for, at least, two meals and he didn't seem to mind going, which made life a lot easier.

Joi needed to save her energy for our trip the next day to Santa Monica to see Dr. Wilson. I was always stressed when we went to see him. Most of the time, I tried not to think about the future. Every second now was precious, so denial, whenever possible, was the easiest path to take. But this time, I was petrified he would say the chemotherapy wasn't working and there was nothing else he could do for my girl.

I set the table, and Joi made coffee, our normal routine. My coffee was less than perfect, and she had a knack for measuring the ground coffee, so it was consistently great. Stan arrived with dinner, and we enjoyed our meal together.

It had been a long and lovely day, and we had every intention of ending it in our favorite way. Well, we've all heard and used the phrase, "The spirit is willing, but the flesh is weak," and that was definitely the case that night. All we were capable of was laughing!

Suddenly, Joi decided to do the one thing she knew would make me crazy. She started tickling me!

"Oh, noooo!" I yelled. She knew I couldn't control my feet or my bladder when she did this. My feet kicked, and, well…my bladder? Guess!

Giggling and gasping for air, I, at last, slipped from her grip and raced to the bathroom. The woman was delighted with her conquest and couldn't stop chuckling. This was a side of Joi I actually loved. Her playfulness always relieved the stress that too often filled our lives. That night, our energies finally spent, we relaxed and slept deeply.

I didn't mind being the focus of Joi's teasing. Seeing her have so much fun made it all worthwhile. Her beautiful green eyes would sparkle with an impish delight, and, after all, I was the lucky one who loved and was loved by this adorable woman-child.

Many of my happiest memories are of those times…times when the stress and strangeness of life in the spotlight would fade and we became just two little girls, sitting in a sunny park, hands joined, talking innocently of always and forever. We had found ourselves in a real life fairy tale, and I couldn't even *imagine* anything but a happy ending.

Chapter 24

The Cliffhanger

We got up a little later the following day because Joi's appointment with Dr. Wilson had been scheduled for early afternoon, rather than her usual late morning time slot. She couldn't eat or drink after midnight the night before having blood work done, so she preferred a morning appointment; however, nothing was available.

As Joi was hypoglycemic, she needed to eat on a regular schedule. When her blood sugar was too low, she became irritable, edgy, and occasionally her whole personality changed. Sweet and lovable Joi would be replaced by a paranoid and sometimes angry person I didn't know. It always threw me.

One afternoon in Las Vegas, she hadn't eaten at all earlier that day, and we were driving to one of the hotels for lunch. Suddenly, her blood sugar must have plummeted, and she couldn't think straight. We were behind a line of cars waiting to enter the driveway, and, disoriented, Joi put the car in park and left it … and me … in the street! She was running to the hotel to get something to eat, and I ran after her, practically throwing the key to the valet, telling him she was sick. Joi pushed her way past the slots and tables and the people playing them until she reached the closest restaurant, where she slumped down into a booth, head on her arms on the table.

I caught up with her and told the host to get her some orange juice fast, that she was going into shock. They saw that things were serious and had a pitcher of fresh juice in front of her within a minute. As Joi gulped it down, the look on her face began to change, and she stopped trembling. The frantic, desperate stranger left, and Joi had returned.

That afternoon, we ate lunch as if nothing had happened. Joi had no memory of what had occurred earlier, no recollection at all of leaving the car running in the middle of the street. I didn't say anything then, but the next time we saw a doctor, we discussed it with him. He told us to make sure she ate regularly and always had some glucose tablets nearby, in case her blood sugar dropped suddenly.

Never wanting this to happen again, that morning we slept as late as possible, so she could tolerate waiting for food until after her one-thirty appointment. I insisted on driving in case she had a problem. Stopping the car in the middle of Wilshire Boulevard would not go over well with the local police! She knew I was right and handed me the keys. We made excellent time and were sitting in the office lobby fifteen minutes early. I asked the receptionist if Joi could have her lab work done sooner, and she said she would try to squeeze her in a little early.

The waiting room was filled, but no one was chatting. It felt oddly quiet. This was an oncology practice that specialized in helping people whose conditions were not very hopeful. They had all been referred by doctors who could no longer provide them with a magic bullet. Drs. Rochlin, Wagner, and Wilson were ahead of the pack when it came to trying new drugs on patients who had no other options. When they ran out of combinations of drugs to try, all that was left were smoke and mirrors.

Most of the faces in this little room had empty eyes staring out into space. They would occasionally try to fake a smile, but everyone in that room had received a death sentence. Everyone but Joi. She alone had not heard those words and, as far as I was concerned, she never would. At least, not any time soon.

Joi and I were friendly and tried to cheer up the room by making light conversation. Joi was one of the few patients who still had most of her hair. Almost everyone was wearing a wig or hairpiece to hide the side effects of chemotherapy. Because of this, Joi felt secure that her health was much better than these other poor souls. There were dozens of questions she didn't ask, and the pathology report and her diagnosis were never volunteered. Joi had hope and a positive attitude which kept her going.

Soon, the receptionist called us, and we moved to the little room adjacent to the lobby. Janet, the lab tech, asked which arm was used last week and Joi told her the right. That answer meant her left arm would get the abuse today.

Four tubes were filled with Joi's blood and then spun in a machine. One of the tubes was then tested to see if her hemoglobin was in the safe range. The type of chemotherapy she was taking could be quite rough on the body, and it was very important to make sure her red cells were not being destroyed along with the cancer cells.

Janet wrote down some numbers and slipped them into Joi's chart. She then looked up at us and said that Dr. Wilson would want to talk with us. My heart fell. Every possible terrible thought flew through my brain, careening wildly like an errant tennis ball. I could barely breathe. I was petrified the chemotherapy had stopped working and that Joi would be told she had very little time left.

Still not wanting Joi to know my feelings or fears, I kept my body from shaking and smiled. I told her, "He must have some good news," and my words seemed to calm her. Just as we were about to sit down in the holding area, Dr. Wilson opened the door to his office and asked us to come in.

Dr. Wilson was a man who rarely smiled, though he had a softness and gentle manner that made you feel that he cared. His job was not a happy one; all of his patients eventually died. He did his best to keep them alive as long as he could by giving them what he knew was poison, but his talent was calibrating the dosage so that it did what it was supposed to do and didn't kill the patient…at least, for a while. I had noticed, at our previous visits, that his sentences were usually only five or six words at the most, and today I was terrified we would hear only two words: "I'm sorry."

Joi and I sat nervously at his desk as he opened her chart. He looked at the numbers that had just been entered, and a big, wide smile came across his face. I was stunned. Could it be?

He looked at her and said not two, but three wonderful words: "You're in remission!"

Yes! I heard my heart yell, and I knew the smile that exploded on my face had never been bigger.

Joi was oddly subdued, but seemed pleased. Dr. Wilson was visibly delighted as he told us she was responding much better than they had ever imagined. Her body was able to tolerate the Cytoxan much longer than most patients and had been able to keep the cancer cells at bay. He also said she didn't need to come in every week, that once a month would be fine for now.

I was thrilled! This meant we could move to Palm Springs as soon as we wanted to live in our new home. It also meant she might be able to work, if she wanted to, and if the opportunity presented itself. To me, it meant we had more time together, and I would still have my love, my best friend, my dear Birdie in my life. The relief I felt was immeasurable, and I couldn't stop smiling.

When we got up from his desk, I thanked him and spontaneously threw my arms around him. I hugged him with all the gratitude I had in my heart. Joi looked at him with tears running down her cheeks. For her, this meant she could start living her life again, not having to turn down work.

It meant we could do more and enjoy our life together.

Joi couldn't quite reach his neck with her arms; he was over six feet tall and very thin. I'd had no trouble because I was almost as tall as he was, but he understood what Joi was trying to do and bent down, so she could hug him and give him a kiss on the cheek. I could hear her whispering to him how grateful she was and that words couldn't express her happiness. It was a wonderful moment for all of us, one that I will never, ever forget.

Walking on air, we made an appointment for one month later and quickly walked out of his office. The door barely had time to close before we threw our arms around one another and held on as if our very lives depended on it. Then... we kissed as if there was no one else in the world to see us... and, frankly, at that moment, we wouldn't have cared if there had been.

We had been "pardoned," and I felt as though the gates of my personal prison had swung wide. I was now free to go home... to my Joi, my love. This was the beginning of a new and wonderful chapter in our lives. Joi was going to live, and we were off to Palm Springs!

Chapter 25

Remission

There are no words to express how happy we were when Dr. Wilson said the magical word—remission. We stood in the hallway outside his office, kissing and holding each other until we heard a group of people walking in our direction. At that point, we didn't really care what people thought, but, wanting to be alone together, we ran to the car.

Whenever Joi and I were excited or happy, we'd act like kids, free and filled with fun. That day, I felt like a colt running in a springtime meadow. We'd run a few feet, jump, skip, and then start running again! We both felt the lifting of the thunderstorm which had followed us for months. The black clouds were dissipating, and a shining shaft of sunlight was streaming through the darkness at last. We ran as if the wind gave us wings.

Laughing, we finally got to the car, completely out of breath. Alone, we looked deeply in each other's eyes…when Joi announced she was starving! She was a natural comedian, her timing superb. She almost put me on the car floor, I was laughing so hard!

After pulling myself together, I realized I was hungry, too. We weren't far from the Santa Monica Pier which had a couple of great restaurants. Joi loved the idea, so off we went. It was time to celebrate and, since we really loved the ocean, sitting near it would be the perfect place to bask on our happy day.

We got lucky and found a parking space right near the pier. The stress and tension of waiting to talk to the Doctor had taken its toll and, even though the news was good, running from the office to the car had sapped what was left of our blood sugar. Neither of us had eaten since the night before, and we were relieved to find a place to park so close to the pier entrance.

The Santa Monica Pier was one of the top tourist attractions of Southern

California in those days. It jutted out over the beautiful blue undulating Pacific on huge pilings that looked like stilts; the pier itself swayed just enough for us to need sea legs. Although it was usually foggy and overcast until later in the day, this time, the weather seemed to be celebrating as well—clear and sunny, about seventy degrees, lovely and warm for early winter.

Now even more hungry, we looked almost desperately for some place to eat. Nothing appealed to us until we came to the end of the pier and noticed a little café off to the right of the foot traffic, behind some fishing poles, nets, and a small rowboat. It definitely was not a tourist trap, but looked like the kind of place the "regulars" at the pier might frequent. In fact, it was kind of funky. But, and this was the deciding factor, the most incredible smells were coming from its open door. "Delicious" would be an apt description if one could describe the taste of food before eating it! We looked at one another at the same time, and Joi said, "Why not?" In we went.

The checkered tablecloths reminded me of some of the pizza places I went to as a kid, and, sure enough, when we looked at the menu on the wall, it was Italian.

It took our eyes a minute to adjust, but the impression was one of warmth and color. Like out of a foreign movie, someone was humming and singing softly in the kitchen, and a friendly older woman was at a small table, clearing the plates from a meal someone had just enjoyed.

"Welcome!" she called out to us with an open smile. Perfectly cast, she also had a lyrical Italian accent! "Come. Sit," she said warmly.

And did we ever. We sat, we ate, and we laughed for over an hour. We were right. The cafe was for locals and had been on the pier for years. It was owned by a family who had never cared about making it "the place" and had kept it comfortable—a homey hangout we'd been lucky enough to find for ourselves.

After a great meal of hot bread, shrimp, and halibut, topped off with terrific coffee, we wandered to the end of the pier and watched the late afternoon sun as it began to sink into the Santa Monica sea.

Our day had been idyllic. We'd been told Joi was getting better; we were happily full with good food and friendship, and we were in love. I put my arms around her and kissed her forehead. Life was good. And I was determined to keep it that way for her…one day at a time.

That evening, Joi recounted our entire day (except for the hugging and kissing part), telling Stan about the wonderful news Dr. Wilson had given her. He couldn't believe what he was hearing. How could this be? They didn't think she would make it for more than a few weeks or a month or two at the most. Joi had fooled them! Her tenacious spirit and will to live had proven them wrong.

I watched her as they talked. She was glowing, and Stan couldn't seem to get enough of the good news. Finally, relieved but obviously exhausted emotionally, Stan slipped a little brandy into his coffee and retired to his favorite chair.

A little while later, we went in to check on Hubby. Fortunately for him (and us), he was down for the count. The combination of brandy and good news had put him into a contented doze. Happily for us, his snoring was predictably…and humorously…loud. This always gave us a perfect sound cover for the rest of our night.

The evening was still young, and we were finally alone. The day that began with fearful anticipation had become one filled with a sweet high that had me almost giddy. I turned the radio to our favorite easy listening station, and the soft romantic music was perfect for dancing. Joi loved to dance as much as I did, and it began the perfect ending to our perfect day.

We lit jasmine candles that left a sweet and delicate scent throughout our room. The song ended, and my dear girl took my hand and pulled me gently toward our bed. Sitting next to me, she softly stroked my face while telling me how much she loved me.

Her sweet words made me cry. She said she couldn't bear the thought of leaving me "to face the world alone." She just "had to get better." There were too many things we still needed to see and do. Kissing the tears on my cheeks, she held me tighter than ever before. She began to cry, too, saying it just wouldn't be fair to have so little time together now that she finally found the love of her life.

I somehow realized I had to pull myself together to help her through this terrible sadness. I said that she wasn't going to leave me, that I wouldn't let her go. Pulling her close, I assured her the doctors had found a treatment that was working and that she didn't need to worry. I told her not to be concerned about me, that she needed to keep her thoughts positive.

I don't know if she believed my words or just desperately wanted us to have a happy ending, but she eventually stopped crying. She closed her beautiful eyes as I kissed them and moved down to her soft, sweet lips, as our mood slowly changed from tearful to passionate. The night was long and filled with tremendous emotion as we made love like never before…as if it would be the last time.

It was almost noon when I finally awakened. I thought we'd be tired from very little sleep, but that was not the case with Joi. My honey had gotten up before I even started to move. With one bleary eye, I could see her zipping around with the energy of a teenager, picking up the clothes that, in our passion, we'd thrown in all directions. I smiled sleepily and told her to stop, that I'd pick up everything "as soon as I could move."

Bending down to give me a quick kiss, Joi laughed and told me to take my time. I didn't want to stay in bed alone, so I managed to stagger up, put on my fuzzy pink robe, and join her in the kitchen. She'd already made a lovely pot of coffee—twelve cups, in fact. Wisely, she knew we would need them!

Stan had left to play tennis with his friend Edwin, and from there he was off to work, so we'd been given a real gift—another day to ourselves. I asked Joi what she wanted to do on this glorious day, and she surprised me by saying she wanted to see *Bigfoot,* our film! It seemed that Bob Slatzer, the Director, had called and told her it was playing in some obscure little theater in Hollywood and asked if we'd like to go with him.

Bob was a really nice guy who seemed kind of lonely. He was never formally told of our relationship that resulted from working together on the film, but he wasn't blind. He had to have picked up on our glances and that I rarely called her Joi. It was always "honey," or "darling," no matter where we were. I watched what I said in front of people in the business, but, around most people we knew, "honey" or "Birdie" was her name.

Joi thought it would be fun to have lunch at Canter's Delicatessen and then meet Bob at the theater to see our "Oscar-winning" performances. She called him and said we'd meet him at the theater for the late afternoon showing. She told me that Bob loved being seen with good-looking women, and we were quite a combo, if I do say so myself.

We took a relatively fast shower, separately. If we'd taken it together, we'd have definitely missed our appointment with Bob! Whoever said that you can have too much of a good thing was quite mistaken.

Joi picked out what she wanted me to wear, and, for herself, she decided on a pair of black cashmere slacks and a red and black cowl neck cashmere sweater. She had a tailored black mid-thigh cashmere jacket to keep her warm in the theater in case it was cold, a probability in that kind of older building.

I put on a pair of black jeans with a gray and pink V-neck sweater. She also wanted me to wear the coat she'd given me the morning after we spent the night talking at Schwab's Drug Store. I can still remember opening the bag as she handed it to me. I was in total shock! No one had ever been so thoughtful and kind to me, especially someone who barely knew me. It was completely unexpected, and I was so surprised that I lost my head and kissed her on the cheek. I guess it didn't frighten her off, though … what a lucky thing for me!

We were ready to go, and Joi took her medications just as we were headed for the door. She was used to taking vitamins by the handful, so one Cytoxan pill, her Methadone for pain, and a few multivitamins were gone in the blink of an eye.

We were both feeling extremely good and just a little frisky. I always tried to follow her lead, and, if she was not feeling well, we'd walk very slowly. If she was feeling okay, we'd pick up the pace. If she was feeling really good, she loved to skip along like a little kid. That day, we skipped!

In the car, she checked her makeup in the rearview mirror, then playfully leaned over and kissed me lightly on the cheek. Nice! We were going to have another wonderful day.

Canter's was on Fairfax, just a few miles from our apartment. We weren't on Beverly for very long before we saw Fairfax approaching, and, as we made our turn, we spotted a great parking place right in front of the deli on the other side of the street. We continued driving almost half a block until the traffic let up and, the second we could make a creative left turn, we did. Joi was good! The way she hung the U placed her at an angle where she could just slide into the parking place.

We didn't jump out of the car because there would be a lot of people who would recognize her, and we had to maintain a semblance of decorum in front of Canter's. We walked in, past several hundred people in the restaurant. This place was a jewish heaven. The food was always phenomenal, and the ambience was like being in New York in the kosher district. We both loved the food and knew this was the place to enjoy some of the best of it.

That day, Joi and I had a great table in the center of the restaurant. The building itself was very old and shaped like a big box. Canter's had been there for many years and still had a lot of the same clientele.

When you looked around the room, you'd see many octogenarians with purple, blue, or bright orange hair, and most of the little old men did the famous three-hair comb-over that was developed and perfected in Miami Beach, Florida. I think they put something like Vaseline on them to hold the hair in the precise location of the head. It was a definite talent that took many years to perfect, and some got it right until there was no hair left to put in its proper position!

The waiters and waitresses at Canter's could be very nice … they could be, but, most of the time, they weren't. You could hear them screaming from table to table and yelling the orders as they approached the deli section. This was a Hal Roach comedy with sound, and great fun to share the experience with a friend who had a similar sense of humor.

The décor was your typical Jewish deli of that era, stark with metal chairs and tables, most of which needed a shim under one leg, so they didn't wobble when the Waitress put an overly full glass of water on the wrong side. There were beveled mirrors on many of the walls to make it seem more spacious and a few green plastic plants in the corners of the room. The linoleum was dingy with years of built-up wax, and the carpeting had a definite path to guide your way. But the décor was unimportant. The food and ambience were the reasons people flocked like starving birds to this nest. The aromas that filled the air, from the moment you opened the glass door, came from all directions and made you want to stay forever.

We finally got the attention of our waitress. She came up to the table and abruptly dropped the menus on the table, narrowly missing the 1960s-style water glasses.

"Whaddaya want?" she barked.

We were afraid to ask her to come back, since we'd told Bob we'd be there on time for the opening film credits, so we ordered.

"Two extra-lean corned beefs on rye with cole slaw on the side," I said nervously.

"Whaddaya wanna drink?" she barked again.

"Two cups of coffee with cream," I barely managed to say before she picked up the menus and stalked off.

Looking back, we'd have been disappointed if she'd treated us any differently. This was part of the ambience that was so great, and you just didn't go there if you were thin-skinned. These gruff old gals were a colorful part of the charm of this wonderful dinosaur. They were delightful in their rough, bossy attitude.

Our sandwiches arrived in very short order, warm to the touch and close to three inches thick. One sandwich would have been enough for us to split, but we could always take a sandwich home to share later. If "magnificent" is a bit strong to describe corned beef, "amazing" would definitely be appropriate. It was exactly what we wanted, not dried out or fatty. The meat was very lean, and the rye bread was just baked and slightly warm. This was Jewish heaven!

The Waitress dropped the check on the table and told us to pay the cashier at the front of the restaurant. When we walked to the cashier, Joi also asked for a fresh loaf of Jewish rye from a stack neatly arranged on shelves near the register. The bill for everything was under $8, and Joi paid with a $10 bill. She took the change, walked back to our table, and put the $2 under the plate. That was one thing about my Birdie. She always made sure she tipped more than the usual amount, especially for people who made very little money.

Satisfied and smiling, we left our memorable epicurean nirvana and walked to the car. Traffic was light, and the theater wasn't very far, so we were right on time. It would have been great if a valet had been provided, but no such luck.

We drove around the block a few times and finally found an empty spot and pulled into it. We had just started our jaunt to the theater when we heard someone yelling Joi's name. I turned and saw Bob (who had become quite portly since we last saw him), trying to catch up with us. We stopped and waited as he huffed and puffed his way along, his face purple by the time he got to us. I thought he might have a heart attack! Needing to rest for a while, he leaned against a building wall for a minute or two.

When Bob finally caught his breath, we started off again toward the theater. Joi didn't want anyone to recognize her, so she'd put her hair up in sort of a bun and, after pulling a pair of sunglasses out of her black suede shoulder bag, she slipped them on just a little before we got there.

At the box office window, Bob bought three tickets, handing one to each of us as we walked by the red velvet ropes to the young male ticket-taker. This theater could never be confused with Grauman's Chinese. A little long in the tooth, it needed a good coat of paint on the wall. You could see some of it chipping in areas where the lighting was a little too bright. This was the kind of cinema that could only afford to show B-quality films. Looking around at the moviegoers, I realized this was probably the cheapest way for them to have a place to sleep for a few hours, provided no one booted them out.

Bob went to the concession stand and bought one of those gigantic bags of butter-flavored, oil-soaked popcorn. This was one time I didn't think I'd be able to eat. Joi looked at it and started to get a little queasy.

We began walking toward the inner doors, which were opening, so people who'd seen the earlier showing could leave. We stood to the side as they passed by. Most were laughing and making comments that were less than complimentary to the film. I hoped no one would say anything derogatory about Joi, but, just in case, I managed to get her attention, so she'd be distracted from listening. There weren't that many people in the audience, fifty at most. While they passed, obviously wanting to leave as quickly as possible, my ears were attuned to some of the things being said. All the negative remarks seemed directed toward the film, and not at her.

Joi did manage to hear some of the cracks people made about how it was a waste of perfectly good film, but she had seen some of the rushes during the filming and knew it was a real "turkey," so this came as no surprise.

As we walked down the aisle, I found myself wishing that we really had been able to "walk down the aisle," but we were living and loving in the wrong era. Joi and I had made our own vows to each other and had promised to be together "until death do us part." As far as we were concerned, we were as married as any two human beings could ever be, and without the cost of the bridesmaids!

We walked carefully down the center aisle. Joi didn't like wearing her glasses, so she preferred to sit midway to the screen. Her vision was pretty good, but was restricted for driving.

There was one time when we went to see my parents, and, on the way back, she was stopped for driving too slowly on the freeway. The cop pulled us over and asked for her license. He was a young, good-looking guy who recognized her immediately. When he saw her license, he knew for sure she was the movie star he'd always dreamed of meeting. He radioed to some of his buddies, and four squad cars and two motorcycle cops pulled up in back and in front of us.

The young cop saw she was required to wear glasses whenever she drove. She wasn't. He looked at her very carefully and asked where her glasses were. She looked him straight in the eye and said she was wearing contact lenses. She wasn't. He looked at all angles to see the little circular line that should have been resting on her pupils, and called each and every cop over to look as closely as possible for those "tricky little contacts" that seemed quite invisible.

He and his buddies knew she was trying to pull a fast one, but they didn't care. They were just having a great time looking into her beautiful green eyes. This little dance went on for over half an hour, and they all finally agreed she was wearing prescription contacts. She happily autographed some of her 8 x 10 photos for the guys, and, from that point on, she wore her glasses whenever she drove. She had almost learned the hard way on that one.

In the theater, there was a row of empty seats with a good view of the silver screen. Bob went in first, and then Joi and I slipped in behind him. The lights were still on, and Joi was making conversation with Bob, telling him how much she'd "enjoyed working on the film," and how he should've been given a much larger budget to make the film the way he wanted it…one he could be proud of. She tried to make him feel appreciated, by saying the right things that might keep him from "falling on his sword" after seeing the film. He was smiling as the lights dimmed and credits started to roll.

Stunned, we sat in total silence and disbelief throughout the film. The few people in the audience were laughing at the acting and the script. Though it was supposed to be somewhat of a horror flick, meant to keep the audience on the edge of their seats, it was being seen as a comedy!

No one shrieked in terror. No one gasped in fear when they saw the Bigfoot "monsters." Little children did not cry out when I kidnapped Joi and took her away with me. All you could hear was chuckling and sounds of derision coming from the seats surrounding us. We were mortified, especially Bob.

The poor guy finally leaned over and asked Joi if she'd mind leaving before it ended. Thank God! We both got up, relieved to be getting away before the lights came on. As we escaped up the aisle, Joi held her head down, hoping no one would see her.

Once outside, "whew!" was all we could say. Bob was bright red again and obviously humiliated, but Joi repeatedly told him it was a good film that was sabotaged by too little money. Hearing her words seemed to soften the blow. Joi joked with him and said that it might become a cult classic; you never could tell.

He laughed and said, "You might be right—stranger things have happened!"

We escaped unscathed, except for a few bruises to the ego. I had a feeling I knew where Bob was heading as soon as he left us. He hung out at the Cock'n Bull, a wonderful restaurant and bar on Sunset Boulevard, which was known as a great place for cocktails after work. Bob did enjoy imbibing, and that night was definitely well-suited for a real bender.

He walked us to our car, and we hugged and kissed him on the cheek, thanking him for taking us. Joi told him we should all go out for lunch whenever he had time. He said he was working on another film with his buddy, Anthony Cardoza, who'd been the producer on *Bigfoot*. They worked quite a bit together, putting out fast and cheap films that made them a few bucks and kept people working. Actually, the cinematographer on the film, Wilson Hong, went on to do some bigger budget films.

Though Joi and Bob were not happy with the film, I was secretly excited to see my name in the credits. I was last and referred to as "Monster," but in my young mind it was in letters ten feet high, and I was delighted! This film was also the reason for the most wonderful thing that ever happened in my life... it was where I met the beautiful Joi Lansing, now my sweetheart. Unwittingly, my friend Aleshia and Director Bob Slatzer had made my most precious dream come true.

Joi, grateful no one had recognized her, was relieved and happy we were on our way home. The only thing that gave her some peace of mind was that she'd had her name up in lights on a theater marquee. On the way home, she also told me how blessed she felt to have gotten that film in the first place, knowing we'd never have met without it. If there was such a thing as divine intervention, the angels had definitely done the casting that time.

Stan was waiting anxiously for our return, but seemed surprised when we opened the door.

"Why are you home so early?" he asked.

Joi told him the bitter truth with her dry sense of humor. She laughed as she told him that *Bigfoot* had to be the worst film she'd ever had the pleasure of starring in. Stan didn't know if he should console her or laugh along, as she told him our experience from beginning to end. She gave him enough cues that he realized he could laugh with her. The experience was actually funny, if more than a little painful. When she told him about the look on Bob Slatzer's face when he realized that people thought it was a comedy, Joi had us all laughing until it hurt.

We all went about our business for a while, settling in after our odd day. Then Stan came into our room and asked Joi if she'd thought about when she might like to move to Palm Springs. She really loved the penthouse apartment, but thought the air would be a lot cleaner and healthier for us in the desert. She was feeling good these days; the chemotherapy was doing a miraculous job, and the idea of getting away from the city made us both happy.

I vowed quietly to myself that our time in the desert would be some of the sweetest we would ever share. It was the very least I could do for my girl...my dear, dear girl.

Chapter 26

The Christmas Tree

Joi decided it would be great to spend Christmas in Los Angeles and then go to the desert at the beginning of February. She loved Christmas and wanted to get a massive tree to celebrate the hopeful things that were happening in our lives. We had a cathedral ceiling that could accommodate a fifteen-foot Christmas tree and, since she'd never lived in a place where she could have such an enormous tree, that was exactly what she wanted.

Stan agreed and would make sure the loan closed before the end of the year. It was November 1970, and we had so many reasons to be thankful. This year, Joi wanted to invite my parents to spend Christmas with us. I knew how thrilled they'd be, especially going to the home of a movie star in her penthouse apartment. They were very impressed with celebrities and had hoped that someday I'd be one, too, just like Joi. They didn't know our relationship but were hoping I was her protégé. The most important thing to me was that they be loving and kind to her, no matter what they might have thought. She deserved to be loved for the person she was, not because of, or in spite of, her celebrity.

We both adored Christmas and decided on not only a huge tree, but one that could be planted after the holidays were over. Thankfully, Joi was still doing well physically and would be with me to celebrate another holiday season. Since Stan and I had been told she wouldn't be around (and I felt it was miraculous that she was), this season would truly be the time for a special celebration. I wanted it to be the most glorious Thanksgiving and Christmas of her life.

I planned to cook our Thanksgiving dinner and was confident I could pull it off. I had always helped my mother prepare a massive feast and knew exactly what to do. It would be an intimate time since Joi wanted to have a quiet celebration with just the three of us.

Two days before Thanksgiving, we all went to the Chalet Gourmet on Sunset to buy the food for our feast. One of the nicest markets in the area, it had the best quality food, and its meat and produce were premium grade. We were able to find a fresh turkey that weighed eighteen pounds. It was, as Stan said, "a honker." I never knew exactly what that meant, but he used the term when something was extra large or extra special, and apparently that turkey qualified!

We selected all the items to make the sausage dressing my mother had taught me to prepare. We also needed fresh sweet potatoes and green beans, and I decided to make fresh cranberries, instead of opening a can. All of these recipes were simple to fix, and the most complicated part of the preparation was coordinating the cooking time for everything, which I had down perfectly. We happily left the market with a serious amount of food for our Thanksgiving feast.

As we drove down Sunset, Joi was singing the way she always did when we drove, and she was feeling good. Stan was in the back, puffing on a favorite cigar, as usual. Joi stopped at a light and noticed a Christmas tree lot on the corner that had popped up for the early birds who loved this time of year. She sat up when she thought she spotted a gorgeous blue spruce in the middle of the lot, towering above all the rest.

So, when the light changed, she moved forward, but slowed down until the opposing traffic went by and then hung one of her famous and totally illegal U-turns to head back to what she had already decided was "her tree." Stan about swallowed his cigar on that one, and I held on while simultaneously looking for a cop, the way I always did when she made that move. Lucky as usual, no one saw her, and she pulled in and onto the lot, parking (she said) so the workers could help load and tie "her" tree on the roof of our car.

The three of us wound our way through the bushy greens and finally came upon her prize. Oh, my! It was not only the tallest tree on the lot, but perfectly proportioned, too!

"That's it," Joi cried with delight. "That's my tree!"

A burly "mountain man" with a black parka, who seemed to own the lot, had seen us pull in and obviously spotted Joi immediately. Over he came, grinning like a smitten boy. Joi graciously smiled, told him about seeing her tree from the street, and asked how tall it was.

Actually puffing out his chest, he proudly told her it was almost fourteen feet tall. He continued explaining—as if he'd grown it himself—that he'd just finished measuring it because someone else had been interested in it but decided it might be too large. Luckily for us, it would just fit! Joi thought there would even be enough room on the top for a petite angel with short wings.

Joi asked Barney (who had introduced himself by then) if he had a tarp or something similar to put on top of her car, so the tree wouldn't scratch the paint. He had a large roll of three-layered plastic he was sure would do the trick.

I then saw an amazing transformation as I watched Joi become a helpless female! Joi almost shyly asked the price of the tree. Barney mumbled a bit and then seemed to settle on a price…obviously a "special" one for this exciting star. (Yeah, it was special all right. Much more expensive!)

"Uh, that would be…$150?" he said, his voice going up at the end as if he were asking for her approval. Stan started to reach into his wallet to pay him, but neither of them had counted on this blonde NOT being dumb.

"Ohhhh, too bad…" Joi said, putting her hand softly on Stan's arm who then, as if on cue, wandered away. Joi spoke quietly, perfectly portraying a fragile, deeply disappointed woman.

"I hadn't figured on spending so much on my tree," she said to Barney with a sigh…a BIG sigh…as she turned sadly away, as if to leave. About to bust, I started to follow her.

"Wait…" cried Barney, in classic, "I'll save you, Nell!" fashion. He kind of shuffled. "Uh, for you, ma'am…I can come down a little." He paused. This was obviously difficult for him. "Uh, would…uh…$100 be all right?"

"Sold!" Joi said, suddenly all business. "Now, can someone please get it on my roof? I want to set it up tonight!"

Joi caught my eye and sneaked a wink. What a gal!

Stan came back and paid "mountain man," who then picked up the tree with the help of several of his workers, first showing us where to pour the water to keep it alive. After laying the tree over plastic sheeting on the roof of the car, he wrapped thick cording in two places around the trunk, then ran the cord through all four car windows. All of us pushed and pulled on the tree to make sure it was secure. It was a little longer than the car on both ends, but we didn't concern ourselves with that because we just wanted to get home. It passed the tie test to everyone's satisfaction, and off we went.

Joi drove, and Stan and I held the rope securely to make sure it didn't come loose, but, as they say, "The best laid plans..."

As we picked up speed, air whipped under the tree, making it bounce. Joi was in her own world, happy and singing up a storm again, while a REAL storm was brewing on the roof! The faster she went, the more the fourteen-foot tree danced. And we both shrieked when she hit forty-five! Stan and I thought we were going to lose the tree and were terrified of being pulled out the window while trying to hold on to it!

Suddenly aware of what was happening, Joi hit the brakes. THIS solved nothing. The tree bolted forward and then backward, then forward and backward until the rope grabbed and tightened with the slip knots Barney had tied to keep it secure. Joi had freaked out by that time while the tree continued to bounce on top of the car. At last, it stopped, and we all exhaled. Joi looked up at the tree and then, glancing back and forth at both of us, asked if we were all right. Stan and I looked at each other, smiled, and, with a sigh of relief, said in unison, "Just fine."

In a little while, we arrived at our building with no damage done, except perhaps to everyone's nerves. Our groceries were getting warm, so we had to rush and put everything in the refrigerator before worrying about the tree.

There was one thing we'd neglected to consider. How in the hell would we be able to get the tree off the car and carry it all the way up to the top floor? Oooookay. We all looked at the tree and then at one another. Then, we all laughed.

Joi spoke up confidently.

"How late does Jack work?" she asked with a definite note of hope in her voice.

I said I thought he'd be there until, at least, five o'clock and told them to wait, that I'd be right back...like they could go anywhere with a fourteen-foot tree on the roof.

It was a quarter to five as I ran to the elevator, hoping against hope that Jack hadn't taken a few days off because of the holiday. I knew he had relatives out of state and that he and his lover often spent Thanksgiving and Christmas with them. But, with relief, I saw that the door was still open. I was almost at the inner door to his private office and caught him just as he was ready to walk out.

Jack and I had become friendly since I'd been living with Joi, and I knew that, if he could help us, he would. I breathlessly explained the drama of our Christmas tree problem. The main question for Jack was whether he had any young and studly males who could hoist, then haul this lovely tree up all those flights of stairs (of course, it wouldn't fit in the elevator), and then help set it up for us.

I explained to Jack that Stan couldn't lift anything more than a tennis ball (repeatedly, in five sets, slamming and lobbing his shots while going in for the kill). In fact, there was no way Stan would touch the tree nor pick up the heavy grocery bags I had just hauled into the apartment.

Jack was my hero! He had a few guys working in the building he would round up to take the tree to our apartment. They would set it up, put something under the base to protect the carpeting, and then fill it with water to keep the needles from falling off. Joi was elated when I told her we'd be able to decorate our tree once that was done and we'd bought some lights and tinsel.

We could finally relax for a few hours; the day had been fun but a little hectic at times. It's the way flying a plane was explained to me. It's ninety-nine percent mellow and easy, and one percent sheer terror. I really enjoyed the mellow and easy part, but the terror with the dancing tree on the rooftop was enough craziness to last me quite a while.

The guys untied the tree and brought it up to the apartment, being especially careful not to bend or break any of the limbs. The tree was so symmetrical and beautiful, it would have been very sad to have survived the Sunset near-disaster only to be brutalized in an elevator. They managed to open the false ceiling panels so the top part of the tree could poke through. This was one part of the master plan no one had even thought about. Without the ability to move those panels, a third of the tree might not have made it.

The tree was placed in the center of the sliding glass doors that opened out to the terrace, with room enough to walk around it to open the door if we wanted. Joi called it the "White House Tree" because it reminded her of the size and splendor of the Christmas tree the President and First Lady displayed. Joi's tree was just as gorgeous and, after we decorated it, would look like the one we'd seen in the Bloomingdale's window when we spent Christmas in Manhattan.

Stan gave the guys an extra nice tip for saving the day. We'd still be downstairs trying to figure out what to do with the mini-forest on top of the Caddy without them. Jack stopped by to make sure everything was taken care of and marveled at the size and perfection of this paean to Christmas.

Joi remembered that Jack had a little house he'd bought in West Hollywood on Westmount Drive. After a quick private talk with Stan, Joi walked over to Jack and asked if he'd like the tree for his yard after Christmas. Jack was delighted and hugged Joi warmly for this wonderful gift. Joi mentioned that if the tree started to look a little "rough," she'd let him know, so he could move it before it turned to timber.

The hard part was now over, and we could begin having fun decorating the tree. We couldn't wait to start shopping for what we needed! Although Joi knew that Stan didn't enjoy shopping, she invited him to join us, so he wouldn't feel left out. He declined, of course.

Joi and I generally spent most of our time alone. Stan was usually only with us at dinner. We'd either have a light meal at home or go out to a favorite restaurant. On our return, Stan would go to his room and light his cigar. It was the same routine night after night. He'd pour himself a snifter of brandy and nod off in his recliner. Joi and I would go to our room and watch TV in bed.

We decided to go to the Rexall Drug Store on La Cienega and Beverly to buy our Christmas decorations rather than a Beverly Hills department store. It was a lot closer; we'd be able to buy four times as much for the same price, and we wouldn't have to deal with the attitudes of some of the sales clerks. Rexall was like a mini-emporium with an amazing selection of lights and colored metallic hanging orbs.

Joi wanted to decorate the tree with solid colored lights and matching glass balls. She loved red, while I was more into royal blue. I wanted her to be happy, and she wanted to do the same for me. She asked me to look around for lights, so I grabbed a cart and, while wandering through the store, filled it with bright red lights and matching balls. In the meantime, Joi had filled her shopping basket with nothing but royal blue lights and balls. We met in the center of the store, almost causing a two-cart pileup, and laughed when we realized what we'd done.

"Well," Joi said, "there's only one thing to do! This Christmas ,we'll have all red decorations with white lights, and next year's will be blue." (I felt too good at that point to allow more than a passing thought about "next year" to enter my head.)

Joi then said we "could use the same clear white lights and alternate colors in future years." She had found some unusually shaped lights filled with a liquid that created little bubbles and was delighted with them. I had seen them before when I was a kid living in Kansas, and they brought back some sweet memories.

Off we went to the cashier, and Joi bought both sets of blue and red balls. The tree was so large that we had to buy dozens and dozens to cover every limb. We bought dozens of strands of white lights with one hundred little bulbs each. We made sure that, if one went out, we didn't have to check every bulb to find the bad one. We had both played the "find the dead bulb" game many times before, and vowed never to do it again!

Neither Joi nor I had really celebrated Christmas in a very long time. Last Christmas, we were in Las Vegas living in a hotel room, and, before that, I was living at the Studio Club. No one had a room large enough to even put in a chair, so forget about a tree! Joi had lived alone for quite a few years on the road with her night club act and, when Joi and Stan were living together, he wasn't into Christmas or putting up decorations.

This year, Joi's illness was obviously the motivation for Stan's change of heart. Frankly, it wouldn't have mattered one way or the other if he did or didn't want a tree or lights or decorations. I would have made sure she had the Christmas she wanted, tree and all. This was our celebration! It wasn't just a holiday; it was a joyous time. I knew that her remission was the greatest present we could have. Though it might very well be the last Christmas we would have together, I was determined it would be the most memorable holiday season of our lives.

We pulled into our parking place, and I went off to find the cart that was usually in the garage. I hoped it would be large enough to accommodate all our Christmas goodies. I brought it back, and we loaded bag after bag of decorations, filling the cart. Then, piling very carefully, we filled it again. The packages were almost teetering, so Joi stayed on one side while I was on the other. Each of us used one hand to guide the cart and one hand to steady it. We moved slowly toward the elevator, legs pressed up against the cart, constantly pushing the bags back to where they belonged.

Just after we got the cart (with its precarious cargo) into the elevator, things got even rockier, but I managed to push our button before it seemed we would lose every last bag onto the elevator floor! Joi deftly reached around and grabbed my hand, making a circle of our arms around the tower of bags. We took tiny little steps to control the cart that had begun to feel as if it had a life of its own, rolling this way and that.

It felt like a scene from an *I Love Lucy* episode! Joi was Lucy, and I was, of course, Ethel. I said something to that effect, and Joi started with one of her laughing fits. The harder she laughed, the harder I laughed, and the harder WE laughed, the closer we came to dumping the whole thing—balls, bags, and boxes—all on the elevator carpet! Finally, at our floor (just in time, I think), the elevator door opened, and we staggered along the hall to the penthouse.

We couldn't let go of one another's hands, so Joi used her shoulder to push the button on the doorbell. She rang several times, hoping Stan wasn't asleep in his chair, in which case he was almost impossible to rouse. No one came. I had a foot free and began kicking the door, once we realized our "knight in shining armor" was most likely out for the count. There was no way either of us could let go and reach for a key without making a very expensive mess all over the hallway.

Finally, though probably in a sound brandy-aided sleep, Stan must have heard the doorbell. We saw his eye when he looked through the peephole and must have seen what looked like contortionists from the Cirque de Soleil! In a fog, he opened the door and saw that we were in a real pickle. Regaining his sensibilities, he gathered up a few of the bags from the top of the pile, allowing Joi and me to finally let go and stand up straight.

We were still in a happy mood even if a little stiff from our travels from the car, and picked up the bags that were beginning to spill over the side. As we disconnected our fingers that were wrapped together in a tight grip, Joi winked at me and said, "Who says women are the weaker sex?"

At least, we had fun laughing at ourselves during and after our little escapade.

Joi grabbed one bag, and I took another. She was better at organizing than I was, so I handed her one bag or box at a time and she made piles of lights, balls, and other ornaments on the kitchen table. In that way, we could easily get to the things we wanted later when we began to decorate our tree.

We were both so pooped from our foray into the colorful world of Christmas décor that I was relieved when Joi suggested we wait until morning to begin our tree decorating adventure. She delighted me further by suggesting we turn in early. "Cuddling," for me, was the perfect way to end this perfect day. Happily, as tired as the world could often make us, we always seemed to find time for love.

Innocently, I didn't realize how important the memories we made that evening and the following day would be for me. I was blind to all but my love and our holidays to come. A Christmas I will never, ever forget.

Chapter 27

Hollywood Revisited

The next morning, after a wonderful night of passion and laughter that kept us going till the wee small hours of the morning, we popped out of bed like a couple of kids. While still in our jammies, we quickly poured our coffee and began trimming the tree.

Stan wandered out a couple of hours later rubbing his head, eyes bleary and looking for breakfast.

"Nope, not this morning," Joi told him with a smile.

It was every man for himself that day. Sleepily, he admired the tree and then toddled away to make himself some toast.

Joi and I were determined to finish our tree before lunch.

That morning, as we only had coffee for breakfast, we were extra hungry. After we draped the last string of lights and put the final big, shiny red ball in the right place, it was time to top our tree with the silver-winged angel that Joi had bought for this special Christmas.

We soon realized the tree was so high that the tip would actually be out of sight, but Joi insisted the lovely angel be attached just below the ceiling hole, where we could still see it. Since I was the tall one, it was always assumed that I could do this kind of thing. I got the job, yes, but I'm not exactly great with heights. Even though I looked like I could do just about anything, I wasn't comfortable climbing anywhere, definitely not up a ladder! Joi saw my face, understood without my saying anything, and went to talk to Stan. We knew he wouldn't do it either, but she thought maybe, with his penchant for "fixing" things for her, he could find someone who would.

Stan was still at the breakfast table, reading the *L.A. Times*. Pages were strewn all around him as he enjoyed the last of his morning coffee. Joi asked if he could solve the problem of her Christmas angel while she and I went shopping. (We wanted to be alone that day, and she knew he'd want to tag along if he learned that Greenblatt's was our destination.) Loving the role of rescuing "his girls," Stan readily agreed to find someone to navigate the thirteen feet or so that would have to be climbed to secure our little angel in her place of honor. Relieved, we hurriedly dressed and headed out.

As usual, the line of people at Greenblatt's standing in front of the deli case was two-deep, and the place was buzzing with Los Angeles's hungriest people. Lots of industry "runners," local artists, actors, and writers, and those just hooked, as we were, on the great food, stood patiently for their turn.

In those days, the only tables were the two at the back of the deli that the Owner had placed there for friends and various celebs who showed up with some regularity. Joi was recognized immediately by the young Host, who was a fan. He gushed while we navigated our way past the hungry patrons to get to our table. Smiling and gracious, as she always was with her fans, Joi told him she would gladly sign an autograph if he'd bring her something to write on before we left.

It was always fun for Joi when she was recognized, so our lunch began on a high note. Suddenly, someone else recognized her.

"Joi Lansing!" boomed a man's deep voice.

We looked up, and Joi smiled brightly and said, "Mervyn!" as she stood and hugged him warmly. I'd never seen Joi stand for anyone, so I knew he had to be someone special to her.

Joi introduced me and then asked Mervyn LeRoy (a Hollywood icon) to join us. Mervyn met Joi when he was Head of Production at MGM and had known her from the time she was a young girl at Metro. He had watched as she was discovered by Arthur Freed, and then he acted as a kind of mentor to her during those years.

The host came over, and we ordered the signature sandwich all around. The two of them continued laughing and chatting and sharing war stories of "back in the day." I sat quietly, watching Joi in her element. It was so good to see her happy and free of pain or worry. In those days, I counted these special moments and pulled them up when I needed to believe that somehow everything was going to be all right. This was a way of coping that became more and more important to me as the months passed.

Though Mr. LeRoy was famous for many things, one skill that set him above the usual Hollywood movers and shakers was his ability to discover talented young actors capable of becoming stars. Several of his "finds" were silver screen successes like Clark Gable, Lana Turner, Robert Mitchum, and Loretta Young. For Joi, his interest in her was a vote of confidence in her talent and beauty, which had meant a lot to her through the years.

When we were about finished, Mervyn mentioned he was in town on business and would be returning to his home in Palm Springs the following day. Talk about a wonderful coincidence! Joi told him of our plans to move to Palm Springs in February, adding that we wanted to spend the holidays in the penthouse. He delightedly gave her his phone number and promised to show us the town as soon as we were settled.

After Mervyn excused himself, explaining that he had an appointment he had to get to, Joi could barely contain herself. Those were the halcyon days in Palm Springs where real celebrities like Frank Sinatra and Kirk Douglas owned one of their several homes, and where seeing a star or two at the local market was not unusual.

Being squired around by the brilliant and famous Mervyn LeRoy would be a definite plus for Joi and her career, something she desperately wanted to get back to now that the chemotherapy seemed to be working so well. She was convinced that meeting Mervyn again was a wonderful sign, that the newest chapter in our lives would not be just a move, but a way back into the industry that seemed to be so callously moving on without her.

Understanding all too well how important keeping a positive attitude was to her health, I enjoyed and encouraged Joi's hope that Mervyn's return to her life would help get her career back on track. As we walked to the car, she practically bubbled with ideas. It was fun seeing her so "up," but, knowing her as well I did, I was concerned with how high she was getting. If she didn't calm down a bit, this high could well turn into a low.

It had been a while since the last horrible emotional episode I went through with Joi. I truly thought it would never happen again, but I was getting nervous. In retrospect, I'm now convinced that, once triggered, these episodes were most likely caused by severe hormonal changes produced by the estrogen that doctors had, for years, prescribed for her. In those days, no one knew how dangerous using hormones could be. When Joi told her doctors she needed "something to keep me young," they assured her that estrogen was the magic elixir.

The traffic was busy as it always is before any big holiday, and Thanksgiving was about as big as it could get in Hollywood. Even though I was cooking, Joi wanted to get a few decorations for the table and house. (We were famous for doing things at the last minute, and this was one of those times.) We spent almost an hour trying to find a place to park and pushing through the crowds bustling around us. It seemed that everyone had forgotten their table candles and special turkey-decked napkins!

By the time we got back to the car with our bags, we were both pooped. Though I knew Joi was probably more tired than I was, she had become almost too quiet. Her chattiness a few minutes before had turned to silence, and I was confused. Had I done something wrong? I was only twenty-one and so new at navigating my own feelings that understanding the complicated emotions of the woman I loved was almost impossible for me. We rode home in silence.

As we pulled into the garage and parked, Joi was still not speaking. I finally had to say something, so, still a little nervous, I cautiously asked, "Is something wrong?"

She turned to me, and I'll never forget the sadness in her beautiful eyes as she said quietly, "I'm getting old."

I was stunned.

Joi's face was flawless. She had always avoided the sun and made sure she cleaned and moisturized it every night, but something had made her feel as though time was taking its toll on her beauty. As I helped her carry the packages to the elevator, my simple guess was that seeing Mervyn had something to do with this. Still, I knew, from past experience, that Joi didn't like it when I pried, so I didn't say anything. I hoped, however, that, at some point in the evening, she would share more.

Chapter 28

Meltdown

Once home, I emptied the bags in the kitchen while Joi went in the bedroom to change clothes. I finished up and followed her. She'd changed into her robe and was lying in bed on her side, looking away from the door toward the windows. I went over to her and, while touching her shoulder, asked if she wanted anything. She turned slightly (I could see she'd been crying), and said, "No," but asked me to spoon with her. At that moment, she was the most fragile I'd ever known her to be.

I lay down and curled around her, slipping one arm under her head and the other across her body. She sighed sadly and snuggled into me. Minutes passed, and we said nothing. As I stroked her hair, she began to slip into sleep.

Quietly holding her close, I was so grateful she could feel safe enough in my arms to rest. This was new to me. For too long, I'd known her to run from feelings that hurt her or touched on her insecurities. In trying to escape them, she would take pills and drink herself into oblivion, striking out at anyone around her (usually me) in her frenzy.

Lying there, I couldn't help but recall a time not that long ago when I almost lost her... and us... because of one of those heartbreaking episodes.

One morning, soon after Stan had bought the house in Palm Springs, Joi awakened to find blood all over her pillow. I hadn't seen it when I got up earlier and had tiptoed out to make coffee. I heard her shriek! Terrified, I ran back to the bedroom, only to find her holding her face and sobbing. The spot on her nose, the one that originally sent us to the doctor, had started bleeding again! She'd been doing so well on the chemotherapy that this completely sideswiped us. We rushed into the bathroom, and I held a washcloth on it, but it continued to bleed. Then, Joi remembered some Styptic she had, and we finally got it to stop.

I tried to hold her, but she shoved me away. Pushing past me, she headed into the kitchen to find the bottle of scotch. There was nothing I could say to keep her from taking a swallow of the golden liquid she hoped would silence the screaming monsters in her head. As she swallowed mouthful after mouthful, there was something this time that was terrifyingly different. She not only wanted to black out…she wanted to be out!

While I begged her to stop, she became more and more incoherent and stumbled around the room. I deftly pulled the bottle away from her and poured the poison down the kitchen sink, but she turned and tried to grab it back from me, her hands flailing in the air, unable to find their mark. Slipping past her, I ran to the bathroom to flush her pills down the toilet. She was more out of control than I'd ever seen her…this was nothing like the drunken episodes in the past. I knew she would die if I didn't stop her.

I had locked the bathroom door behind me and she beat on it, her fists thumping weakly, barely making a sound. I was terrified she was already dying. I found another bottle of a new prescription Ted had sent her by mail a week ago, and I counted the pills. I knew she hadn't touched any of the sixty Tuinals before today, but now there were only fifty-five in the bottle. My heart sinking, I realized she must have taken the five pills either before or after she started drinking. The scotch was down the drain now, and there was no more in the house.

Angry, I threw the rest of the pills down the toilet and flushed them on their way to hell, where they belonged. Temporarily relieved, I suddenly realized she had stopped pounding on the door. I pulled it open, only to find her in a stupor against the wall next to it.

Quickly, I checked her pulse and watched her chest as she inhaled and exhaled. The only thing I thought to do was watch her respiration and call an ambulance if she started to have breathing problems. I'd been here before and understood that the longer she went without any more liquor or pills, the sooner the poison would leave her system.

Joi was "nodding," and I knew she couldn't move without help, so I left her long enough to call Stan and tell him what happened. He didn't sound alarmed, said he was in the middle of a meeting, and would be home within an hour or two at the most. I was afraid to be alone with her, but I guess he'd been through this often enough to assume she'd be fine, and turning his world upside down one more time was just not worth it. I hoped his assumption was right, but was still worried. This time was not like the others, and it scared me.

Time passed, and, as Joi became a little more lucid and kept fighting to wake up, she mumbled, demanding I bring her more pills. She was in obvious anguish and staggered past me, into the living room. I followed quickly, trying to keep her from falling. I got a strong hold around her waist, hoping I could steer her back to bed where she might finally pass out.

As I tried to lead her back toward the bedroom, the swaying of her body suddenly pulled both of us down toward the glass-topped coffee table. I pushed her as far away from the table as I possibly could, and she landed on the floor, barely avoiding a crash through the deadly glass. A crystal ashtray that Joi had bought me was right in the middle of the table and, as our bodies glanced off the edge, the ashtray went flying and shattered into dozens of vicious glass shards. One cut like a razor just below Joi's elbow; another cut into my leg. Both wounds bled slowly.

Joi lay on the floor in a semi-conscious state, wanting to get up, but unable to do so. Seeing that she couldn't walk, I left her for a moment to find a few bandages. Fortunately, I found some large Band-Aid bandages that Leslie, Stan's daughter, had given him, and they would protect both of our wounds easily. Neither of the cuts were really deep, just messy and very painful. We were very, very lucky.

I hurried back to wrap Joi's arm. She was still out, and I was too shaken from the tumble to worry about cleaning up the blood stains. There would be plenty of time to deal with that later.

Joi slept fitfully on the floor, mumbling incoherently. I wondered what would happen next, especially when she discovered I'd dumped her scotch and flushed her pills. I had kept two pills, mostly to sedate her if she became too difficult to control.

As her eyes began to open, she mumbled something about her arm hurting. I told her she had fallen and cut herself on the ashtray. She started to get up, and I held on, trying to guide her away from the shards left in the carpet. I had picked up two large pieces of crystal, but numerous little glass spikes were sprinkled around the rug, still ready to do damage if either of us fell again.

I used my body weight to push Joi away from the broken glass, and, suddenly more awake than I realized, she jerked out of my arms, thinking I was pushing her around! She started shouting, telling me to take my hands off her and to leave her alone. I tried to calm her down and kept telling her how much I loved her and that no one was trying to hurt her. This just made her furious. Her arms started thrashing as she told me not to touch her. She became violent, and I couldn't hold on to her. She pushed me away, yelling that she wanted to die, that she didn't want to live like this, and that I should leave her.

Her voice became shrill and unrecognizable as she began to weave toward the sliding glass doors that opened onto the terrace. Terrified, I knew I had to stop her before she got to them...before she got to the short balcony wall, the only thing between her and a deadly fall to the pavement hundreds of feet below.

The penthouse overlooked La Cienega and Sunset Boulevard, and the distance from the balcony to the ground was guaranteed to kill anyone who fell that far. As Joi turned to hit me with her clenched fists, I caught her just feet away from the patio's edge and picked her up in my arms. Struggling at first and still moaning that she wanted to die, she finally stopped when she realized she had very little strength and couldn't get away. As I carried her toward the bedroom, still shaking from the knowledge that my girl had been inches away from killing herself, she curled into my arms, sobbing.

I gently laid her on the bed as she continued to sob quietly, begging me to "let her go." She said she couldn't take living and wanted to die now, not sometime in the future. I was still shaking as the thought devastated me, but I held back my tears, knowing I mustn't fall apart.

Finally, she stopped mumbling and began to slip into sleep. I lay down next to her, holding her until she was breathing normally at last. She slept as the poisons in her body began to wear off and the terror in her mind began to fade. Exhausted, but relieved, I saw that the woman I loved was starting to come back to me, little by little. Opening her eyes for a minute, she half-smiled at me and went back to sleep. I knew that my girl had absolutely no recollection of what had happened during the past three hours.

I heard Stan open the front door, walk into the living room, and gasp at the sight of blood on the rug. He rushed into our room, finding us on top of the covers, Joi asleep in my arms, and both of us bandaged.

Quietly, I told him that finally everything was okay now and that Joi would, at least till next time, be all right. He seemed awkward and rather embarrassed as he left the room to make some coffee, probably because he'd been so cavalier when I called him. This time had been different, as I told him, and he'd not been there to help me. I think he was ashamed.

As I lay next to her, breathing deeply to stop the shaking inside, Joi moved slightly and slowly sat up. I watched her closely…looking into her eyes. I exhaled. Yes, my girl was back.

Confused, she noticed her arm and asked what had happened. At that moment, I made a decision I'd never made before—this time, I was going to tell her the truth! She would know every single sordid, tragic detail. Until that day, Joi hadn't realized what kind of real pain she put me through (and sometimes Stan) when she went off the deep end with drugs and alcohol, usually without warning. But this time, she would know…and what would happen to us, would happen. This time it was either me or her demons, and I was going to let her know this, no matter how hard it would be for me to do it.

I told her we'd talk about it after she had something to eat. As we walked into the kitchen, I realized I'd forgotten that Joi was also taking methadone along with the rest of her cocktail! Fortunately, she hadn't abused this medication and would just take a pill every four to six hours whenever she started feeling any pain. I realized, though, that the extra pain medicine in her system had only added to her blackout and uncontrollable emotions and could well have triggered the different reaction I'd noticed this time.

Stan was in the kitchen heating a big bowl of chicken soup that Joi and I had brought home a couple of days earlier from Nate 'n Al's in Beverly Hills. We had shared a huge "chicken in the pot" with matzo balls and kreplach, and filled our to-go container with half a chicken and little, tiny noodles. This was just the ticket to bring Joi back to herself again.

At this point, Joi was able to stand and walk without losing her footing. As she sat down at the dining room table, Stan brought her the hot bowl of soup which she ate with gusto. Soon she was feeling a million percent better, except for the pain from the cut on her arm. She didn't remember either taking pills or drinking alcohol…the whole day was just a blur to her.

When Joi went to the bathroom, I followed to give her the one pill she usually took about this time. She took it and lay down. Things were finally peaceful. Her thoughts were still a little jumbled after all the crap she'd as-similated, but she was as sweet as could be when we cuddled in bed. Then, when she remembered what she'd asked me earlier, she sat up in bed and said, "Honey, I need to know what happened today. I need to know it now, so I can sleep, okay?"

I knew this was it. I took a big breath and began to explain, detail by sor-did detail. Her eyes slowly filled with tears as I told her how she'd screamed at me and pushed me away, how we'd both fallen and cut ourselves on the ashtray she'd given me...how she'd tried to jump from the balcony...tried to end her life and our life together. By then, she was sobbing softly as I talked. When I finished, we were quiet for a long time, it seemed. Finally, she took both my hands and began to speak.

Her eyes were wet from tears of shame and sorrow. As I wiped them away, she told me she couldn't imagine ever lifting a finger to hurt me, especially since I was the one who loved her more than anyone in her life. She told me she would never, ever take another drink again...that she'd found out the hard way how alcohol turned her into a monster and unlocked the door to her own personal hell. She finished by telling me that door would be closed forever. We held one another, and she cried for what seemed like a long time, as she whispered to me, "Baby, I'm so sorry. I'm so very sorry."

Alcoholics and addicts are famous for saying those kinds of things but, all too often, there is a next time. In this case, Joi meant everything she'd prom-ised, and that pivotal day was the very last time her beautiful lips ever touched a drink.

Joi stirred and I came back to reality. Those terrible memories were old news, and I realized the sweet woman I held so close, still sleeping safely in my arms, needed me more than ever, now that she was willing to face her fears, rather than hide from them. With a heart full of love, I watched her sleep, knowing in the deepest part of my soul I was more than willing to be all she needed me to be. Not until death...would we part.

Chapter 29

Thanksgiving Day

Thanksgiving was truly a time to give thanks for every day and night Joi and I had spent together, as well as each precious day to come. I felt so blessed as I quietly slipped out of bed at the crack of dawn to get the turkey stuffed and into the oven. Joi rolled over, sleeping like a baby, as I crept from the room.

I started with the stuffing. All the ingredients in my mother's recipe blended so perfectly that I couldn't stop nibbling as I stuffed the "honker" turkey until it looked like it would pop! As I put it in the oven, I guessed it would take most of the day to cook.

Everything else was ready to cook or bake and would be easy to coordinate later in the day. It was way too early to stay up, so I went back to bed and spooned with my sweetheart. The drapes were closed, but the daylight peeked in through the little space beneath the hem. Fortunately, I was deliciously tired from the day before and drifted back into a dreamland where we were invincible.

A couple of hours later, I woke to hear Stan rustling around in the kitchen. Again, I stumbled out of bed, this time throwing on my fuzzy terry cloth robe. As I tiptoed from the room, and, just as I turned the doorknob, Joi stopped me by drowsily asking, "Where are you going, honey?" I told her I wanted to see what Stan was getting into in the kitchen. "But I want you to stay," she purred.

Suddenly wide awake and smiling, I turned back to the bed when we heard a loud noise coming from the kitchen. I told her I'd be right back, rushed out, and found Stan bending over the oven, peering inside. The noise had been the oven door slipping from his hand the first time he tried to open it. I asked if everything was okay, and he said the aroma was "driving him crazy" and he "had to check it out." With his Peck's Bad Boy grin, he stood up, acting for all the world as if HE were the chef! Yawning, he left the oven and wandered over to make coffee. His was always a little too strong for me, but it really didn't matter since I drowned it with milk and sugar.

I checked to be sure the turkey was still covered with aluminum foil, and was relieved that Stan, in his enthusiasm, hadn't "undressed" it. (Naked turkeys never cook quite right!) He asked if he could help, and I told him to relax, that I was taking care of everything, and his only job today was to sit and watch TV. He seemed pleased and toddled off with his coffee to turn on the Macy's Thanksgiving Day Parade. We all loved the gigantic balloons, the marching, and the music.

That year, there were anti-war protesters picketing the parade, trying to get some media attention and make a statement about our presence in Vietnam. Joi and I were both against the war. Some of the guys I'd known in school had been killed; others became so messed up mentally they'd never be the same. Joi had gone to cheer up the troops with Bob Hope and would have been happy to do it again. The guys loved her, yelling at the top of their lungs when she came on stage. She felt horrible for the kids sent into a war of futility and hell and wanted to do anything she could to help.

Stan sat with his feet propped up on an ottoman. I hoped he could relax and enjoy the day without the need to start hitting the brandy. Joi's mood and the stability of her health affected the amount he drank during the day. She was doing great, which would definitely put a rosy complexion on this Thanksgiving.

I went back to the bedroom and opened the door quietly, hoping Joi had been able to go back to sleep. To my delight, she was quite awake and very happy to have me back in the room. My lovely girl was lying on our bed with the top sheet barely covering her ankles! Though I felt a little strange with Stan only a room away, it wasn't enough to keep me from dropping my robe and falling into her arms with total abandon. The TV was loud enough to muffle our "playing," and we shared a wonderful morning for which we were appropriately thankful.

Joi and I hoped that Hubby was enjoying the parade and not wondering why we were still in bed. Life had been going smoothly without him suspecting our relationship. Though Stan and Joi were no longer romantically involved, just the thought of us together might spark a little too much interest.

Dressing hurriedly, we casually walked out of our room sporting the comfy fleece outfits Stan had bought to surprise us. Joi looked great in yellow, so that was her choice. I love blue, which just happened to be the second choice. It was a win-win for all of us. Stan was a "hero," and we had soft, fuzzy outfits to keep us nice and warm. It was winter, and, even in California, it could still get pretty nippy at night. Joi looked beautiful in her bright yellow sweats with its little hood draping like a miniature cape down her back.

The aroma of food cooking made us all hungry, especially Joi.

"When will the food be ready?" she asked. "I'm hungry as a tiger!"

Stan and I were happy when she was the "tiger." That meant her appetite was good. One of the positive side effects of chemotherapy was that it kept her appetite strong, so she wouldn't lose a lot of weight with the disease. She needed the nourishment to keep on fighting.

Fortunately, the turkey was almost finished cooking, and it was time to remove the aluminum foil tent, so the skin would turn a beautiful golden bronze color. My job was in the kitchen, so I told them, "Hold their horses. Dinner will be served very soon," and left them to enjoy a marching band from New Orleans.

Back in the kitchen, I basted the turkey with the rich juices that covered the bottom of the pan. All I cared about was having a moist turkey with crisp brown skin, and making sure that Joi got a little food now, so she wouldn't go into a hypoglycemic crash. There was one good and fast solution. Being certain it was done, I cut a slice of turkey from the breast and brought it to her on a little plate. It was in her hand on the way to her mouth before I could hand her a fork! She ate it voraciously, leaving nothing on the plate. Realizing she needed more, I went back to the kitchen and cut a few more slices. Stan looked dejected watching Joi's enthusiastic snacking, so I made a plate for him as well, and another little piece for her. They both seemed very pleased and kept asking for more.

As I was hungry myself, I snagged a chunk of the crispy golden brown skin, my favorite part of the meal, except for the dressing. OMG! It was wonderful! No wonder they wanted more! I sliced a little piece of white meat for myself and ravenously enjoyed the succulent morsel. I had assumed we would have a regular sit-down meal, like most other people, but here we were, eating a little here and a little there, as I brought it out in waves from the kitchen. I realized it didn't really matter how we ate our meal as long as we were together. It was our Thanksgiving, and we would spend it any way that made us happy.

In that spirit, I asked how they wanted it served…if they preferred to be seated at the table or to "rough it" in front of the TV. A resounding and unanimous decision from my twentieth-century pilgrims, they were quite happy to eat in front of the television! Besides, a tennis match was just starting, and it would be almost impossible to pry Stan away from watching it.

There was plenty of room on the coffee table for their plates, and I could even bring a few serving dishes with extra food, so they could serve themselves. The fresh green beans with bacon pieces were pretty much ready, and so were the sweet potatoes mixed with mandarin oranges and covered with baby marshmallows. I needed to drain the cranberries that were boiling on the stove. They didn't take that long to cook, and all I had to do was add a ton of sugar to make the fresh cranberries taste delicious. I pulled the pan off the stove and drained it in a colander. They looked and smelled exquisite. I put them in a bowl and threw them in the freezer for a quick five minutes to chill enough to make them enjoyable.

I brought my hungry little Tiger Team more turkey slices, sweet potatoes, and green beans, along with plenty of dressing in one of the serving dishes. That was a good enough start. The cranberries were chilling, and I just needed to fix the mashed potatoes and gravy.

Joi and Stan were like little kids at a family reunion, sitting at their own table and eating only the things they really wanted. No one had filled their plates, so they could take as much or as little as their hearts desired. My dressing (rather, my mother's dressing) was a big hit.

I had been catching a bite here and there each time I went in and out of the kitchen, so I was eating just as much as they were, but more like a happy carhop than a chef!

Finally, the potatoes and gravy were ready and, as I brought the missing link to the dinner, I realized something was not quite right. Joi and Stan both had a look that was hard to mistake…that very uncomfortable look of those who couldn't eat another bite for fear they'd explode! I brought them coffee, hoping it would calm their stomachs. After a few sips, they seemed to feel a bit better. Though I was thrilled the dinner was a success, I felt badly they were bordering on misery. Time was the only solution, along with the Alka-Seltzer tablet I put in a glass of water for each of them. I hoped the bubbles would give them a little relief.

I continued to pick at the food, enjoying every bite, but I knew when to stop eating, tempting as it was. There was one last siren to lure Joi and Stan to total misery—Joi and I had bought a homemade pumpkin pie from Chalet Gourmet with fresh whipped cream on top! Happily, their good sense took over, making them leave the pie for another time.

A while later, after removing most of the tasty temptations, I sat cuddled next to Joi, feeling happy that my girl was content with the meal I'd made for her. Stan had gone into his post-meal repose. He had excused himself and moved to his recliner, cigar lit and resting in the ashtray next to his half-filled brandy snifter and flask. It wouldn't take long for the burning stogie to die out. In fact, Stan was on the way to burning out himself!

Noticing that Stan had gone off to dreamland (eating pumpkin pie, no doubt.), Joi got up, flicked the burning ash from his cigar, and closed the door to his room. He would probably sleep for the next four or five hours, at least. A true creature of habit, he was always predictable.

Joi and I loved spending peaceful evenings together, at times watching old movies on TV, other times quietly reading books in each other's company. Often, when a particular passage or story would strike Joi's fancy, she would read out loud to me, creating beautiful moments I would treasure forever.

Tonight, as Joi snuggled close to me, we watched the great old holiday classic *It's a Wonderful Life*. I avoided thinking this would most likely be our last Thanksgiving. It was a passing thought, and I let it go almost immediately. All I knew, really knew… was that the love we had for one another was timeless… and that this Thanksgiving would be the one I'd remember as long as I lived.

Chapter 30

Roses in Cincinnati

It had been a great Thanksgiving, and I was pleased that Joi had enjoyed my cooking so much. After watching *It's a Wonderful Life* while cuddling on the sofa, we went to our room and started our nightly routine of removing makeup, brushing teeth, and getting into fresh jammies. Then, bouncing onto our big pillow-top bed, we were snug as two proverbial bugs in a rug.

Neither of us was in the mood for more television. Lately, we'd been reading a popular book of the day, *The Godfather*, which Joi had purchased in paperback at a little bookstore in the middle of Hollywood. Not feeling too tired, she offered to read to me tonight since she knew what delight I took in listening to her. I snuggled next to her, head on her shoulder, as she began to read.

The book was fascinating to her, but I found myself becoming more uneasy the longer she read. It brought back memories of a ghastly episode which occurred not long after the beginning of our relationship. It was a true nightmare for both of us, and it had to do with another Godfather.

When Joi and I first found one another, and we had one of those long-into-the-night "getting to know you" talks, she told me that she once dated a guy named Lenny. He was "one of the boys," a term used in those days to indicate a Mafia connection, and was considered the Boss of Cleveland.

Joi had dated him for a while, but things had not worked out the way he wanted. He was much more interested in her than she was in him, which didn't make him happy at all. She never told me what caused the breakup, but I can't imagine her as a gangster's moll. Judy Holliday had played the part very well, but Joi was way too bright and definitely had a mind of her own. That was probably the reason it ended.

Soon after our talk, Joi was offered a one-night booking at a little club in

Cincinnati called the Bedroom. It would be an easy gig that paid a thousand dollars for only one show. However, when her agent, Stan Scottland, disclosed where it was, Joi told me she was nervous about going anywhere near Cleveland, and Cincinnati wasn't that far away. She accepted the job, though, thinking that Lenny wouldn't find out she was in the same state. At least, she hoped he wouldn't.

She mentioned that Lenny was still "smitten" with her and wasn't too pleased when she decided to break it off. She'd used the excuse that she was still in love with Stan and they had reconciled. Being married had its advantages, since she could have her dalliances, which Stan seemed to have no trouble with (maybe he was doing the same thing), and have the perfect reason not to commit. Her marriage license was the ideal life raft when the romantic seas became a little too rough and choppy.

The day we arrived in Cincinnati, we went directly to the club. The Owner, Jake, showed us around and took us to the showroom where she'd perform and where the band would set up later that day for their one rehearsal before going live for the audience that night.

Joi didn't make enough money to bring her own musicians, so she had to rely on the club owners to hire guys from the local union. She'd always been lucky with the three- to five-piece bands that shared the stage with her, since she brought her own arrangements, which were easy to read and not that complicated. If the band was good, they could always improvise and add things to spice it up, and, if they were mediocre, it was simple enough to wing it.

We planned to stay in town for one night and fly out the following morning. The club had provided a hotel room not too far away, and transportation had been arranged to pick us up and take us back to the hotel at the end of the show.

We were tired from the flight and decided to rest until the rehearsal at four in the afternoon. The show started at eight-thirty, which gave us time to go back to the hotel and take it easy while waiting for room service to bring our dinner. This would help Joi conserve her energy for the show.

We walked into the hotel lobby when suddenly Joi stopped and barely whispered, "It's Lenny!"

The very person Joi had been afraid to run into was sitting not thirty feet away from us in one of those overstuffed hotel chairs. There he was, the King of Cleveland in all his gory glory. There was a huge bouquet of red roses in a crystal vase sitting next to him on the end table.

Looking up as we entered, he smiled a snaky smile and stood up. Joi told me quietly to stay there, that he was very jealous and could be incredibly dangerous, and that she'd be right back. Then, taking a deep breath and smiling confidently, she walked toward him.

"Lenny! How nice to see you…" I heard her say.

Thinking she was just going over to talk to him, I turned and made my way to a couch by the window, overlooking the pool where a family was splashing. I sat down and then peeked carefully over my shoulder at Joi and Lenny. They were talking, but it didn't look like a reunion of old friends. Joi's back was to me, but I could see Lenny's face perfectly. It was hard, yet expressionless.

Then, roses in hand, he took her elbow and steered her to the hotel reservation counter. Joi said something, and the Clerk handed her the key to our room. I stood up and almost walked after them until I remembered what Joi had said. To stay here. To trust her. I watched the elevator doors close as my mouth went dry.

After an hour passed, I had a stomach-sinking feeling. She had asked me to trust her and I did, but I didn't trust him for a minute. I went into the bar and ordered a Seven Up just to do something, and then came back to the window, still pacing. I looked at my watch again. An hour and twenty minutes was too long. Too long for just a talk.

Suddenly the elevator doors opened, and Lenny came striding out, again expressionless. This time, though, that look scared me. I know he saw me, but he strode past without a glance and pushed his way angrily through the swinging doors.

As he turned onto the busy street and out of sight, I rushed across the lobby to the elevator, hit the button to the second floor, and started praying, "Please, God, please make her okay. Please make my baby okay."

I found our room and tried the handle, grateful it was unlocked. There she sat on the edge of the bed, disheveled and crying. Of course, I knew what had happened. She looked up and reached for me, her face wet with tears.

Wrapping her tightly in my arms, I began rocking her. "It's all right, baby, it's all right. Honey, you're all right now… I'm here… I'm here."

I laid her back on the pillow, lay down beside her, and held her for a long time. I kept soothing her, but we said nothing about what had happened, though she continued to sob quietly.

That bastard! Though Joi was in a tough business, she herself was anything but tough. She had an innocence about her, not unlike the innocence projected by the then-popular and eventually iconic Marilyn Monroe. At times, it was almost as though she was a very young girl in a woman's body, and this was one of those times. She had stopped crying but seemed deflated, flat. I continued to stroke her hair slowly and whisper how much I loved her, that she was safe now, that she was okay. She began to relax and then buried her head against my breast. Her breathing was becoming regular.

I had never felt the kind of rage that I felt that day. Yes, I was young, but my feelings had always run deep, even as a child. Of course, Joi's needs came first, and I knew showing my anger would not help her in any way. I comforted myself by knowing she was safe now and that my love would help her heal over time.

When I felt she could handle it, I led her into the bathroom, turned the water on in the shower, and began to wash every inch of her beautiful body. There would be nothing left of that monster's touch by the time I was done. As I helped her dry off, we didn't talk about it. I didn't ask her what happened; she didn't offer to tell me. Words weren't needed … at least not then.

I knew we couldn't sleep in that room, so I called the front desk and asked to be moved to a different room. The Desk Clerk asked if there was a problem, and I told him it had been taken care of. In a few minutes, a bellboy came up, took our bags, and moved us to the new room.

Eventually, we realized we'd almost forgotten the club rehearsal and, if we didn't get dressed, we wouldn't make it. The band had been hired and would soon be waiting for the star to arrive. The professional in Joi knew she had an audience to please that night and, though I had no idea how she was going to pull that off, I understood there was no way she wouldn't give them her very best.

We dressed for the show and went to the lobby where we waited for Jake, the owner, who had decided to be our driver that day. On the way to the club, he told Joi what a huge fan he was and how greatly he admired her. He continued nonstop, reciting all the television shows she'd ever been in and thanking her for coming to his "little club." He said it would be standing room only because all of his family and friends were so excited to meet her.

Hearing how thrilled everyone was about her appearance, Joi couldn't help but feel better. For some years, she'd been afraid she was slipping in the business because, as she grew older, the television parts were fewer and fewer. But, on stage where she could sing her heart out, Joi had never been better.

Already dressed for the evening, we got to the club just in time to run through the songs once before the show. The band was made up of some great local union boys who probably knew how to read charts in their sleep. They, too, were excited to be playing for such a beautiful and famous singer, and the rehearsal went on without a hitch.

Joi thanked them graciously, evoking smiles (and a shy shuffling of feet by the bass player), and we left for the green room, where all performers gathered before and after a show. As we waited for the band to start, I took her hand and asked gently, "You all right?"

She squeezed it and sighed, "Honey, I have to be. Okay?" I knew what she meant, and "the show must go on" rang truer in my mind that night than it ever had or ever would again.

A few minutes later, we were surprised when Jake came into the room and asked Joi to come out and meet the audience. Well, this was a new one. Usually if that ever happened (which was seldom), it was after the show.

This time, though, the audience asked for her autograph on the photos of Joi that Jake had printed up. Ever sweet to her fans, Joi walked from table to table, thrilling the audience before she'd even sung one note! Finally, after her successful meet and greet, we slipped backstage to wait for the first notes from the band which would herald the beginning of her performance.

I was amazed at how poised she was. Joi had never sounded better. She went from song to song, filling the room with melody, rhythm, and love. Whatever her feelings had been that afternoon, she'd put them away to give the audience one hell of a show. When it ended, they gave her a standing ovation of the kind that every entertainer in show business dreams about … one we could still hear as she left the club in the waiting car and drove back to the hotel.

On the ride back, Jake thanked her over and over for the "greatest night" in his club's history. Always a lady and a pro, Joi graciously thanked him, saying it was her pleasure to be in his beautiful showroom, and thanked him for asking her.

Once back to the hotel, we kicked off our shoes, dropped our dresses, and, relieved, wrapped ourselves in our robes. We ordered and split a BLT, which we ate quietly until I finally felt it was all right to ask how she was doing. She nodded and said, "Okay," and then, "I'm beat…bed time."

That night, I slept lightly in case she needed me, and, at one point, I thought I heard her crying. I looked down and saw that she was actually still sleeping. The dream must have passed because her breathing became steady again. Relieved, I wiped a tear from her sleeping face and then slipped into slumber myself.

The Concierge called the next morning to let us know our cab was there, and we gathered up our things. Someone, thinking we'd forgotten them from the other room, had brought the roses over to our room. As we left for the lobby, I picked them up and, as we passed the garbage chute in the hallway, I threw them away as the trash they were. I silently hoped, as we stepped into the elevator, that in time the garbage that had brought them to her would receive the same fate.

On the trip home, we seemed closer than ever, and we never spoke of it again. That chapter was over, and we went on to live the life we were meant to live. Together and in love…no matter what.

Joy Rae Brown
at 5 yrs

"Joi Lansing" at 16 yrs with Aunts and Uncle

Joi with "Grampy" Raymond Shupe and Grandma Grace

Joi when she was with
Creative Management Agency (CMA),
Hollywood, Ca. 1969...

(left and below)
In New York from
photo session
with world famous
Photographer, Maurice
Seymour. 1969

Another of Joi's "fave" shots from the session with Maurice Seymour, NY 1969

Joi's favorite PR photo from a 1960 session with
famous Photographer Maurice Seymour. New York

Another favorite shot of Joi's from that same photo shoot
with Maurice Seymour, New York, 1960

Joi having fun with a spunky pose at a special photo session with Super- Star
Photog, Maurice Seymour for her new 1969 Portfolio. New York

Stan Todd and Joi's
Wedding 1960

Joi & Mickey Hargitay
(Mariska's Daddy!)

Joi when she starred in
"Come Blow Your Horn" with
Jackie Coogan & Selma Diamond. 1970

Joi with Ron DeSalvo "Come Blow
Your Horn" 1970 Thunderbird Hotel in
Las Vegas

Joi flirting with Bill Hayes "Come Blow Your Horn"
1970 Thunderbird Hotel in Las Vegas

On the set of "Bigfoot" with Producer Anthony Cardoza in 1969

Joi and Will Hutchins in her tv series, "Sugarfoot". 1958

Me at 19, two years before I met Joi. I was doing some teen modeling and was made up to look much younger than I was.

CALIFORNIA STATE BOARD OF EQUALIZATION

Seller's Permit

THIS PERMIT DOES NOT AUTHORIZE THE HOLDER TO ENGAGE IN ANY BUSINESS CONTRARY TO LAWS REGULATING THAT BUSINESS OR TO POSSESS OR OPERATE ANY ILLEGAL DEVICE.

ACCOUNT NUMBER

6-70 SR EH 18-618705

JOI & RACHEL LANSING

███████████

Palm Springs, California

№ 905888

IS HEREBY AUTHORIZED PURSUANT TO SALES AND USE TAX LAW TO ENGAGE IN THE BUSINESS OF SELLING TANGIBLE PERSONAL PROPERTY AT THE ABOVE LOCATION

STATE BOARD OF EQUALIZATION

THIS PERMIT IS VALID UNTIL REVOKED OR CANCELLED BUT IS NOT TRANSFERABLE
Not valid at any other address
BT-442-R REV. 5 (6-67)

DISPLAY CONSPICUOUSLY AT THE PLACE OF BUSINESS FOR WHICH ISSUED

One time we got the "bug" to do some designing for friends. A sweet memory.

---

western union   **Telegram**

1969 JUL 24 AM 8 21

SYB032 SSA117 SY LTA003

(L VEA072) CGN PD PDF=SANTA PAULA CALIF 23 412P PDT=

MISS JOI LANSING DLY 75 DLR IMMY=

WEDGEWOOD DINNER THEATER 1016 CEDAR SWAMP ROAD

GLEN COVE NY=

LOVE AND BEST WISHES CONGRATULATIONS ON ANOTHER TRIBUTE

TO YOUR GREAT TALENT BEST WISHES TO RACHAL=

CARLTON AND MOM=

MARCH 1972 IND. 50¢ 33620

Glamor girl Joi Lansing posed with her little sis (*you* guess which is which) who also hopes to launch film career.

Joi and me at the premiere of "The Indomitable Dr. Phibes" with Vincent Price in 1971

Chapter 31

Sweet December Birthday

My birthday is five days before Christmas, the twentieth of December. When you're born this close to Christmas, it's usually treated as just an ordinary day of the week. Everyone's broke buying Christmas or Hanukkah presents, and the last thing they want to think about is another gift.

Late December babies usually have their birthdays celebrated in conjunction with the holidays, and I was used to being told, "This is your Christmas and birthday present." Joi understood this and always made sure my birthday was the biggest event of the year.

I was awakened by Joi on Sunday morning, December 20, as she carried in a tray filled with my birthday breakfast. I sat up in bed with pillows propped behind my back and, as she placed the tray on my lap, I saw she'd prepared my favorite breakfast meal.

There were eggs over medium, cooked just right, and sausage patties without a lot of grease. She'd gone to our favorite little French bakery and bought fresh croissants that were still warm to the touch. Joi knew I enjoyed coffee served in a glass, so she found a special Irish coffee mug that was absolutely perfect. I couldn't have been more pleased!

I didn't want to eat alone, so I asked her to share this feast with me. There was more than enough for two, so we split everything in half. I did eat a little more than half of the croissant, which I think she expected. Even now, I could live on them and get as big as a rotunda, but good sense prevents me from eating them too often.

We finished breakfast, and then she asked how I'd like to spend my day. I thought for a minute, then told her I'd love to just get in the car and go for a ride. I didn't care where we drove but wanted to spend as much of the day as I could alone with her. Stan had promised to take us out for dinner any place I'd like, but we'd still have all afternoon together.

"Well, let's get going," she said, and we hurriedly got dressed.

Stan was already out playing tennis with a buddy from the Beverly Hills Health Club he'd recently joined. Joi left him a note saying we'd be back close to dinner time.

Just to be as comfortable as possible, we put on sweats. Joi had filled the gas tank when she went out for the croissants, so there was nothing to do except get in the car and go.

Joi asked which direction I preferred, and I said I'd love to drive down Sunset Boulevard. I actually didn't feel like doing much of anything, except be in the car holding hands with her. That was celebration enough for me on this beautiful day. We pulled out onto La Cienega, went up the hill to Sunset, and made a right turn, putting us on the way to downtown Los Angeles. Suddenly, I had a brainstorm and told her I'd like to go to Chinatown for lunch. She smiled and said, "Great idea... it'll be lots of fun on a Sunday afternoon!"

Midway to downtown and being typical Sunday drivers, we took our sweet time looking around. There were interesting little shops all along the streets, and a few were even open. The morning was a little brisk, with no clouds in the sky, but the sun took the chill out of the air as morning turned to afternoon.

We had the music turned up, listening to the most popular song on the radio. Joi was singing, *"This is the dawning of the age of Aquarius, age of Aquarius... Let the sunshine, let the sunshine in."* The song was so happy and upbeat; it made our drive delicious fun. We rocked side to side with the beat, keeping time by hitting our hands on the dashboard.

As we looked around to see if we could find a fun little shop to explore, we spotted the most amazing and unexpected creature walking down the street. I couldn't believe it! I yelled at Joi to pull over, and she spun the steering wheel to the right as fast as she could. She had the good sense to look in her rearview mirror before she pulled this stunt, since we'd been poking along and had more than a few drivers a little frustrated with us. She made sure no one would rear-end us, even though it would definitely be our fault.

There was a parking place halfway down the block, but I asked her to stop first, so I could jump out. She hit the brakes, and I threw open the door, stepping quickly out of the car to the sidewalk where our little mirage was strutting.

As Joi went on to park the car, I couldn't stop smiling as I followed this special little guy as he waddled down the street in his formal black tuxedo. He was obviously taking a leisurely Sunday stroll. Perhaps he knew it was my birthday and had dressed for the occasion!

I stayed a few feet behind because I didn't want to startle him, but, when Joi caught up with us, I spoke to him quietly, saying, "Hello, little fellow. Where ya' goin'?"

Not frightened at all, the sweetest little penguin turned around, looked us over, and—I swear—smiled at us! We were absolutely charmed. What a magical creature this was! Who would believe it? A little penguin toddling along Sunset Boulevard! And on my birthday yet!

I was afraid he might waddle into traffic, so I reached down and picked him up. He was the most adorable little penguin with the sweetest disposition who seemed happy in my arms, not wiggling or squirming to get away. He nestled like he was used to being hugged, and we realized he must have been lost from someone or some place where he was very happy. As entranced as we both were by then, I knew we had to find his home…wherever that was. We walked along in the direction he'd been going and, sure enough, a few stores down the block, we saw a pet shop with pictures of fish on the windows. Its door was wide open.

Joi and I peeked in and saw a young man who looked up at us, smiled, and then casually said, "Thanks for bringing him back."

He explained he was the Shop Owner and that "Timothy" lived there and occasionally decided to go for walks. He came over, took Timothy gently out of my arms, and put him in the little pond which was built just for him in the middle of the store.

It seemed Timothy had total freedom to walk around the neighborhood, acting as a mascot for this tiny little store. Because of the traffic dangers, Joi and I weren't thrilled to hear this, but so far the little guy had been safe. Since he wasn't ours, we could only hope he would continue to be fine and safe on his community tours.

Joi and I stayed a little while longer, enjoying Timothy's antics. For a minute, we wished we could take him home, but, after seeing all the penguin poop, visions of our white carpeting loomed, and we thought better of it!

We said good-bye to him, but not until we promised to return with a fresh fish or two some day. Then off we went to Chinatown. It was time to continue our birthday adventure, although I couldn't imagine what would top this sweet and amazing experience.

We were not that far away from our colorful destination, maybe another twenty minutes. Back in the car, Joi picked up the pace after people started honking their horns and flipping us the bird as they passed. I guess they didn't understand that Sunday is meant for lollygagging, not for rushing around. We felt they should stop to smell the roses, or, at least, stop saluting as they passed by!

Joi knew downtown very well and had no problem finding the signs that said, "Welcome to Chinatown." We parked and walked through the arches which marked the beginning of the touristy part of this interesting place. There were small stores lined up one after another with sarongs and flip-flops, kites, and thousands of other things in the windows and on the sidewalks. It was a sure thing that tourists would find a plethora of goodies to bring back to wherever they called home.

As we wandered, there wasn't anything in particular that I found interesting, that is, until we glanced in the window of one of the little clothing shops and saw a beautiful satin brocade robe in royal blue. I stopped and smiled, thinking how good it would feel on my skin in the morning. Joi saw me musing and asked if I wanted it. Of course, she already knew by my smile that I did.

We went in the store, and Joi asked the Shopkeeper if they had it in my size. The tiny woman replied, "You don't worry… it fit; it fit," as she handed her the largest size. Joi took it out of the bag and looked at it, and then looked at me, trying to get a sense of how I would look without trying it on. The Shopkeeper insisted we take it, writing up the sales slip before we even decided. I laughed at her determination and told Joi not to worry, that it would be just fine, so she bought it and handed me the bag as we went on our way.

Realizing it was lunch time, we looked for a place to eat and saw a cute little restaurant hidden in the corner of the plaza. After checking the menu posted outside, and peeking in to see if there were other people inside, we were pleased to see it was almost full. This made us both feel a little more secure about our selection.

The room was very dark with paper globes hanging from the ceiling. The clientele was mostly Chinese, with very few tourists, which I thought was also a very good sign. Separating the lobby from the dining area were folding screens made of hand-carved dark wood and a gigantic aquarium with brightly-colored salt water fish in unusual shapes. A puffer fish followed us as we walked with the Hostess past his glass house.

We were both pretty hungry but didn't want to spoil our dinner with Stan since we'd be going to the Luau in Beverly Hills for my special birthday meal. The food was Polynesian style, and they had delicious curried shrimp that I loved. A light lunch would take the edge off, yet still sustain us till dinner.

We decided to split an order of wonton soup and pork fried rice. This showed no imagination on our part, since we could have had the same thing from our local Chinese joint down the street, but it wasn't the food we were looking for; it was the ambience of Chinatown, a world that spoke of faraway lands and had a kind of mystery all its own.

We ate our lunch at a quiet table away from the din of families with little children. We were far enough away, so we could chat to our heart's content, without the drone that so often accompanies a successful eating place. The food was excellent and the company spectacular. Joi had never been more beautiful, and I had never been happier. I couldn't think of a better way to spend my twenty-third birthday.

As the afternoon passed, we sat and talked for hours. There was nothing I enjoyed more than our conversations. Joi was well-read and knew a little about almost any subject. We never ran out of things to talk about and, even during periods of silence, we were still communicating.

Finally, it was time to go home, and we hoped to take a nap before it was time to go out again. Joi drove back with a little more enthusiasm on the gas pedal, and we were home in what seemed like no time. Stan's car was in his parking place as we pulled in right next to it. In the elevator, Joi gave me one of my birthday kisses, and it was lucky for me that we lived so far up! If that was any indication of what was to come, I was in for one of the best birthdays of my life.

Stan was watching a tennis match when we walked in. He asked how my birthday had been so far, and we told him about our escapade with Timothy and lunch in Chinatown. At first, he didn't believe a penguin was walking down Sunset Boulevard, but, after we went through the whole production detail after detail, he finally realized we were telling the truth. It must have sounded pretty implausible, but stranger things have happened in Hollywood, and especially to Joi and me. We certainly had a knack for finding adventure everywhere we went. I don't know if it was the energy combination of the two of us, but I'd been a magnet for unusual situations in my life even before I met her.

In fact, I'd made up my mind to tell Joi a little story about one of my misadventures after our dinner that night. It happened in Palm Springs, where we planned to move shortly. But now it was nap time, we were both sleepy, and our tummies were full enough to send us to dreamland for a few hours. We started to cuddle. That was the last thing I remember.

Fortunately, Joi had set the alarm for six o'clock, figuring that would give us plenty of time to get up, shower, and get dressed. After a couple of hours, the alarm jolted us out of a sound sleep, and it was time for my birthday shower, one of my requests on this special day.

We had a nice, big shower which made moving around very easy and, while steam from the hot water clouded the glass enclosure, we pretended we were in Tahiti. Delighting in the warmth and feel of the water on our bodies, we made love under the sultry, tropical waterfall of our imaginations. Finally, the water began to cool, and, relaxed and smiling, we reluctantly said good-bye to Papeete, at least, until next time.

Joi had a lovely black knit pant suit that fit me perfectly, and she asked if I'd like to wear it to the Luau. It would look great with the beautiful black Italian loafers she'd bought for my birthday last year. Since I didn't have the occasion to dress up very often, I told her I'd love to borrow it. Joi watched me as I put it on, then kissed me gently and told me I looked beautiful. She wore a red mini skirt and matching sweater with three-inch pumps that would've made Joan Crawford green with envy!

That night, we both did our makeup perfectly. Joi had shown me some shadowing tricks she'd learned as a protégé at Metro. I loved creating a bit of illusion with a few pats of powder and a shadow here and there. A little darker powder can make your cheekbones appear higher and better defined. I have a strong square jaw and an Irish nose which can be softened or made to look more prominent. Joi loved to play with makeup and try different looks on me. Tonight I was going to be glamorous, just like "my big sister." We had so much fun playing sisters, thinking no one would ever question it. Fortunately, we looked enough alike to get away with it.

Even Stan dressed up that night in a navy blue sports jacket and navy pants, instead of his usual sweats and polo shirt. Most people didn't pay much attention to his wardrobe because his charm and energy distracted them. In fact, he expected people to accept him for who he was, not how he dressed. He added a white turtleneck sweater with his favorite navy and white saddle shoes. Joi was in shock when she saw how he was dressed. She wanted someone to take a picture, so she could remember how nice he could look when he wanted to!

Although Joi liked driving and Stan liked sitting in the backseat smoking his cigar, that night she politely asked him not to smoke in her car. She never complained about my smoking habit (that now I so wish I never had). I guess her nose was probably so used to his cigars that a silly little cigarette wasn't that offensive.

Joi pulled up to the valet in front of the Luau, one of the hot spots in Beverly Hills. A polite and handsome young man opened her door and recognized her immediately, addressing her as Miss Lansing and wishing her a wonderful evening. Another valet opened my door…with far less fanfare, I might add!

When we entered the restaurant, I felt like I'd walked onto the set of *Adventures in Paradise*. Joe, the maître d', was very well-known in town. He'd worked in the same capacity at Stefanino's and knew Joi as a customer, as well as a celebrity. She told me that he always made sure she had the best table in the house. I doubt that anyone would seat her next to the door to the kitchen or against the back wall in a corner, since having Joi as a guest in a restaurant was great for business. Men would slip the Maître d' fifty bucks just to sit near her. I saw more waiters almost drop plates of food as they walked by, looking at her "eyes" instead of what was in front of them.

Joe escorted us to a table in the middle of the room where Hugh Hefner and a bevy of his lady friends were seated at a large table about twenty feet from us. The moment Hugh saw Joi, he smiled and waved at her. She smiled and waved back, in spite of the nasty looks the "ladies" at his table gave her. She told me that he'd tried unsuccessfully for years to get her to do *Playboy*. She didn't mind dressing with low-cut gowns or being seen in a sexy bikini, but that was the most she would undress. Joi refused to do any nudes, which seemed to make her even more sought after and desirable to the media honchos in town. She told me that Hugh had offered her an amazing amount of money if she would appear, but she still refused.

Few people understood how shy Joi really was. When she appeared in seductive clothing, in her mind, she was just playing a part and that wasn't who she was in real life. At home, she was playful, a girl who wore funky sweats and bunny slippers with big floppy ears that I bought her one year for her birthday. I'm not saying she wasn't sensuous—she had an intense, seductive allure that was all-woman, but with the sweetness of an innocent. I always felt incredibly protective of her, and only wish I could have been in her life years earlier to keep her from some of the dreadful experiences she had as a young actress in HorribleWood.

That evening, Joi made sure that Joe knew it was my birthday. I heard her whisper it to him as he hugged her hello. I always felt like a queen being with her. There are no words that can express what it was like to sit at a table next to her, knowing I was the one to whom she'd given her heart.

Dinner was filled with all sorts of tasty treats that she'd ordered for me to try. I didn't have a sophisticated palate, but Joi was going to make sure I eventually would. I was raised on meat, potatoes, and gravy like most kids from the Midwest. She wouldn't even let me ask what she put on my plate until I had tried it, making sure I swallowed it before she'd tell me what it was!

My birthday dinner was a wonder. We ate like it was our last meal, leaving only shrimp tails on the empty plates. It was great to see Joi eat, and I hoped in my heart that her appetite would continue to be strong. When the plates were cleared, and just as I thought we were getting ready to leave, Joe came over with a beautiful exotic dessert of mangos, pineapple, and passion fruit, covered with a fruit sorbet and sprinkled with fresh coconut. One lit candle was placed in the middle of the dish, waiting for me to it blow out.

Joi said, "Make a wish, honey," and I inhaled and held my breath.

My wish was to keep all my memories of her alive till the end of my days. Then, breathing deeply, I blew the candle out. She asked with an impish grin, "Okay, what did you wish for?"

Squeezing her hand under the table, I said, "You know I can't tell you, honey, or it won't come true!"

We all laughed. Then, Joi and I ate a few bites of the lovely fruit, and Stan helped polish it off.

"I can't keep eating like this, or I'm going to turn into a water buffalo," I told her, as I play-waddled out of the dining room sideways, trying not to bang into the birds of paradise lined up along the little foot bridge on our way to the door. She laughed as loudly as she could without bringing too much attention to herself. We were both feeling silly, and I know she would have tickled me, just to watch me squirm, if she could have.

The Valet started rushing to get our car when we came through the doors, but Joi told him to wait. She suggested we take a walk to get our digestion going, which we often did, especially after a big meal. I loved the idea, so Stan just went along and lit up his after-meal cigar. He'd made the concession to Joi not to smoke in her car, but that was all.

Beverly Hills was a very safe place to walk, and the storefronts were fun to look into when no one else was around. Joi loved looking in the windows of the very chichi shops, the ones where you need a second mortgage to buy a T-shirt. She loved to dress well and wasn't cheap, but would not pay the prices hanging from the mannequins. Joi had many of her gowns made by a talented seamstress she knew, which saved her a lot of money that she needed to support herself. She'd learned in the business that work doesn't always come when you need it, so you'd better conserve and spend your money wisely.

We walked by the gallery that represented Leonardo Nierman, and she showed Stan the painting she wanted. This was one of the times I hated the fact that I had no money. I would have bought the painting for her in a heartbeat. I hoped Stan would buy it for her for Christmas, but there were things he just didn't get. Subtle suggestions didn't work with him—you needed to hit him upside the head with a two by four for the message to get through. She hinted that it would look great in the Palm Springs house, but he just changed the subject.

I wanted to say, "Why the hell don't you get her the damned painting? It's the only thing she's ever asked from you!" It wasn't as if he couldn't afford it. He threw away a lot more money on some of his get-rich-quick schemes, but I knew I couldn't force him or do anything to embarrass him. He was being very good to her, and to me as well, so I'd just have to keep my mouth shut and hope for the best. I realized it was my own frustration and feelings of inadequacy in not being able to do the things for her that I wished I could. I hated that Stan was able to, yet didn't do it. And I didn't know how to tell him.

Walking back to the car, we felt a lot less miserable and bloated. Taking a little stroll after dinner was one of the pleasures we most looked forward to when living in the desert. There the nights are sweet with the smell of honeysuckle, warm and balmy. Twinkling stars light up the sky as the moonlight guides your way. We'd be there in a little over a month, and the excitement was starting to get under our skins.

We were home within fifteen minutes, and it felt wonderful, especially after such a long and delightful day. This had been a very special birthday with all the details taken care of, and I could hardly wait to be in our room to spend more time alone with Joi. Fortunately, Stan went directly into his room and turned on the television, lighting up one of the last Cuban cigars Joi had bought him a few months ago. I knew he would be a happy camper and eventually nod off.

Joi went in the kitchen and made us both cups of Constant Comment tea with a slice of orange floating on top. We loved it because of its soothing effect, and it had just the right amount of refreshing spices. She brought a tray to our bedroom with cups and a ceramic pot filled with two tea bags steeping in hot water. This would be more than enough, so we wouldn't have to venture out of our room for the rest of the evening.

I'd been wanting to talk to Joi about Palm Springs, but was waiting for the right time to broach the subject. Once, I casually mentioned to her that I'd been cast in a film that was to be shot there, but had not gone into all the details. It would soon be our new home, so it was important that we talk now.

Since we'd been together, we'd shared so many things about our pasts, dredging up both good and bad experiences. I knew that tonight was as good a time as any, so I said I wanted to tell her about "my wild exploits in the desert." She could hardly wait, knowing that I'd managed to get in and out of unusual circumstances most of my adult life. I assured her that she'd enjoy the story. I began by asking if she might like me with dark hair.

She asked me, "Why dark hair?" and I proceeded to tell her the story.

Chapter 32

Miss Ivory Hunter

Joi settled in next to me, sipping her tea, as I began my story...

I was living at the Studio Club in 1968, pursuing my career in films, when I went on an audition advertised in the paper. I had an agent, but she hadn't sent me on any decent interviews, except the one where the guy dropped his pants, and, since that was "in-decent," it didn't count!

This time, I went on my own to the address in the ad, which was a very small office in the middle of Hollywood. At least, twenty young blonde women were sitting on old wooden fold-out chairs in the reception area which spilled out into the hallway. The nondescript furniture looked like it came from the Salvation Army, a worn receptionist's desk with lamps and cheap reproduction prints that were old and dusty.

Every one of the girls had light blonde hair and were, at least, five foot seven, as requested in the ad. I asked one pretty girl if she knew what this was about, and she thought it was for a "lead in a movie." The ad had mentioned "legitimate film work, non-union can apply," and, naturally, we all believed it.

I'd been trying to join the Screen Actors Guild, but it was the old Catch-22. You had to be in a film to be able to join, and you couldn't be in a film unless you were in the union! I never did understand that logic.

That day, I was wearing one of my few "interview" outfits, a teal blue sheath dress with matching three-inch heels. They were obviously interested in stature, so I presented myself with all six foot two of me (with the spiked heels, of course).

Eventually, a tall, thin man in a navy blue suit and burgundy tie came out of his inner office. Striding down the hallway, he eyeballed each of us girls, looking us up and down. He didn't seem like a creep, though, more like a businessman there to do a job. His look was serious, not especially friendly, and his features were sharp, even a little severe. After appraising each one of us, he seemed to have made a decision. Turning, he walked up to me and asked if I'd join him in his office.

As I walked ahead of him, I could feel him watching my every move. I had always been secure in my looks, especially after being in beauty pageants and one of the winners of the TV show, *Dream Girl of '67*. I loved being tall and felt good about myself. I knew you only had one opportunity to impress on an interview, so I made sure I stayed calm and composed.

He introduced himself as Bill Free. After we talked a while, he seemed to warm up, even smile a bit, though barely. He said he thought I might be right for the part, and then went out to the waiting room to excuse the rest of the girls, thanking them for their time. He told them to leave their headshots, and he would call them if he thought he could use them in a future project. He also gave them the old "Don't call me; I'll call you" line that was famous in the business. I'm sure they all recognized the brush-off and were disappointed.

I started to get up and thank him for his time, but he asked me to stay for a few more minutes. He made a quick call to someone he said was the Director, inviting him to come to the office because he had "found the perfect woman to play the part."

While we waited, he looked at my 8 x 10s and said they were pretty good, but not great. He mentioned he had a photographer he wanted me to use, and I also needed a more exciting name than "Nancy Hunter." The "Hunter" part was okay, but the "Nancy" had to go.

"See?" Joi interrupted, smiling. "Joey Bishop and I were right! Nancy isn't a good name for you. Rachel is!"

I agreed with her since I loved my name "Rachel," but said that Bill had an entirely different take on what it should be. She started guessing, "Marilyn? Lana? Alexandra? Elena?"

"Not exactly," I teased, "but you're close!"

"Well, what was it?" she asked, having fun with the guessing game.

Knowing exactly how she'd respond, I said, "Ivory Hunter," and she cracked up!

Laughing, as I knew she would, she hooted, "In Hollywood that kind of name usually ends up on a stripper or go-go girl!"

It sounded so Hollywood that it was actually funny.

As soon as Joi regained her composure, I started telling her how "Miss Ivory Hunter" became the star of an untitled film. According to Bill Free, they had the script written, but hadn't yet come up with a working title. I didn't care. After all, I was going to be the star of a real Hollywood film! I knew it was legit. It had to be because he didn't "come on" to me. At least, that was what I thought.

Joi slowly shook her head, thinking she knew where the story was headed. She urged me not to be embarrassed about what I was about to tell her, that she'd been in a lot of bizarre circumstances during all the years of her career. She'd started out very young with a bit part in *The Wizard of Oz* and then was recruited to be in the young actors program at MGM. She was aware of all the wackos and pretend producers out there and tried to make me feel unashamed of being naive. That really took the pressure off and made it much easier to explain what happened next.

I'd never done a film and didn't know the first thing about the correct protocol involved. I asked for a script, so I could start learning my lines, but was told it would be provided when we went on location to Palm Springs. I'd never been to Palm Springs, either, and found this incredibly exciting. Bill told me not to worry about bringing a lot of wardrobe, as I'd be given everything I needed. Shooting would start in a few days. I couldn't wait to let everyone at the Studio Club know I'd gotten my first starring role!

There was a knock on Bill's office door and in walked the director, Al. Bill asked me to stand up, so Al could see how I looked, and I got up and stood next to him. He was a small, short, finely-boned man wearing baggy khaki trousers, a long-sleeved button-down khaki shirt, and greenish-brown suspenders. His wire-rimmed glasses, which seemed too large for his face, emphasized his deep blue eyes. *Hmm*, I thought, *So this is Al, the director, who's going to make me a star.*

While we talked, I eventually asked about a contract, and Bill explained it would be ready for my signature in a few days, that the lawyers would draw it up and make sure it was to my liking. I asked how long we'd be shooting, and they both piped up, "A few weeks."

This was definitely too good to be true!

As I questioned when we'd leave and where I'd be staying, Bill said we'd leave that Friday, in three days' time. Al said we'd stay at the Spa Hotel in Palm Springs, and, since I'd have my own room, I could invite a "few of my friends from the Studio Club" to keep me company. I never imagined this! What fun, and that put me totally at ease, allaying any fears I might have had.

I didn't want to jinx it by asking how much they'd be paying me, but I finally blurted it out.

"How much can I expect to be paid for my work?" I asked very quietly.

Bill answered with a reassuring smile, "The way it looks right now, Ivory, you'll be getting more than scale per day."

"That's great!" I said, smiling, though I had absolutely no idea what "scale" would be.

They said they'd call to let me know when I'd be picked up and even congratulated me, in unison yet, as I shook their hands.

Well, needless to say, I left the office with wings on my heels. I was so excited, I could have flown right out of there and back to the Studio Club. I had heard about Lana Turner being discovered at Schwab's, but never thought that I'd be so lucky. I'd always had a feeling I was destined for something special, but didn't think it would be quite this easy.

I got back to the Studio Club and told everyone I saw about the movie, and how I was going to Palm Springs in just a few days to shoot. I practically danced up to my room. I saw my friend, Coral Kerr, a wonderful artist working at Hanna-Barbera. I told Cathy Marks and Molly Fleming and Koko Tani and anyone who would listen. I went to the office to let Mrs. Fortier know I'd be gone for a couple of weeks and would pay my rent in advance. I called my parents in Covina, telling them my wonderful news, and they promised to visit me in Palm Springs. I also invited Coral and a few other friends to stay for a few days. Coral said she'd take a few days off from work because she wanted to be there for me if there were any problems.

Frankly, the word "problem" didn't even enter my mind. I thought I'd asked all the important questions and had received perfectly reasonable answers. How could anything possibly go wrong?

Joi looked at me, obviously wondering what would happen next, and hoping nothing terrible had happened to me in my Pollyanna pursuits. I assured her I'd always been very lucky, that I had a guardian angel who plucked me out of difficult situations and helped me land on my feet. And I told her not to worry. She nodded, and I continued with my story

Bill and Al picked me up in the lobby of the Studio Club on Friday as promised. I wanted the ladies in charge and some of the girls to see that I wasn't making up a story about starring in a film. I also had a little premonition that told me to make sure people got a good look at them "just in case," though I really didn't think I was in any jeopardy, and besides, some of my buddies would be with me, wouldn't they?

I had one small suitcase filled to capacity with all the necessities for two weeks. I didn't need a lot of makeup since there was always a makeup person on a set, and my hair would be done by a stylist hired by the film company. Stars just needed to show up and say their lines, right? At least, that was what I thought.

We'd been driving for about an hour on I-10 when Al started looking at exits as if he were searching for something close ahead. Before I knew it, we were off the freeway and heading down a bumpy gravel road. When I asked where we were, they said there was a small resort they wanted to check out and we'd "have lunch and stretch our legs a little before we got back on the road." Lunch sounded like a great idea. We drove a good fifteen minutes before we came to a barbed wire fence with what looked like a walkie-talkie near the lock. A little note taped to it said, "Push button to gain entrance."

After Bill pushed the button, we waited a few minutes until an old beat-up Jeep came flying down the road, bouncing hard as it hit each bump. The dust was like a wall following it, with rocks and dirt flying everywhere. The driver, an old guy with a leather cowboy hat, slammed his Jeep to a stop just behind the gate and leaned out to look us over. He asked if we knew where we were. Bill said, "Yes," and, glancing at me, the driver kind of shook his head and told us to follow him to the lodge. I didn't know what he meant by, "Do you know where you are?" It struck me as a little strange, but I was still thinking the best about my adventure in showbiz.

The gate swung open, and soon we, too, were bouncing all over the road with shocks that weren't as good as those on a Jeep. We were in an older model Cadillac that was well taken care of and in fairly decent condition. I thought it had a lot more trips left in her unless we hit a rut a little too hard and tore out the undercarriage. But I wasn't going to open my mouth. These people were in charge and could fire me since I still didn't have a contract. I had to walk on eggshells until I felt a little more secure.

We pulled up in front of what looked like a little desert oasis, though we were out in the boonies with nothing but scrub and cactus and an occasional palo verde tree. The parking places in front of the building were mostly full, but we pulled into an empty space right near the entrance. Bill took my hand as we got out of the car and told me not to be alarmed at what I was going to see, that this was a private club for members and their guests only.

I didn't have any idea what he was talking about. Not, that is, until Al opened the door, and I walked into the lobby. *Oh, good Lord*, I thought. *Everyone is naked!* This was a nudist resort, and no one had told me where we were going. Now, I considered myself open-minded (you had to be in Hollywood, or you wouldn't last), but I never imagined myself walking around in my altogether in front of strangers!

With this bit of information, Joi's jaw dropped. She wasn't a prude by any stretch, but would never put her body on display for anyone to ogle. I continued...

I told Al and Bill that I didn't have a problem being there, but was a little too shy to walk around in my birthday suit. They acted as if they understood, but hoped I wouldn't be offended if they went along with the style while we had lunch. They promised we'd only be there for an hour or so and then get back on the road to Palm Springs.

Bill explained that he loved the nudist life and tried to participate whenever the opportunity presented itself. He said this was a famous nudist colony only known to people so inclined. It takes a lot to offend me, and I'm not one to judge anyone, especially something I think is perfectly normal and inoffensive, so I happily went along with the program.

We ate a delightful lunch at a table under a large sun umbrella, beside a massive free-form pool. Dozens of people were enjoying the water—couples with young children and men and women who appeared to be together. Bill explained that very few singles were allowed because they would be more suspect as someone there just for kicks. True nudists pay no attention to one's body parts, especially the parts that gravity had a habit of moving as they walked. They were not looking for fun and games, but for a clothing-free lifestyle, just like their ancient ancestors who played in trees thousands of years ago.

This was certainly an education, especially since I hadn't seen many dangling participles in my life. (Come to think of it, I was probably one of those single people looking at all the things I wasn't supposed to!) It was fascinating to watch the laws of physics as I observed people playing tennis, watched how the muscles in the body stretched and flexed while bending and jumping. Several of them had trim and muscular bodies, and the aerodynamic beauty of their bodies in motion was quite spectacular.

We finished lunch, and Bill and Al went back to being puritanical. They put their pants and shirts on, and it was time to go. We had less than an hour to drive and, though the vegetation was sparse, it had a simple and pure beauty.

It was late afternoon when we arrived in one of the most beautiful places I'd seen in my life. Palm Springs had a special feeling that hit me the minute we turned the corner around the mountain. I felt a serenity like no other place I'd ever been.

The Spa Hotel was on Indian Canyon in the middle of town. We pulled into the portico where a valet took the car and carried in our bags while we walked into the lobby. Bill went up to the front desk to check in. They knew we were coming, and the Clerk welcomed me by saying, "Hello, Miss Hunter, welcome to Palm Springs and the Spa Hotel. I hope you enjoy your stay with us."

I couldn't believe it! This was really happening and not some crazy con. I loved hearing "Miss Hunter." It was like music to my ears. The Clerk handed me the key to my suite and showed me how to sign for room service or other services in the hotel or gift shop. I was new to this kind of treatment, but took to it like the proverbial duck to water. I hoped no one would pinch me and make it all disappear, and I was determined to enjoy this until the last day of shooting…whenever that was.

No one had yet given me a shooting schedule, and I was still waiting for my script and, most importantly, my contract. When I asked Bill about them again, he explained he'd have a shooting schedule as soon as the crew arrived from Los Angeles. They were doing a few rewrites on the script, and the contract was still in the lawyer's hands but would be ready soon. He told me not to worry, to enjoy myself until we started the actual production, and asked if any of my friends were coming to keep me company. I told him, at least, a few would be in town tomorrow.

"Then, why don't you just rest and order room service for dinner?" he suggested with a smile.

I had no problem with that. I'd been to hotels before, but nothing like this beautiful resort. I'd never been alone in a hotel room, and, at first, I found it strange and a little lonely. Having my friends stay with me would make things a lot more comfortable and fun. Besides, I wanted to share my good fortune with some of the people who were dear to me. Coral had been a loyal friend, and we'd been close since I moved to the Studio Club. Sue Spratt was also a good friend. I knew we'd all have a great time, and Bill had even said I could sign for all of our meals!

Joi couldn't take the suspense and said she kept waiting for the other shoe to drop, but I assured her that, at this time, everything was going along without a hitch. She sighed, then said, "Okay. Go on."

Unexpectedly, Bill called my room and said we'd be going to a local Cadillac dealership to pick up an appropriate car to use in town. At the dealership, Bill made arrangements to get a beautiful limo, one of the most exciting things that ever happened to me. I'd never even been near a limousine, and now I had one at my disposal. Bill either bought or leased a few other cars for the production company, and it didn't take him long to take care of the negotiations.

Upon returning to the hotel, I had people asking for my autograph, and I was more than happy to oblige. Feeling great, I finally began to relax and enjoy my first night alone in a beautiful hotel room. The furniture was all light-colored wood, and a tall armoire held a large TV on a swivel pedestal. I made sure it faced my side of the enormous king-size bed and had the remote right next to me as I looked over the room service menu for dinner.

I was in shock when I saw the prices, but I guessed this was normal for a fancy hotel in a resort town. I decided to order something not too expensive nor too cheap, so I found a turkey dinner that sounded good. I was trying to ease into this newfound bit of heaven without rocking the boat.

I took a shower in the bathroom that was larger than my room at the Studio Club, and I couldn't understand why anyone would waste so much space on a bathroom! In fact, there was a lot of "getting used to" that I needed to do. I hoped Bill and Al would be mentors and give me a little guidance. This was a wonderful new world, but I didn't have a single road map to help me find my way. I would just have to play "follow the leader," watch how everyone else answered questions, and hope for the best.

During my first few days as Ivory Hunter, my only responsibility was to sit around and enjoy the hotel. Bill and Al had me join them for lunch in the dining room when they had guests who were interested in investing in the film. My role was just to sit there and look pretty. I only spoke when asked a question, and rarely engaged anyone in serious conversation. I was more a prop than anything. When the men started talking business, it became obvious that Bill was short on production cash. I was being treated like a star, so it didn't matter to me what was going on. I had a lovely suite, and my friends were on their way to keep me company. I had anything I wanted to eat and was in proverbial hog heaven.

When Coral arrived, I was excited, since we'd always had a great time together. Although I still hadn't seen a script or received my contract, I was having too good a time to worry about that anymore. After all, I'd been a nobody a few days ago, and now I was a movie star…in name only, of course, but I was the only one who knew that.

I'd been chosen to be queen for a day on a much more exciting level. Everywhere I went, people looked at me like I was a Grecian goddess who'd reincarnated in the form of a blonde, green-eyed amazon named Ivory Hunter.

In a few days, my other friends came and were having fun at the hotel swimming pool. I saw them periodically during the day while I enjoyed being the big shot and sharing my good fortune. Coral spent more time with me, being a little more inquisitive about when the film would start shooting. I had no idea, and every time I'd ask Bill or Al, I was told we were waiting for the rest of the crew to arrive. This seemed like a reasonable answer, so, at least for the moment, I'd stopped asking questions.

One afternoon, Bill took me to the hotel gift shop to buy a few things I needed. I saw a gorgeous silver evening dress with a low-cut v-neck. It was considered a mini dress, hitting me about five inches above my knees.

It wasn't as short as some of the other minis hanging in my closet at home, but I didn't bring them because they were a little too sexy for the image I was trying to portray. Bill wanted me to look more elegant than sexy, and I liked that idea.

I found a pair of exquisite silver dress shoes with a slingback heel and beautiful bead work on the top. They were the most expensive shoes I'd ever seen at over $150. The dress was over $250, which seemed like an insane amount of money to spend for such a small amount of fabric, but I showed the outfit to Bill, and he said they fit the image he wanted me to project. He signed for them, and I took them to my room before he changed his mind.

Taking it all really seriously, I even developed a different walk and practiced my Miss America speech pattern. "You always hesitate before you answer a question," was pounded into the heads of beauty queen participants. Whenever one of Bill's business associates would ask me something, I'd stop and hesitate for a few beats and proceed like I'd been taught. I even practiced this when a waitress asked how I wanted my eggs cooked!

When I called my parents, I told them everything was great and asked if they'd be coming to the desert to visit. Bill said he'd make sure they had a room to stay in if they decided to visit for a day or two, so they planned to come down for the weekend. I couldn't believe how generous and kind Bill was to me and my parents and friends.

Meanwhile, I was having a glorious time as the gracious hostess, telling my parents to enjoy themselves and sign for any food they wanted to eat. They got into the role of "parents of the star," and told anyone they met that Ivory Hunter, a new young Hollywood star, was their daughter.

I was happy being able to spoil them a little, since they'd worked hard all of their lives. My dad was a career Navy man who had enlisted when he was just seventeen, a few years before World War II broke out in Pearl Harbor. He was stationed on an aircraft carrier just a few miles out of harm's way when the Japanese attack wiped out most of the ships in the harbor. He put in over twenty-one years and worked his way up from swabbie to lieutenant-commander.

It was a great opportunity for me to give back to them for all they'd done to encourage my interest in acting. They never discouraged my desire to be in the limelight, and I think my mom enjoyed living vicariously through all my pursuits. I had no idea how long this would last, but was living in the moment.

My folks stayed for the weekend and were included in dinner meals with Bill and Al. My friends had enjoyed their Palm Springs getaway but were also going home after the weekend. I was happy that Coral could stay a little longer to keep me company.

Bill said he wanted to introduce me to some lovely people who had a mansion just outside of Palm Springs. He asked me to wear my new dress and shoes, and he would meet me in the lobby at seven that evening. I could hardly wait to wear my luxurious silver outfit and was excited to meet these new people.

Joi was getting more and more intrigued with every word I said. She said she was waiting for the punch line. I explained that she'd know soon enough and to just enjoy the story. I promised I wouldn't drag it out and keep her on edge, that the fun parts were in the details I'd explain soon enough. She was content with my explanation, and began again to listen curiously.

That night, Bill and Al took me to an amazing home high on the side of a mountain on the way to Palm Desert. The road up was winding and steep... lucky for me it was dark, so I couldn't see how steep the sheer drop was just a few feet from the road. I'm petrified of heights and especially of going up a severe incline. It doesn't bother me looking forward, but completely freaks me out looking behind at the road below. I didn't dare look back as we were climbing the hill.

The road took us to a large circular drive in front of a beautiful two-story home. My nerves had calmed a little, and my nausea had begun to subside by the time we entered the house. A huge room was filled with, at least, thirty guests, all of whom looked like they were having a wonderful time. Bill told me to "mingle and enjoy" while he and Al were busy talking with the host and hostess. The party had actually been given in my honor to introduce me to the high society members of the community! Bill walked me around and made sure everyone had an opportunity to meet Ivory Hunter, the up-and-coming new star on the horizon.

A staff of four professional waiters served enticing shrimp cocktails and finger sandwich appetizers. The best part of the evening, however, was the spectacular view of the Coachella Valley seen from the floor to ceiling windows on all sides of the living area. I stood in awe as I watched the majestic lights spread for miles and miles against the blackness of the desert night.

We were there for two to three hours at most. From eavesdropping, I got the distinct impression that Bill and Al were extolling the virtues of the film we were in the process of finalizing. Frankly, it felt like a fishing expedition, in search of a big "catch" to infuse capital into the coffers of Bill and Company, but the evening seemed to go well, and everyone was more than pleasant.

When we went down the hill, I kept my eyes squeezed shut. I was still dizzy, but hoped we'd reach the flatland before the pretty little shrimp and finger sandwiches came back for a second appearance! We made it just in time.

I went to my room right after our return to the hotel and said goodnight to Coral before I got ready for bed. I slept like the world was my oyster and my dreams had finally come true.

The following morning, I got up around ten, and a tray with coffee and orange juice was sitting outside my door. I called Coral to join me. Nice.

Around noon, Bill called and said we'd been offered a better arrangement at a different hotel and would be moving in about an hour. I told Coral to get ready, and she packed the few things she'd brought for the short visit. Bill had a bellman pick up our things and transfer them to the limo waiting in front of the hotel.

Coral joined me in the stretch limo and kept asking questions about when filming would start. She'd worked quite a bit in films and had a lot more experience than I did. She felt something just wasn't right and was concerned about the razzle-dazzle going on.

As we rode, she continued to focus on the script and my contract. I explained that the script was supposedly on its way after a few rewrites, and the lawyer had finished the contract and mailed it from New York. I said everything seemed to be aboveboard, but, in my heart. I had to admit I was beginning to worry.

We moved to the Canyon Hotel, a little further out from the main part of Palm Springs. The area was a bit desolate but had a quiet and peaceful beauty, and the hotel was nice. It wasn't as chichi as the Spa Hotel, but I still enjoyed being treated like a queen, without a care in the world. Again, I was given a lovely suite with a combination living room and bedroom. The couch made into a bed, where Coral would sleep.

I didn't see Bill or Al on the day we checked in, but we made plans to meet in the hotel bar the following morning at eleven. I dressed in comfortable blue slacks, a white linen jacket, and a pair of nice white loafers, then knocked on Coral's door to say I'd see her a little later.

The bar was on the opposite side of the spacious, plant-filled lobby. It was dark inside, and it took a few minutes for my eyes to adjust. I didn't see Bill or Al, so I sat near the entrance where I'd be able to spot them as soon as they arrived. The Bartender asked if I'd like something to drink, and I ordered a cup of coffee with lots of cream. When he returned with my coffee, I asked if two gentlemen had come in looking for me. He pointed to two tall men at the far end of the bar who didn't look the least familiar.

As I turned back to take a sip of coffee, the two men stood and slowly walked over to me, standing one on each side. The taller of the two asked if I was Ivory Hunter. I said I was, and asked if he was an associate of Bill Free. He replied that he knew of him, but they were not connected in any way. I started feeling uneasy, wondering why they weren't going back to their seats.

The man on my left took out his wallet, flipped it open, and showed me a shiny brass shield that said "Police" on it. My mouth went dry. He said they wanted to ask me a few questions, and would like me to come to the police station with them. I think I gulped, then stood up and walked out of the bar between the two cops. Me. Ivory Hunter. A star.

Joi's face turned pale. Just talking about this part made me uneasy and, seeing this, she began rubbing my back to relax me. As she gently rubbed, I continued my "Tale of Palm Springs."

The officers walked me to their unmarked car where they told me they were special detectives in the Palm Springs Police Department assigned to obtain information regarding Bill Free. At the station, they took me to an interrogation room and said they hoped I could fill in some of the blanks and would appreciate my cooperation. They were very nice and assured me that they didn't suspect me of any crime at that time. I, in turn, promised to tell them anything I knew.

I was frightened out of my mind because I didn't know why they were after Bill. I knew I hadn't done anything wrong, but innocent people sometimes get caught up in the wake of sharks being pursued. I asked one of the detectives what

Bill had done to create this investigation, and he replied that he couldn't go into details, but it was regarding unpaid hotel bills and the fraudulent purchase of automobiles from local dealers. My jaw dropped with the realization that this had all been a hoax to defraud local business people and to get investors for a film that didn't exist. And I'd been used as a front for their sneaky little enterprise!

Suddenly, I was furious! I asked the Detective for some paper and told him I'd write a book if it would help stop these men. He brought me a handful of notebook paper and a pen and left me alone in the room to write everything I remembered from start to finish. I wrote every detail I could recall from the first moment I met Bill Free until the police took me to the station. It took me a few hours, but I hoped what I wrote would make them understand I had no part in this scam.

When I finished, they both read what I'd written, and their attitudes seemed to soften. One of them left the room and brought back the Chief of Police, who told me they'd suspected that this was a three-person team. He said they were also concerned that prostitution might be a part of the scheme, but had found no evidence I'd been involved. I just about lost it when he said those words. It was the furthest thing from the truth. I couldn't believe they thought I'd been "hooking" in their city! Besides, I was way too busy being a star, and, although I couldn't say it, I wasn't into men anyway.

I was visibly shaken, and the Chief told me not to be upset. He said they only wanted Bill, and I was free to go. I explained I had almost no money because everything had been provided, and I didn't have a car because I'd come with Bill and his friend.

The Chief decided there was only one solution that would make everyone happy... I'd have to leave town, and it would have to be now. They arranged for one of the officers to drive me to the Greyhound bus station, where he handed me a ticket, told me to take the bus back to Los Angeles, and to forget about coming back for a while.

It seemed that Bill had ripped off the local gentry for thousands and thousands of dollars. They had interviewed people in the hotels and businesses where Bill had done his fancy footwork, including all the guests from the party on the hill. Bill had tried to con them into investing in the proposed film, using me as proof that they'd already hired an actress to star in the production.

The police had not been able to find Bill and Al, but they had the full intention of prosecuting both of them for fraud and conspiracy to commit fraud. Although I was free to go, being in their shadow had sullied my reputation. Now I knew what it was like to be "rode out of town on a rail," and told you're not wanted there anymore.

The most embarrassing part of the story was when the police called my parents and asked them to pick up my things at the Canyon Hotel. I'd left everything in the room when I was plucked from my place in Hollywood history. My parents drove from Covina to the hotel and offered to pay for my expenses, but the Hotel Manager was more than kind, saying I had been a victim also and that they would pursue Mr. Free for what he owed them.

When I got to the bus depot in downtown Los Angeles, I called one of my friends to pick me up, then suddenly realized Coral might still be sitting in the hotel room! Back at the Studio Club, I received a frantic call from her saying she'd planned to leave Palm Springs that same day to take a flight back to the city. When she couldn't find me to say good-bye, she called the front desk and was told "Miss Hunter was no longer a hotel guest."

After Coral's return to the Studio Club, we talked non-stop, and I was so relieved this ordeal was over. We could both sleep well in our tiny little beds in our jail-sized rooms, knowing we were back safe and sound under the protection of the ladies of the YWCA. I really should have discussed my "big break" with them beforehand, but I thought I was invincible and knew exactly what I was doing. I told Mrs. Fortier after the fact, and she smiled and said, "You really need a keeper."

She knew I was full of adventure, complicated by being horribly naive.

Slowly, Joi's face broke into a smile, and then we both started to laugh. I felt so much better having told her my deepest and most embarrassing secret. I'd been so afraid that, when we moved to the desert, we'd run into someone I'd met when I was an infamous movie star. Joi told me not to worry, that people forget, especially if the name is changed and the association is totally different. She said I definitely didn't have to disguise myself with dark hair. I'd be Joi's little sister, and no one would question my respectability. She said that "Ivory Hunter" was now deceased, and Joi and Rachel Lansing were upstanding pillars of the community.

Joi knew exactly how to make me feel comfortable. I knew I could tell her about anything in my life, no matter how bizarre or ridiculous it might have seemed. The trust I felt between us comforted me. That night, in her arms, I slept the sleep of the innocent. Safe ... and in love.

Chapter 33

Christmas

I had finally finished the pastel portrait of Joi I'd secretly worked on for months, just in time for our Christmas celebration. Now it was Christmas Eve, and I was getting ready to start prepping for tomorrow's feast. My parents were coming for dinner, so my girl and I had gone through the same drill as we did for Thanksgiving. Off we'd gone to Chalet Gourmet, picked up a gigantic turkey, and bought the same veggies and sweet potatoes that were such a success at our last holiday meal. Joi wanted to help, and having her by my side working in the kitchen was my idea of a real Christmas treat.

The next morning, we got up at the proverbial crack of dawn. Joi was already filled with the excitement of Christmas, and her eyes lit up when she ran to the living room to see what might be under the tree. Her childlike wonder and genuine glee overtook her when she saw the portrait, tied with a big red bow. (She had no idea I'd been working many nights after she'd fallen asleep, getting it ready.)

Joi picked it up and gently untied the large red satin bow, letting it fall to the floor. She held it out and looked at it, then put it on the floor and looked at it from a distance. Twirling and laughing, she started doing her Birdie dance, which she only did when she was extremely happy. This was the highest compliment she could have paid me, and I was delighted.

Laughing, she came over and hugged me, telling me how much she loved it and how beautifully I'd captured her smile. She said there was a place in the living room where she'd have Stan hang it temporarily until we moved. For now, she leaned it against the coffee table, saying she wanted to be able to see it when she first walked into the room.

Then, still obviously tickled, she walked to the tree and picked up a small box. Smiling, she handed it to me, saying it was important she give it to me when no one else was around. Loving the mystery, I opened it slowly. Inside was a beautiful blue velvet box, the kind you see in the fancy jewelry stores. I felt my heart begin to pound.

Carefully, I lifted the small lid and gasped. My eyes fell on the most beautiful ring I'd ever seen in my life. The quality was unmistakable. The wide yellow band was made of 18-karat gold in an open honeycomb design, while seven sparkling stones were sprinkled along the top, three beautiful diamonds surrounded by four rich blue sapphires.

Joi lifted it carefully from its box and then, gently taking my left hand, slipped it on my ring finger. Looking directly into my eyes, she said softly, "I'm in love with you, Rachel…and it's time I gave you a ring. With this ring, I thee wed."

My eyes filled, and it felt like my heart would burst. I whispered the same words to her, wishing I had a ring for her as well. Then, as if the angels had planned it, I saw exactly what I needed. Stan had left a cigar band on his tray and, picking it up, I smiled and slipped it on her ring finger…telling her I loved her deeply, and promising I would buy her the real thing as soon as I sold one of my paintings.

Her smile was beautiful. It was as if I'd given her the Hope Diamond, the way she kept staring at it. We held one another, and I vowed I'd wear my ring "until the day I died," knowing I would never break this promise to her. She needed to know that she owned my heart, a gift I had given willingly. Then, we kissed as passionately as if someone had just told us, "You may now kiss the bride."

Knowing that Stan might be coming into the room at any moment, Joi wiped my happy tears and led me in the Birdie dance! Minutes later, laughing and winded, I cried, "Uncle!" Then, regaining whatever composure this special Christmas morning would allow, we headed for the kitchen hand in hand.

It was time to put the turkey in the oven, which we had prepped the night before. I had learned from Thanksgiving what I had to do and in what particular order. Joi took pride in helping me, and I, more than ever before, knew we were "family." I was "home," and so was the woman I loved. And I would never forget this day.

I was excited to be spending this very special Christmas with Joi, since it was not one that was particularly expected, and it meant more to me than ever because of it. Though her last checkup was very good and she was still in re-mission, the Doctor couldn't predict how much longer this would last. He had cautioned me to live each moment. It was clear that was all he could suggest.

The morning went too quickly between all the food preparation and get-ting dressed in our best holiday garb for the day ahead.

Dad and Mom (or Ivan and Doris, as they preferred to be called) were at the front door at precisely two o'clock, allowing the perfect amount of time for us to chat for a while before we served dinner at three-thirty. Joi answered the door and hugged them both as they came in the apartment. Dad handed her a bouquet of fresh pink and white variegated carnations, and she thanked them as the lovely hostess she was. Joi had been to my parents' home, at least, three or four times before, but they'd never visited us here until this Christmas.

Seeing my mother again reminded me of how terribly selfish she'd been just after Joi and I returned from New York and Joi had been diagnosed. I hadn't realized how long it had been since I'd called her, and, when I tried to tell her about Joi's health and how difficult it had been, her dismissal of my explanation made me angry enough not to want to call her ever again. We were finally speaking again, though, thanks to my dad's intervention. He had called to say how sorry he was about my "friend," and that my mother was really upset at the time and wasn't thinking clearly when she tore into me. I asked to speak with her and then invited them to our home for Christmas.

My parents had never been to the penthouse, and they were obviously very impressed as Joi took them on a nickel tour of the place. She made a point of showing them our room, and emphasized "our" as she showed them around. I said a silent "Yikes!" to myself and watched their faces to see if they reacted to the unusual sleeping arrangements. Neither of them even winced. Stan's room down the hall was the next stop on the tour.

I knew they thought Joi and I were like sisters and had hopes that she would be instrumental in furthering my career. Little did they know that I had found the life I wanted to live … a happier life just being with Joi … a bliss that show business could never provide.

Dinner was just as good, if not better, than Thanksgiving. My parents had brought a few presents for Joi and me, and even a box of cigars for Stan. Joi and I had bought them a sterling silver lazy Susan for their dining room table, which they absolutely loved. The afternoon was very relaxing. My mother helped with the cleanup, letting Joi sit down and rest, which she needed to do more often these days.

All of the excitement we'd experienced in the past month had started to take its toll. Joi was beginning to tire a little more easily lately. I watched for this and encouraged her to rest whenever I noticed the strain on her face or how she moved.

Finally, the "folks" began to worry about the heavy holiday traffic and left, happy and full, with their lazy Susan in tow. It was only eight o'clock, and things were back to normal and very peaceful. We looked at one another and both smiled...and exhaled! We laughed at our stereo moment, and Joi took my hand as we headed for our room. Time for Christmas TV to watch a holiday movie.

It had been a big day. Stan adjourned to his room and resumed his usual routine. His cigar was lit by the time he adjusted his recliner to the maximum position. We hugged him and thanked him for his part in making the day a happy one. He'd hung my painting of Joi in a place of honor where it was enjoyed by all.

We got into our jammies and turned on the TV. Joi's favorite film of all time was just starting—*The African Queen* with Spencer Tracy and Katherine Hepburn—and we hoped we could stay awake till the end.

Joi and I took turns getting up and peeking in at Stan, making sure he didn't torch himself and us with his cigar. His habit of falling asleep with the stinky thing in his mouth was a dangerous one. That night, I checked on him frequently, letting Joi rest and watch the film.

Stan had always been careful. Careful, that is, until brandy was added to the mix. Since Joi's diagnosis, it had become habitual for him to take a nip every few hours throughout the day. It never made him drunk exactly; it was more like a sedative to help relieve his anxiety. We each handle our pain in the best way we know how, and his comfort came in a bottle of Christian Brothers brandy.

I went back into our bedroom and brushed my teeth. Joi had already finished her nightly ablutions while I was on fire patrol. I got in next to her, pulled the sheet up to my chin, and snuggled against my girl as she pulled me close. We continued to watch the tube, and I remember Joi managed to stay awake until the best part of the film when "Bogie" and Kate blew up the "Louisa," a German gunship, with their makeshift torpedo. Then, content, she fell asleep peacefully in my arms.

Looking down at my girl's beautiful sleeping face, I traced her cheeks and chin with my finger. *The perfect ending to a perfect Christmas*, I thought. I yawned and then looked at my hand adorned with my exquisite new ring. Smiling, I added sleepily, *and our perfect love…*

Chapter 34

Home in the Desert

As soon as Stan closed escrow on our new home, Joi and I made preparations to move on February 8. Stan arranged for a truck to take the few pieces of furniture we wanted to keep, so we didn't have much to move, mostly personal items like clothing, some kitchen stuff, and a few things we'd need right away, such as bed linens and towels.

We had happily navigated Thanksgiving and Christmas and decided to bring in the New Year quietly at home. It was a night of quiet celebration and love. We went from laughter to tears recalling the past twelve months and the many changes we'd endured. I'd kept hoping a miracle would happen and they'd find a cure for the awful disease that was slowly taking my Joi away from me. As the ball dropped that night in Times Square and the New Year officially began, I held her in my arms and sadly realized that the same hope I'd clung to for so long would still be my only way to cope with the mounting sorrow in my heart.

Joi had a doctor's appointment a week before we were set to leave town. It was time for her regular blood test to make sure the chemotherapy was working, and Dr. Wilson would do a short examination as well. They didn't keep us waiting this time, and, once in his office, he told Joi that he was a little disturbed by her blood count and would add another drug to her chemotherapy cocktail. She'd been on Cytoxan, and he was adding a new drug called Oncovin, which was in the same family.

Knowing how important it was to keep Joi's spirits up, Dr. Wilson also told her how good she looked and to continue doing the same things she'd been doing right along. He was surprised to see how well she was tolerating the chemotherapy, since many of his patients suffered with terrible side effects, such as uncontrollable nausea and vomiting. I knew she'd already outlived her prognosis by many months, and I was ready to help her with the new chemo-therapy cocktail, hoping against hope it would continue to keep her with me.

With a smile, Joi told Dr. Wilson she was "feeling pretty good, just a little more tired" than she'd been a month ago. He asked about any pain, and she told him it seemed to be under control, that the methadone was working. He was pleased and encouraged her to get a lot of rest, adding that he was happy she'd decided to move out of the city. As we started to leave, he took Joi's hand and said he hoped her life in the desert would be filled with peace and tran-quility. He then gave her the new prescriptions and said to come back in a few months, unless she experienced any changes. Smiling kindly, he told her to call any time and congratulated her again on the move.

We got up very early on February 8 and said good-bye to our dear friend Jack, who was still the manager at the penthouse. He was sad to see us leave, but said he'd remember us every day when he looked outside at his new tree. We were happy to give him our first live Christmas tree in appreciation of how good he'd been to us.

Jack would soon be taking over another job at a new project in Marina del Rey, a massive residential apartment complex that was just being built. At his invitation, Joi and I had driven down to see it a few weeks earlier. Jack grinned and said, if we got bored with the blistering summers in the desert, we might think of getting a second place by the water "to cool off." I could see that Stan registered what Jack was saying, and I hoped that something might come of his interest. It would be good for Joi to have some place to go near the ocean which she so dearly loved.

We then checked the penthouse from closet to pantry, making sure noth-ing was left behind that shouldn't be. We'd loved living here and would leave with some wonderful memories…well, most of them were good. Joi had stopped taking pills and drinking alcohol, but, with all the unknowns of her illness and emotional complications that might develop, I was glad to be leav-ing that treacherous balcony high over the city.

Stan was down at the cars, rearranging the clothes and suitcases, and was in a good mood. As we brought the last bunch of clothes and laid them in the trunk, he announced it was time for the caravan to head out. Joi and I were a bit sad to be leaving our little love nest, but we knew that our new home would be even better.

Driving down I-10, we passed the off-ramp to the nudist colony from my "Ivory Hunter" days, and I pointed it out to Joi as we zoomed by. In a serious tone, she asked if I wanted "to go back and play a little tennis." We both laughed as I choked on my Seven Up. She had a way of catching me with a one-liner that put me on the floor laughing. When I got my breath, I told her I really wasn't in tiptop shape for such an exciting match, but I'd let her know when I was. Laughing again, she jacked up the music, and we spent the rest of the trip singing our way to our exciting destination, Palm Springs—Playground of the Stars.

We arrived in our new hometown in less than three hours from the time we left Los Angeles. We were supposed to meet the Realtor to pick up the keys, so we pulled into a little convenience store on the corner of Palm Canyon and Racquet Club. Stan went in, got us all something cold to drink, and called the Realtor from the pay phone outside. (This was before the era of cell phones.) They arranged to meet at the house in a few minutes. Excited, we drove up Racquet Club to the charming Little Tuscany area and pulled into our new driveway on Tuscan Road.

Smiling, Joi and I sat there admiring our little house. Stan was driving behind us and had missed a light, so we had a moment alone. She took my hand and squeezed it as if to say, "We're home, honey." I returned the squeeze, grateful to feel her strength and love at that special moment.

Our new place looked just as beautiful as the first day we'd seen it. The stucco was painted a cool white with a dark green wooden trim, and the driveway was surrounded on both sides with waist-high evergreens. A lone Mexican fan palm tree was on the other side of the front yard, adding balance and giving the front of the house a tropical effect.

Stan and the Realtor arrived just a few minutes after we did. As he turned the key in the lock, Joi and I looked at one another and grinned. It felt like another Christmas! He opened the door with a bit of a flourish, knowing how excited we were. If it had been a movie, the script would have read, "Ahhhh-hhh," for both of us!

The first thing we noticed was how sparkling clean it was. It was late afternoon and shady, but the lights were on, and we could see how beautiful everything was. I took Joi's hand and led her across the room to the large sliding glass doors that looked out onto the backyard. I remembered it had a lovely covered patio surrounded by pink and red hibiscus plants, with an area suitable for building a small kidney-shaped pool. The view was the best part of all. With no buildings to interfere with the city lights at night, it would be truly breathtaking. Joi sighed. We were finally "home" in a place of our own.

Since neither of us were at all handy when it came to anything mechanical or electrical, we knew there would be challenges without someone like Jack to deal with the usual homeowner issues, but I did know how to change a light bulb and an air-conditioning filter, and, coming from Kansas, I, of course, knew that plants and trees needed to be watered! That would be one of my jobs, which really appealed to me, but I was a little afraid for these living flora, since my thumb had been black from birth. I hoped there would be someone to advise me, so they'd last longer than a few months!

Conveniently, the house came with a stove and refrigerator. Grateful the electricity was on and the refrigerator was cold, we made some iced drinks. (I'd never had one that made its own ice before, and I loved it!) We sat on the floor, relieved and happy to be there. Stan sat outside on the short block wall surrounding the patio, smoking his cigar. The late afternoon air was warm and sweet, with a light breeze. Our first night was beginning on a lovely note.

Just an hour later, the first delivery truck arrived. It was our new and wonderful bed, a Beautyrest mattress, the coziest one we could find. It was perfect for both of us, not too hard, not too soft, "just right," as the three bears were known to say. We'd also bought new goose down pillows, so our first night's sleep would be like floating on a cloud.

Jack's buddies moved all our things into the house, putting each thing in its proper place. They even took our clothes out of the car and brought them in and hung them in the closet. We really had very little to do, except to give simple directions like, "Here," "There," "Yes," and "No."

Our living room furniture was supposed to arrive within a week of our move, but no one ever guarantees the exact date or time. (It's always just a little bit vague.) Stan had his adjustable bed and portable TV, so he was set until such a time as our sofa arrived.

While Joi was organizing her clothes in our huge walk-in closet, I pulled the plastic off the new mattress and slipped the clean sheets I'd washed the night before onto its comfy surface. We'd had a very long and exciting day, and it was time for Joi to rest before dinner. Stan was out like a light in his own room, so Joi and I decided to repeat what we'd done when we moved into our penthouse.

Hand in hand, we tiptoed past Stan's room to the front door. I opened it quietly, and, as we stepped out into the soft desert breeze, Joi turned and put her arms around my neck. Lifting her easily into my arms, I carried her across the threshold, hoping that our new life would be filled with peace and health, especially for my dear girl. We held hands as we walked quietly into our bedroom. Now "officially home," we slipped out of our clothes and under the covers of our wonderful bed. There was time to cuddle for an hour or so and then rest up for our first dinner out in our new little town.

But, "the best laid plans often go astray," as they say. We fell asleep within a few minutes and didn't wake until eight-thirty that evening. Stan was already in the kitchen fussing around, looking for the coffee pot and cups. He finally found them after tearing a few boxes apart and made us all a nice big pot of coffee. Joi and I got up and had enough of it to get things rolling, knowing we still had to shower and get ready for our evening out.

Palm Springs was a very laid-back town, where people are as relaxed as possible. Very few restaurants, even very nice ones, demand a coat and tie. Otherwise, they'd probably be vacant, especially in the warmer months. Joi showered first while I drank a little more coffee since the excitement and apprehension of coming back to the Springs had sapped my energy. Though, officially, Joi was the one who was ill, she was bouncing around like a bunny, while I, on the other hand, was barely able to drag my pooped body into the shower. Luckily, the coffee got me going, and I hurriedly got dressed.

None of the three of us had talked about what we'd wear, so it was a surprise when we gathered in the living room to find we were all in navy and white! Joi had on a navy sheath dress with white piping around the neck and sleeves. I wore a navy pantsuit with a white collar and trim on the pockets, and Stan was in his standby navy dress trousers and navy sports jacket. His shirt was white with a navy collar and cuffs. We all laughed when Joi said it looked like we planned to spend the evening on a yacht!

Actually, Joi was pleasantly surprised to see that Stan looked handsome and dapper. Getting him to wear anything but his sport sweats was usually a challenge, but this time he'd risen to the occasion and was going to take his girls out in style to a fine dinner.

I usually played the secretary role whenever we wanted reservations at a nice place. I would announce myself as "Miss Lansing's assistant," and we were always given preferential treatment, whether it was the right table, or finding us a place when they were booked solid. That night, I had called ahead to Jilly's.

Jilly Rizzo, the restaurant's owner and namesake, was one of Frank Sinatra's best pals. Not having reservations at Jilly's that night wasn't a problem, since Jilly had known Joi off and on over the years, especially while she was dating Frank. I called and said we'd be there at about ten, and would be a party of three. Jilly's was less than ten minutes from the house, and we could have walked if we'd been feeling a little more energetic.

When we walked into the restaurant, every head turned. Joi was stunning, especially that night. The excitement of the move made her glow even more than usual. Her skin was flawless, soft and peachy white, and her hair was exactly in place, blonde and flowing. And her body? Well, yes… her body. When she walked into a room, even though she was truly beautiful, she put everyone at ease with her radiant smile. (Joi was known as one of the nicest people in the biz.)

The Maître d' took us to a table and seated Joi and me together side by side with Stan opposite Joi. As we got comfortable, we noticed a large empty table for ten, just a little over from ours. The waiters had already begun pouring the water and putting little plates with ice and butter at strategic locations around the table.

Joi and I both loved shrimp cocktails, so we each started with a jumbo prawn appetizer. Stan liked green lip mussels, so we were all set for a bit of seafood nirvana.

Our appetizers were served as the guests at the mystery table began to arrive. The room was buzzing. The first few people seemed a little familiar, and I asked Joi if she knew who they were. She said she seemed to recognize one or two, but couldn't place where or when she might have met them. The next wave of guests entered the room, and it all became quite clear. It was the Chairman of the Board himself, Frank Sinatra, and some of his guests that included Robert Wagner and Tina Sinatra.

As he sat down, Frank spotted Joi and nodded respectfully. He saw she was with Stan and remained the perfect gentleman. Joi had dated Frank on and off after his breakup with Mia Farrow in 1965. After Joi, he'd dated (and later married) Barbara Marx, who was at one time married to Zeppo Marx of the Marx Brothers.

Coincidentally, we'd seen Barbara at the Tennis Club on our last trip to Palm Springs. There had been a little stink because she was wearing a tennis outfit with color on it. The club had very strict rules, demanding that all tennis wear be solid white. Barbara stuck by her guns, stating there was nothing improper or illegal about proper tennis clothing with a color accent. Nonetheless, she was asked to change her attire or leave, which she did—in a huff—and the whole incident created a bit of a scandal. Everyone at the club knew Barbara was dating Sinatra, and the buzz was this had not been a smart move. I heard an apology was immediately sent and that, soon after, the club changed its rules.

Frank was one of the most powerful residents of the desert. Palm Springs had always been a movie star magnet, drawing celebrities such as Liberace, Ginger Rogers, Keely Smith, Loretta Young, Bob Hope, Dinah Shore, James Garner, Sonny Bono, and even the lovely Marilyn Monroe. The climate was (and is) ideal during most of the year, still drawing tourists and Hollywood icons alike.

Joi had told me she'd heard that Sinatra put up the cash for Jilly to open up his new eatery in the desert. He was known to be extremely loyal to his friends, and Jilly Rizzo had been one of his closest throughout the years.

After our main meal, we each had a slice of New York cheesecake which was light and delicious, similar to what we ate at Reuben's Restaurant in New York. Sighing with satisfaction, Stan asked the Waiter for our check.

We sat for a little while, drinking one last cup of coffee while savoring the evening. Then, our waiter returned with a surprise, handing Joi a note addressed to her. It was from Frank. He wrote how nice it was to see her, hoped all was well in her life, and he'd taken care of the check. Well, this was completely unexpected. Joi said, if she and I had been alone, it wouldn't have been unusual, but she was totally surprised he would include Stan in his generosity.

Joi had warm feelings toward Frank…even more now that they were friends, instead of lovers.

Frank's party was still seated as we got up to leave the restaurant, and it was impossible to reach the exit without passing right by his table. On our way out, Joi stopped briefly to say hello to Frank and his guests. She introduced me to him as her sister, Rachel, and, as I shook his hand, he referred to me as the "other beauty of the family." Smiling, Joi leaned forward and kissed his cheek, whispering something in his ear. Whatever she said to him made him smile, too. He stood up and took one of her hands and one of mine, and wished us "a great life in the desert." (I never asked, but I think I know what she told him.)

Still glowing from the great food and delightful ending to our evening at Jilly's, we left the restaurant and decided to walk down Palm Canyon for a few blocks. The weather was still balmy with a light breeze, and the sky was jet black, sprinkled with thousands of tiny sparkling stars. There is no place like the desert when it comes to the skies or air. Even now, they always clear my mind and quiet my soul.

We strolled for about half an hour, looking in the windows of the cute little shops. Joi and I had fun deciding on a few places we'd like to come back to during the day. Our home was so close that we even considered walking back to the house while Stan drove the car home. However, we reconsidered when we realized what shoes we were wearing. Heels in those days were HIGH heels, and "high" definitely meant not taking long walks.

Joi drove while Stan, as usual, sat in the back with his nightly cigar. In those days, most restaurants would tolerate cigarettes and occasionally a pipe, but frowned on cigars, especially if the place was small. He lit his Garcia y Vega and inhaled the first few puffs as if they were a gift from the gods.

The day had been perfect from beginning to end. The drive from Los Angeles was smooth and unremarkable, and our bed had arrived in time, giving us a cozy place to sleep for the night. All was ideal, especially meeting Frank Sinatra and having him graciously guest our dinner tab…not to mention his flattering comment to me, and then his warm and subtle support for "us." February 8, 1971 was a picture-perfect memory and one that will always be mine.

The next morning, as Joi and I were sleeping soundly, the phone rang, startling us. It was before seven o'clock, and I couldn't believe anyone would have the nerve to call at that hour. In those days, they didn't have phones with Caller ID, so you took your chances. I picked it up on about the fourth ring. It was Mervyn LeRoy, so I shook myself awake and managed to be pleasant.

Joi had kept in touch with Mervyn, knowing he'd be a good contact when we moved to Palm Springs. He'd said he was looking forward to squiring us around town, and one of the places he wanted to take us was to see the big fight between Muhammad Ali and Joe Frazier. It was very expensive to see the fight live in New York, but an entrepreneur had rented the auditorium of Palm Springs High School and made arrangements to show it on closed circuit TV. Mervyn planned to buy tickets and asked if we'd like to be his dates. Since we both liked Cassius Clay, even when he became Muhammad Ali, Joi gladly accepted and said she'd call as soon as we arrived in the desert.

That morning, though, he wasn't calling about the fight or a date, but to let us know about the major earthquake that knocked him out of bed earlier that morning! I hadn't felt a thing and neither had Joi. Apparently, the quake was in Sylmar, in the San Fernando Valley near Newhall and Saugus, not far from Los Angeles. It registered 6.5 on the Richter scale and had done a lot of damage. Mervyn had spoken with friends in Los Angeles. who were quite shaken by the major quake and the beginning of the aftershocks.

 Horribly, as the news unfolded in the hours and days that followed, over forty people had been killed in the Veterans Hospital when a few floors pancaked, crushing the patients who were there. At the decades-old Hall of Justice, where Charles Manson and three of his followers had been on trial in the Sharon Tate murder case, fourth-floor walls were laced with cracks, and chunks of plaster littered the corridor. The new Los Angeles Police Building had numerous cracks and serious damage to the facade.

Just the thought of still being in the penthouse when this occurred made me shiver. I am petrified of heights, and the newer buildings were constructed to sway from side to side if a sizable earthquake hit. I kept thinking about all the glass from floor to ceiling in our bedroom where we would have been when it happened.

My love and I had left town with only one day separating us from terror, possible injury, or worse. It may have been Divine Providence or, at the very least, amazing luck that kept us out of harm's way. Whatever force it was that made us choose one day over another for the move was definitely a blessing for all of us.

That morning, Mervyn wanted to make sure we were all right, and that the temblor hadn't done any damage to us or our new home. Joi spoke with him for a few minutes while I got up and made coffee. It was going to be a long day for all of us, and I didn't think Stan would be driving back like he'd planned. Toward the end of the conversation, Joi waved to get my attention and mouthed, "He wants to take us to lunch."

I nodded "yes," thinking it would be good to have friends there in town. You never know what might happen, not only with natural disasters like that day, but especially with Joi's health as tenuous as it had been.

There were only a few people who knew how ill she really was: Stan and I and his daughter, Leslie, who had been very good to Joi through the months after her diagnosis. Then, of course, her doctors. Stan's attorney, Milt Golden, knew, and so did my parents. Joi did tell her mother and half-brother, Larry, after her surgery, but it was the sugar-coated diagnosis with a strong possibility of a "happy ending" that she herself had been told. Stan and I understood her need for privacy and would never betray her secret.

Joi wouldn't tell Mervyn, of course. Her only friend who knew a little about her surgery was Marjorie Meade, whom we'd run into earlier in the year in the parking lot of Cyrano's Restaurant. Joi had only seen her a few times after her surgery, and revealed simply that she'd had a growth on her ovary and was under a doctor's care, which had helped immensely.

Once in Palm Springs, Joi hoped to become a lot stronger and wanted to resume working in the business. She knew how even rumors of illness could end all hope of being considered for another part. No one wanted to hire an actor who might not be able to finish the project or disrupt production schedules, all of which could put the budget through the roof. Joi realized her career could be over if her illness became known.

Stan was still groggy when Joi told him about the earthquake, and, at first, he thought she was joking. Then, he realized no one would joke about something so serious and got on the phone right away to his office. There had not been a tremendous amount of structural damage in downtown, but he decided to go to Los Angles, just to be sure everything was okay.

Joi and I sat on the patio drinking coffee, looking out through the trees to the valley in the distance. We were feeling very close. "Timing is everything," they say, and, for once, it was on our side. We knew we'd been given a break. Our unspoken but completely understood vow was to savor every day we had as lovers and partners and friends…"as long as we both shall live."

Chapter 35

And the Heat Goes On...

Stan left for Los Angeles later that afternoon, anxious to check on his business and then meet with Jack to see the new property at the Marina…if it was still there, that is. It was, and Jack made arrangements to let him stay as a guest for a few days to see if he'd like to lease one of the new apartments. Stan would be able to stay for up to a week, with everything comped, including the use of their health club and tennis courts. His buddy, Edwin Stanley, was already a tenant, so his tennis date card was filled, and Stan was definitely interested, since it was one of the most prestigious residential properties in Marina Del Rey.

When Joi and I had seen the property a few weeks before we left for Palm Springs, we found it to be a monstrous grouping of three round cement buildings with cement bunkers at the base, looking out onto the water. Neither of us was impressed. We thought it looked like a combination of Sing Sing and Stalag 17…not exactly homey.

However, Joi did notice another property nearby, one that was a little closer to the ocean. It was beautifully landscaped with lush vegetation and waterfalls. We drove all through the grounds of Mariner's Village, and decided it reminded both of us of Cape Cod—of course, without the lunatic ruining the ambience. Thank goodness!

Joi told Stan about these condos the day we saw them, just in case the other location didn't work out and the summers were insufferable in the desert. He said he'd check out both, just in case we needed a plan B.

We did need another option if the summer was too difficult for Joi to tolerate, or in case her health began to fail. The Marina would be a good location because of its proximity to St. John's Hospital, and the soothing effect of the fresh salt air could help Joi with any side effects that might occur. Besides, Joi loved the Pacific Ocean and dreamed of a time when we could live on a tropical isle without a care in the world.

But now, it was only the beginning of February and the weather in the Springs was very close to heavenly. The days were in the seventies or a little warmer, and the nights were cool and crisp. We had, at least, three or four months before the sweltering triple-digit days would arrive. For now, there would be no reason to leave unless Joi needed to be closer to her doctors. Anyway, Stan was enjoying the little research he was doing, courtesy of Jack Rawley.

Back in Palm Springs, we waited a few weeks for our furniture to finally be delivered. Living in our bedroom wasn't torture by any means, but having a big plush sofa to stretch out and cuddle on was going to be a treat. Joi loved the silvery-beige sofa and the two dark olive green overstuffed armchairs that swiveled and rocked. The 1970s were a time of hedonistic pleasures and creature comforts. The softer and more plush, the better.

To complete the look, we'd selected off-white and gold-leaf accented end tables and a large square matching coffee table. Our bedroom end tables were on the same truck, along with our crystal lamps with beige silk shades.

The only other pieces we needed were a dining room table and chairs and a couple of barstools for the breakfast bar, separating the kitchen from the dining area. Mervyn had told us of a place in town where we could find exactly what we needed for the house, and we decided to go there the following day. There was a lot of excitement happening in our lives, but Joi was holding up very well, and we enjoyed the peace and quiet of our sleepy, wonderful town. Life was good.

Joi no longer had any problem with pills. She had banished the specter that had haunted her for years, and the only medications she took now were her chemotherapy and methadone for pain. Dr. Wilson had given her scripts for the new cocktail she needed, but, now that we were in another area, we had to find a new pharmacy to fill her prescriptions. Joi was almost out of methadone, and, since there was a small pharmacy close to where we lived, we decided to try it, instead of an impersonal national chain store.

As we entered the shop, the Pharmacist stood at the counter, a thin, older man with beady eyes peering through wire-rimmed glasses. Joi walked up to him, smiling, and handed him the only script she needed to fill at the time, which was the methadone. He looked down at the script and then looked at her. An eyebrow went up, and deep lines formed a scowl on his ruddy face. Then, he actually snarled at her and said, "If you want methadone, there are clinics for junkies like you where you can go to get your fix!"

My jaw dropped, and Joi looked at him as if he'd stabbed her in the heart! I was instantly furious and stepped between them. It was everything I could do not to grab him by his shirt and shake him till he fainted! I told him that if he knew his stuff, he would know that methadone is often used for extreme pain and not just to wean addicts off their heroin.

I asked Joi to go back to the car, and, after she left the store, I turned and told him that she was a cancer patient fighting terminal pain and that, at the very least, he should be ashamed of himself. His mouth went slack; his face had turned a pinkish-gray by that time, and his beady eyes were bugging. I snatched the prescription from his shaking hand and slammed the door on my way out. How dare he!

Joi was absolutely crushed. I got to the car and put my arm across her shoulders. She'd never encountered this kind of arrogance and cruelty before, and she was quivering, almost crying. That fool's stupidity and ignorance of the ethics prescribed by his profession were inexcusable, and I promised myself this would not be the last time he'd have to answer for what he'd done to my girl with his gross insensitivity.

After pulling ourselves together, we went to a Sav-On Drugs, which was not too far from home. There, the Pharmacist was not only pleasant and filled Joi's prescription without comment, but read the script that said it was for severe pain and notated that the instructions be written on the bottle.

As we waited for the meds, I told him what happened at the other pharmacy. He couldn't believe it and was angry that someone from his profession had violated their basic ethics so blatantly. He assured me that he would do something about it, and apologized for the unconscionable behavior of someone who should have definitely known better.

The kindness and professional attitude of this gentleman greatly helped Joi get over the personal affront she'd received from the imbecile with RPh after his name. From that evening on, we always used Sav-On pharmacies whenever possible.

Palm Springs was and is a wonderful little town with mostly good and kind people living there. Our experience with the local gentry was seamless, except for that one occasion.

Life in the Springs was pleasantly lazy. No one ever seemed in much of a rush to do anything. The big night of the Muhammad Ali fight was approaching and, as much as we enjoyed our lazy days, we were looking forward to a little excitement.

We had gone to lunch a few times with Mervyn, and he was always a consummate host. It was obvious he loved having a blonde duet on his arms. Joi had mentioned to me that he was quite a player when he was the all-powerful head of production for MGM. He came up from working in the costume department in silent films, paid his dues along the way, and enjoyed all the power and perks when he was at the top. He could make or break someone's career depending on how he felt about that person. In that way, he was no different from the other powerful moguls who enjoyed the benefits bestowed on them by those yearning for their names in lights, but that wasn't the sweet guy I met. He had obviously mellowed in his elder years and was always the perfect gentleman to both of us.

Fight night finally arrived, and Joi and I were elated to be with Mervyn to see the battle between Muhammad Ali and Joe Frazier on closed circuit TV. The tickets were sold out, and it was standing room only.

I nudged Joi when I recognized the Chief of Police and, when she asked Mervyn to introduce him to us, I thought I would choke! She caught it, whispered to me to relax, and said, "The best defense is a good offense."

Mervyn got up from his chair and walked over to the Chief, asking him to come over and meet two of his very good friends. The Chief followed him, and Mervyn introduced him to Miss Joi Lansing and her sister, Rachel. He shook our hands and said he was so pleased to have such lovely ladies as new residents of Palm Springs. I silently gulped, remembering my ride out of town. "What a Difference a Day Makes" kept going through my mind, and I felt so relieved!

The only person who might have remembered me and possibly caused a problem was now a new friend of my "sister" Joi and me. I couldn't have prayed for a better ending.

The fight lasted fifteen rounds, and Muhammad Ali lost the bout to regain his heavyweight title. I was disappointed because I'd always enjoyed his boxing ability and humor. We left along with the rest of the throng, and, since Mervyn and Joi were both tired, we called it a night.

As the days passed, our lives became more and more relaxed and uncomplicated. We especially enjoyed our evening walks to the coffee shop about half a mile from our house. We'd start out a little after sundown and take a slow and easy stroll, talking all the way. It took about twenty minutes or so to get there, and, by that time, we were thirsty and hungry for our evening meal.

The Hostess usually gave us the same booth, perfectly placed and great for people-watching. We'd have numerous cups of coffee and, most of the time, a salad for dinner. Chef salads were perfect for us because I didn't like hard-boiled eggs, and Joi didn't really want ham, so we traded. The coffee shop was our fun little daily outing and a break from hanging around the house.

Stan came down almost every weekend and also enjoyed his new and more relaxed lifestyle. He was able to cut back on the booze when he was in Los Angeles, because not seeing Joi every day helped him avoid thinking about her illness. Then, the reality would hit him again when he walked into the house and saw her face.

I watched him, weekend after weekend, go into his room and open the zipper on his shoulder bag. His door was open and visible from the living room where we sat. He'd pull out his flask and take a quick swig, then screw the top back on and throw it back where it belonged. Through the evening, I could see how his face would change from his big wide grin and slowly fade into a sad, forced smile.

One weekend, Joi wanted to go to the Ocotillo Inn, a popular resort a few miles away. It was owned by Jerry Buss, who also owned the Lakers basketball team. Stan knew him casually and agreed it sounded like something we'd enjoy. Stan could wear his regular outfit, sport sweats, which was like his own personal uniform, while Joi and I dressed in nice pantsuits and mid-height heels. I wore my favorite blue outfit; Joi wore bright red, and we could hardly be missed.

We pulled up to the Valet at the Ocotillo, who opened Joi's door, then mine, and stepped away from the car as he filled out our ticket. Suddenly, he heard a cough, and, embarrassed, he realized someone else was in the back seat! The Valet fumbled apologetically and opened Stan's door, quickly enough to get a decent tip.

Laughing at the gaffe, we went inside and were shown through the bar area where a jazz trio was playing some great old songs. We were seated in a booth in the small dining room, close enough to hear the music and far enough away to hear our conversation.

After we ordered, I realized I needed to use the facilities, since I'd been drinking coffee all day. The ladies' room was set up very strangely, with the inner door opening into a small area, and the edge of the door barely missing the sinks in its pathway. I slowly opened the inner door and saw women waiting for stalls. There was no place for me to stand, except next to the sink.

Cramped into this small space, I had my back facing the door when a woman threw it open with the weight of her body, rushing to get into the bathroom as fast as she could. She hit the side of my spine right on the edge of my vertebral column, and the force threw me across the small room and onto the floor. I almost knocked a woman down as I crashed. The woman who hit me said, "So sorry!" and ran into the stall.

I was physically stunned, and a lady who was also waiting helped me up. I felt weak as I stood, as if I would fall again, so I leaned against the sinks and tried to steady myself. The woman who helped me up asked if I was okay, and I said I wasn't sure but wanted to report it to the Manager in case I had a problem.

While she left the restroom to find someone, I limped back to our table and told Joi and Stan what happened. Joi was quite upset and took me to speak with the Supervisor. When I described to him what happened, he said he'd write a report, but didn't ask if I needed anything or wanted to see a doctor. When we asked about their insurance carrier, he claimed he didn't have that information. Obviously fearing a lawsuit, he avoided looking either of us in the eye, especially me. Joi took down his name and said she would deal with this later.

After dinner, we left and went home, or, more accurately, I limped and we went home.

A few days later, I went to my own doctor who said the force of the door had torn muscles in my back and had weakened them pretty badly. I had physical therapy for a while, but it really didn't do much good. The insurance company settled for a lot less than if I'd hired an attorney. Live and learn, unfortunately.

The good part was that I now had a little money and was able to buy Joi some new clothes and, finally, a beautiful ring. It meant so much to me to be able to do something for her, at least, once in our short time together. (Not having money to buy her flowers for our anniversary or her birthday is one of the sad memories I have.)

The day I got my check, we went to a local mall in Palm Springs, and I told her to choose what she wanted. She loved that, and had fun picking out dresses with my help. Although the dresses were beautiful, it was the ring that meant the most to her.

The minute Joi found the white gold ring with the pear-shaped diamond, her eyes became big as saucers as she zeroed in on the sparkling rock. That was the one she wanted. Nothing else she saw changed her mind, and I was thrilled to be able to buy it for her. She wouldn't take it off her finger long enough for the Jeweler to steam clean it and put it in a pretty little gift box. She told him it was new and didn't need to be cleaned, to just put the box in a bag, and we'd be on our way.

Joi seldom took the ring off, and I loved looking at it, remembering the day I'd finally been able to put a little bit of my love on my darling girl's hand.

Except when on stage performing her nightclub act, Joi rarely wore any jewelry. For those appearances, she had some pretty exotic and flamboyant rhinestone jewels, created by some of the best costume jewelry designers of the day. She also had some chandelier earrings that dripped all the way down to her shoulders.

We spent most of our days walking around town and getting our exercise. It helped Joi to handle the chemotherapy blend. Mervyn had pointed out Liberace's home, which was only a few blocks from where we lived, so we'd walk by his house, hoping that one day she'd be able to stop and say hello. Joi had known him over the years and enjoyed going backstage to see him while she was doing her show at the Thunderbird.

There were a lot of celebrities living in the desert, but most lived toward Palm Desert and a sleepy area called La Quinta. The big money lived "down valley," where the winds were a lot less active than where we were living. People complained about the wind in Palm Springs, but we never found it to be a problem. Oh, there would be an occasional gust of wind or a mild windstorm in the late afternoon, but it was never severe enough to cause us to mind it. The beauty of the sleepy little desert town right up against those strong, wild mountains more than made up for a little wind, and we were very happy there.

As the weeks passed, I was having a lot of pain and weakness in my back since the bathroom door episode at the Ocotillo Inn. I was given exercises which I did religiously, but, though they helped a little, the weakness and sometimes the pain is still with me to this day. We loved taking our evening walks, but it became more and more difficult trying to work through the pain. The walks turned into twice weekly strolls, and, every so often, Joi would have to walk home alone and pick me up in the car.

We were spending more time in the house, watching TV and enjoying the life of a happily married couple living in suburbia. There was no rat race or traffic jams, only days filled with going to the Tennis Club and watching the VIPs who happened to stop by, lots of cuddle (and lovin') time, and, since we both really liked to eat, lots of good food!

In the summer, business in the desert dies quickly and at the same pace as the temperatures heat up. Initially, we were able to handle the sweltering heat by living primarily inside during the daylight hours. Until about four o'clock, people didn't leave their air-conditioned homes to go outside. As the sun sank slowly in the west behind our mountains, I swear you could hear doors opening all over town. Earlier in the day, however, it was so hot you could actually cook an egg on the sidewalk to make the point.

Chapter 36

Marina Respite

The heat was beginning to bother Joi, so she started dropping hints to Stan on the phone, asking what the weather was like at the Marina, or if he'd spoken with Jack recently. He knew what she was hinting at, since the cable station listed the temperature as 114 degrees at the Palm Springs airport.

Stan had done his homework and had already checked out a few places near the water. The place Joi had liked the most turned out to be the best deal, with the prettiest location, and he was able to get a gorgeous two-bedroom apartment with a water view from every window. Right outside the living room sliding doors were the boat slips for the largest yachts in the Marina. The view was beautiful.

Although Stan usually came to the desert on the last weekend of the month, this time was special. He'd rented our new apartment and was keeping it a surprise for Joi. I didn't really know anything specific because he hadn't told me, but I surmised something was up when I caught him smiling to himself once or twice. It was the same smile he always had when he was about to do something fun for Joi.

When he arrived, he asked us to pack some things, so we could stay in Los Angeles for a week or two. He told Joi that Jack Rawley would let us stay in one of his apartments for almost nothing as an incentive for us to rent there eventually. Joi was happy and excited to be leaving the "oven" (as she'd begun to call the desert.), even for only a week or so.

We secured the house and made sure all the plants and trees were well watered. Stan even paid a neighborhood kid to watch the place and make sure the water hose dripped into the little moat I'd dug around the palm tree. A timer on the drip system also had to be checked to keep the evergreens and hibiscus from drying up and crumbling. It would be money well spent.

Stan took all the perishables from the fridge and a few of the clothes from his closet, and we were ready to go within a few hours. We were back on the road, Joi and I leading the caravan, with Stan right behind us as we sped toward the Marina. Going back to Los Angeles seemed so much faster than the trip we made in February, perhaps because we were just so thrilled to say good-bye to the hot, dry sand, and hello to the cool, blue sea.

We took the I-10 to the Santa Monica Freeway, and, once we were in town, we cut across the city in less than half an hour. The sky was a light baby blue with a few cirrus clouds floating lazily here and there, a delicious day to be near the ocean. We were on Lincoln Boulevard headed straight for the Marina City Club, when Stan started honking at us to pull over. A bit flustered, Joi looked for a side street where we could stop and find out what was so important.

Joi thought either Stan had a problem with his car or was concerned we had something wrong with ours. As we pulled over and Stan pulled up next to us, he told Joi to follow him a few more blocks and not ask any questions because it was going to be a special surprise. He had that Peck's Bad Boy grin from one ear to the other.

Since Joi loved surprises, she did what he said and kept quiet while he pulled out in front and led the way. She turned to me and asked if I knew anything about this, and I said that I didn't have a clue. Stan had kept his secret even from me.

In a few minutes, we saw the little Cape Cod sign saying, "Mariner's Village, Turn Left." Stan used his turn signal for a change, which was a surprise in itself, and we followed closely. The Village was a very large property, spread out over many, many acres, and it was so nice to have our windows down, feeling the wonderful ocean breeze blowing through our hair. Stan kept going down the little lane until we were at the last building nearest the water. He guided us to a parking place and parked right next to us.

Jumping out of the car, Joi ran up to him.

"What's the surprise, Hubby?" she laughed. "Do we get to stay here for a while?"

Stan got the biggest kick out of her childlike excitement.

Grinning, he asked if she'd like to live at the Marina in the summer and Palm Springs in the winter.

"Oh, yes, I'd love to!" she cried.

Then, handing her the key, he said he'd already signed the lease and the place was ours, starting that day. Joi was thrilled, and I, of course, could hardly contain myself!

The building was beautiful and new with an unusual architecture. It wasn't really woodsy like Cape Cod, but fit into the surroundings as if nature itself had created the green oasis with waterfalls, tall ash trees, flowering jacarandas, and a verdant carpet of perfectly groomed grass.

Walking into the lush lobby, we admired the large plants that seemed to be everywhere, and then took the elevator to the second floor. We were delighted to find the elevator was only a few yards from the front door to our apartment.

Playfully, Stan took Joi's key, and deliberately pretended to have a problem opening the door. He loved to tease her, but this time she was too excited to play, and, smiling, she firmly took the key out of his hand and opened the door herself. It worked perfectly, of course, and slowly the huge wooden door swung open.

We stood for a moment, looking into the large living room and the charming décor. It was lovely! The living room was beautifully furnished, modern, with grasscloth wallpaper throughout. A faux fireplace filled the back wall, its gas burners hidden by ceramic wooden logs. At the flip of a switch, it created flames that warmed the room with a cozy and inviting effect.

Across the living room, glass doors opened onto our balcony, with a stunning view of the ocean. Several yachts were moored just below our balcony, and we didn't know it then, but this was the point where all boats going beyond the breakwater would pass on their way to the ocean. The channel where we lived was protected against ocean swells when the Marina was created. We could see sailboats hoisting their sails as they motored out past the buoys that showed them safe passage out to sea.

Back in the living room, we noticed the walls and ceiling had brown wood accents, while the grasscloth wallpaper totally matched the green colors in the thick shag carpeting. Stan had furnished the place with overstuffed chairs and a matching sofa from a friend of Jack's who ran a furniture rental company.

Joi told me later that Jack must have chosen the furniture because everything matched so perfectly.

Stan or Jack had made sure that Joi and I had a wonderful king-size bed, flanked with walnut lamp tables and dressers. The entire condo was washed with rich, warm earth tones that made us feel like we were home. Stan's room was in the same motif, with a huge dark brown leather recliner that opened up almost flat and looked very comfy. From the looks of that chair, Joi and I doubted he'd ever sleep in his bed.

In addition to the two bedrooms, there was a small den we could use as a TV room. It was furnished with a cute little love seat and coffee table, plus an extra recliner for Stan to use while watching the tube.

While Joi and Stan watched the boats coming in and going out of the harbor, I brought some of the clothes and perishables up from the trunk of the car. We hadn't brought much food, so we'd eventually have to go to the market to buy some of the basics we'd need for the following day.

After I finished organizing, I came back to the living room to find Joi floating around on a cloud, deliriously happy with her new summer home. I could feel the Birdie dance coming on, but she was saving it until we were by ourselves. (Certain things were precious and for my eyes only.) My back was still hurting from the injury, but I'd carry her over the threshold as soon as we were alone. Looking at her face as her eyes surveyed every inch of the place was like seeing a little girl at her surprise birthday party, filled with amazement and wonder.

Joi went out to the veranda, waving at people on their boats as they waved back. I could see this environment would be great in lifting her spirits and would also provide much more activity than the desert. Of course, both places were wonderful in their own special way, a good balance of yin and yang—one brought her peace, and the other would energize her. If anything could help support her health, it would be the healing rays of the winter desert sun and the coolness of the ocean breeze. I was very hopeful for my girl. Coming here together could only be good for her and "us."

Stan called maintenance to see if someone could help us bring a few things up from the car. He was told that one of the guys would be right over and not to worry about a charge. If he wanted to tip the guy, it would be greatly appreciated, but their job was to assist the residents, and it was all part of the rental agreement. My aching back was very happy with this wonderful news. It just might have a chance to heal, and I was looking forward to getting my strength back.

Everything in both cars was in the apartment within fifteen minutes of George's arrival. I was going to remember his name and keep his phone number taped to the refrigerator. A little shorter than I was, George had arms as large as most people's legs, a back as strong as a tree trunk, and a manner as gentle as a fawn. I don't know where he was from, but his accent seemed Eastern European. He was obviously not from the United States, but had a work ethic filled with pride in doing even menial tasks.

We all thanked him profusely for his help, and Stan gave him a $20 tip, which was a lot of money in 1971. While George was very grateful for the tip, he had trouble accepting such a generous amount of money. Stan told him to take his wife out to dinner and that we'd be seeing him soon because Joi and I always had projects and would need his help quite often. George shook our hands and left with a smile.

The salt air and slight breeze were so soothing that all we wanted to do was lie down and take a nap with the sliding doors and windows wide open. We'd been living with air conditioning 24/7 for the last few months, and having fresh air caress our bodies as we lay on the bed was wonderfully sensual, especially after the oppressive desert heat that made us feel lethargic. It felt as if life had been breathed back into us again, making us quickly forget the sweltering Palm Springs summer.

We slept with the pleasure of sweet abandon, letting go of all thoughts and worries that clouded our thinking and cluttered our minds. We slept like babies who knew nothing of the trials and travails in this world of ours. We just simply let go.

Because the sounds of the Marina lulled us, we slept peacefully for over two hours. Stan snoozed in his recliner, probably resting in the satisfaction that he'd done something wonderful and special for Joi, something that would make her life more comfortable and ease her pain. I think he was trying to make things as easy as possible, knowing there was very little quality time left for her to enjoy. He was actually thinking with his heart this time, which was all Joi had ever wanted. For a long time, their relationship had not been a real marriage.

Through time, he had ceased to be a husband, but now he'd become a good and true friend who appreciated Joi for the sweet and kind person she was.

Frankly, it was fortunate for me that Stan was a failure as a husband, or I would never have been part of the equation. I came into Joi's life at a time when she was ready for the all-encompassing love I was able to give her. I think our love, the love I brought to her as a woman, was softer and safer than the experiences she'd had with the men in her life, and, as her lover, I was committed to keeping it that way.

When Joi woke up, she was filled with energy and excitement and could hardly wait to go for a walk along the water. She told me how happy she was to be feeling so good, but also mentioned she was ferociously hungry. She wanted to go to one of our favorite places called the Black Whale, a delightful little seafood restaurant that seemed like it was plucked from New Bedford, Massachusetts, and plopped right down in Santa Monica, California.

Joi asked Stan if he'd mind going to the Black Whale, which was only five minutes from the apartment. He said he'd love to go, and was happy he could wear what he had on. Joi and I were also going casual, but a nice warm shower and clean clothes put the icing on the cake.

Though Joi didn't often wear jeans, this time, she decided to, and they looked really good on her. The chemotherapy had been very kind to her, helping her to gain and keep her weight stable and letting her keep most of her hair. She was feeling great and had amazing energy, never complaining about pain, and, luckily, she was not at the mercy of the usual devastating side effects that could have made her life miserable.

Her appetite was also tremendous, which helped keep her from losing weight. This was one of the most encouraging signs as far as the doctors were concerned—that as long as she had a good appetite, she could fight the good fight.

We made it to the restaurant in less than five minutes, but there was a waiting list with, at least, ten parties ahead of us. Stan handed me a folded $10 bill and asked me to work my magic with the Host, who was taking down names for the list. I waited until no one was really paying attention. Then, I went up and spoke with him. While batting my eyes, I explained that my sister wasn't feeling very well and was terribly hypoglycemic. He seemed to understand my concern, especially when I held his hand and left the bill for him to slip into his pocket.

It was amazing how the names on the list got confused and ours seemed to be next in line! Smiling, the Host came over and escorted us to our table, where I told him how much I appreciated his gracious treatment and hoped I'd see him again very, very soon. I heard a few people grumbling in the background, but I hadn't really been lying. It truly was important that Joi get something to eat, and soon.

The Black Whale had some of the best steaks in town, along with wonderful seafood. I always ordered the rib eye and so did Joi. The food was phenomenal! One of their specialties was gigantic shrimp scampi in a rich garlic butter sauce, served with warm sourdough bread to soak up the extra juices. Guests could order large buckets of clams that were priced at "all you can eat" for under $15 per person. The waiters were running around with their arms filled with these metal buckets clanking as they banged against each other on the way to their destination.

Stan was a bucket guy who loved fresh clams. By the end of dinner, he had eaten two full buckets and had started on the third. Joi and I had demolished everything on our plates, including the sprigs of parsley used as a decorative garnish! We both liked the taste of it, so why not?

As usual when we ate a big meal, we decided to take a walk. We loved walking along the water, so we drove to the Lobster House parking lot, just a few blocks away from the Black Whale. It had a lovely walkway where you could stroll along about five feet above the bay and enjoy the fresh salt air.

It was fun to watch the few fishermen sitting along the edge near the water. Most of them didn't have a traditional fishing pole, but used a spool of fishing line with a hook attached. Their gear cost them almost nothing, but they seemed to be having pretty good luck. We saw a guy pulling in a fish that looked like it weighed, at least, five pounds. One little old man asked if we'd like to join him and offered to let us use some of his fishing line. Smiling, I thanked him, and explained that we were just out for an evening stroll, but maybe next time. He was sweet.

As we walked toward the short picturesque pier, we heard someone yelling for help and saw some people standing near a smallish, older man who was waving his arms frantically. As we got closer, we heard him call out that he couldn't swim, and that his dog, that had fallen from the pier, was treading water, and he couldn't get him out! When he saw us, he begged us to help.

Of course, Joi and I hurried to the edge of the walkway and looked down at the poor little thing splashing desperately. We stepped onto the pier. At this end, the water was, at least, five feet below us, and the splashing dog was obviously beginning to weaken because he kept sinking and fighting his way to the surface. His frightened owner said Buddy had been swimming for almost an hour and was close to drowning. We couldn't believe that no one had offered to help.

As usual, I was the tallest person there and realized the only way the little guy was going to make it was for someone to reach down to the water and lift him up and out. Then, making one of those decisions we don't really think about until later when we realize how dangerous or foolish it might have been, I figured that if I'd lie down and hang over the edge, I just might be able to do it. Actually this wasn't as foolish as it might sound since I had been the star of my gymnastics class in high school and was still quite supple.

While Joi held my legs, I laid down carefully on my stomach (there went the new blouse) and slowly scooted forward on my belly. Buddy's dad, Gus, had joined Joi in stabilizing me. I could feel them straining to hold on because we all knew that, if they didn't, I would quickly join the frantic little fur ball in the briny deep.

Wriggling a few more feet forward, I was actually hanging from just above my hips with Joi (and now Gus) apparently sitting on my legs. They hurt like hell and seemed just about ready to go to sleep, but I tried not to think about it and called to the little dog, who was now about ten or fifteen feet away. It wasn't working. Because he didn't know me, he wasn't coming my way.

Beginning to feel lightheaded and realizing it was now or never, I instinctively began doing that dog-kissing noise all dog lovers know. It was, fortunately, something he seemed to recognize, and he slowly turned toward me and began to paddle in my direction. He was obviously exhausted and kept sinking, but he was determined. A few paddles later, he made it as far as my arms would reach and I caught him by the scruff of his neck.

While yelling "I've got him! I've got him! Pull me back!", I held on with all my might. Though Buddy probably wasn't that heavy when dry (only about fifteen pounds), his struggling, the weight of the water, and his exhaustion made it almost impossible to hold him. I knew that, as strong as I was, my hands and arms were just about to give out. I was slowly being pulled up, but I was worried. It was too slowly. Then, suddenly, I felt four strong hands pulling at my waistband and ankles. Thank God, a couple of guys from the pier had stepped in to help us!

Seconds later, I was finally flat and safe on the ground, Joi kneeling next to me, and Buddy shaking cold water all over anyone within ten feet! Gus, quickly kneeling, gathered Buddy into his arms. Joi did the same with me, and Stan put his jacket over my shoulders.

Gus, laughing and crying, wrapped a shaggy, dry blanket around his dog and gave in to the endless doggie kisses he was getting. I was shaky but standing and being hugged by my girl, as the small crowd that had gathered to watch our drama cheered and clapped. A couple of them even patted me on the back! (I admit I liked that very much and, even now, get a little kick out of telling my story.)

Feeling really good about everything, I thanked and hugged both of the guys who had actually saved the day, and then we all headed back to the car and a warm fireplace. Joi said quietly, out of Stan's earshot so it was just between us, that something more than chance had to have brought us to the pier that night. I agreed and said I'd been thinking the same thing. She took my wet arm and hugged it close as we hurried toward the car and a fire and two lovely fluffy robes that, with any luck, would be coming off later that night in the sweet warmth and comfort of our own bed.

Joi and I both loved animals and always wished we could have one in our lives. I'd always had a dog as an adult and missed having one now, but Joi was on the road so much that it was out of the question.

Seeing Gus and Buddy that day, and the obvious love they shared, brought up all the feelings both Joi and I had known as children, but, at this stage in our life, and though Joi loved dogs as much as I did, even without her traveling, it would be way too difficult to have one, especially with her health issues. It was just a matter of time before she might have needed to go back into the hospital to readjust her chemotherapy or have a transfusion if her red blood count went too low.

As we drove home, after a few minutes of silence, Joi asked if there was any other kind of animal I'd like to have, other than a dog or cat. I thought a minute and then remembered that, as a child, I'd had parakeets for many years and really loved them. She said she'd never been around birds, but would think about it.

At home, when we were finally dry and sitting on our sofa, warming ourselves in front of the fireplace, Stan came into the room and, clearing his throat, told us how impressed he was with both of us. He then seemed a little awkward and, clearing his throat again, explained to us that he had been afraid to get close to the water. He said that the pier was wet and, knowing how easily his back went out, it would have been too easy to slip and fall. Realizing how uncomfortable he was, we assured him that he had done the right thing. He seemed to be relieved somewhat and trundled off to have his pre-bedtime cigar.

My back was starting to hurt after I hyper-extended it leaning over the walkway to grab the little dog. Though he hadn't weighed very much, the bad angle had put my lower back into a nasty spasm. The Ocotillo Inn accident had done more damage than I had imagined, and, looking back, I realized once again that I should have had an attorney deal with it, since it could (and probably would) be an ongoing problem.

As we sat on the couch in front of the fireplace, enjoying the warmth and romantic feelings it conjured up, I was reminded of the first time we kissed in front of the fire in her old apartment at Fountainview West. I still hadn't carried Joi over the threshold and was hoping to do it as soon as Stan fell asleep.

Finally, Stan came in to say goodnight and went back to his room for the night. Now, we had time alone to just sit and hold hands, and I was starting to feel a little better with the warmth from the fire. I took her hands and asked her to follow me to the front door, opening it and looking around to make sure we didn't have company. We walked outside, and I picked her up in my arms and carried her into our new home.

Joi kissed me all the way through the door, which was lovely, but actually a little tricky since I always closed my eyes when we kiss. Somehow, we managed to get inside without any bodily injury to either of us, laughing at how silly we must have looked as I carried her precariously through the doorway. I was just happy that we'd continued our "newlywed" tradition which had been a part of every place we lived.

We made it in without any trauma until I started to relax after putting her back on her feet. Suddenly, my back went into a severe spasm that just would not let up. We went to bed, and Joi massaged my back and put on some Absorbine Jr. to help with the pain. Since I had a few pain pills the Doctor had given me when I first had the accident, I took a codeine pill, which helped immensely.

Joi and I were able to sleep because the pill knocked me out, and she could finally relax. We slept well with our windows halfway open, letting the ocean breeze soothe our bodies with its gentle embrace. There was nothing very important we needed to do, so we slept until eleven in the morning.

Stan was up and out very early, and on his way to work. Joi and I got up and had coffee and a little fruit we'd brought from the Springs. We'd have to go to the market to buy staples, but Joi decided we'd do that later in the day after a little shopping excursion in Santa Monica. We completed our normal morning routine and were ready to go within an hour.

Joi said we were going on a little adventure, and though I had no idea what she had in mind, we always had fun doing even the most trivial things. Joi drove us to Santa Monica, not far from the Marina, and seemed to know exactly where she was going. With no hesitation, she pulled into a parking place and told me we'd arrived. I didn't recognize any store we'd been to before, so I just got out and let her lead the way.

Taking my hand as we walked past a few storefronts, Joi abruptly turned and opened a door. As we walked in, I couldn't believe my eyes! It was a pet shop, the likes of which I'd never seen before. The only pets in the shop were beautiful birds, chirping and peeping and squawking at the top of their little lungs—tiny finches, magnificent macaws with bright red and blue plumage, and birds of every size, shape, and color in between. It was enchanting!

I went straight to the parakeets that I'd always loved so much and asked Joi if we could really have a "birdie." As she laughed affectionately at my childlike hope, she said, "Of course, we can."

I saw the most beautiful little baby blue and white boy budgie and, when I asked Joi what she thought of him, she agreed he was gorgeous and seemed very sweet. These birds had all been hand-raised, so they weren't afraid of people.

When the Store Owner came over, I asked to see the baby blue bird, so she took him out of his cage and sat him right on my finger. That was all it took…

it was love at first sight! Joi told her we wanted him, and then we found a wonderful cage and all the toys and food he would need. She put him in a little box that would protect him until we got home.

Before we left, the Owner trimmed his little wings, so he could be trained more easily. I've tried to train birds without clipping their wings, and it was impossible, and I remember chasing them all over the house trying to catch them. There are many hazards for a little bird; it's just too dangerous to let them fly around and possibly zip out the door or hit a window. The Owner clipped the little bird's wings just enough, so he couldn't fly any distance, no more than a foot or two at most.

I was so excited to finally have a little bird in my life again. Joi seemed very happy, too, even though she didn't yet know how wonderful they could be. Unless you've had a parakeet, it's hard to imagine how much love and happiness they can bring in their tiny little bodies. I told her they are just a bunch of feathers surrounding a tiny package of love. She believed what I said and could hardly wait to get home and experience it for herself.

Back at the apartment with our little bird, we got everything set up. Not wanting to frighten him, we put him in the cage, so he could acclimate himself to his new surroundings. Joi asked what we should name him, and, at that moment, he made his first poop in the new cage. I suggested "Mr. Pooper," and she laughed and totally agreed.

Joi and I spent hours talking with him and gradually putting one finger in at a time, so he would get used to being around us. It didn't take long before he was jumping on and off both of our fingers and seemed very happy in his new home. Joi fell in love with him and he with her. He went to her immediately and even hopped up on her shoulder, apparently deciding he was her "little birdie."

From that point on, they were pretty much inseparable. The only time he was in his cage was when it was time for sleep. Otherwise, he was either on her shoulder or on top of her head. She talked to him constantly, and, as he started to learn words, Joi soon understood what I meant about a small bunch of feathers filled with a lot of love.

That first day, Stan came home after work and saw the new addition to the family. He actually thought the bird was adorable, especially the way he'd taken to Joi. Stan said it was because she was a "birdie," also, and Mr. Pooper recognized her as a member of his family.

The little guy brought a lot of happiness to our home and gave Joi a small creature to care for and love. He would sit on her chest when we'd watch TV, dance around, and even serenade her with a song she'd taught him. He'd whistle and sing and bob his little head as he'd look at her and say, "I love you, Joi baby." The first time he said it to her, she was surprised and delighted! It meant so much to her that she had such unconditional love from this beautiful little bird. She declared he was her guardian angel because "angels have wings, and so does he."

Chapter 37

Florida Excursion

We were enjoying our lives together at the Marina and loved our beautiful seaside apartment. On those days when heavy fog rolled onto the Southern California beaches, we stayed in and cozied up near the fireplace with our coffee or hot chocolate. On one such foggy morning, Joi received a call from her agent, Stan Scottland, telling her she'd been offered an engagement in Jacksonville, Florida, acting in a dinner theater play.

Joi really wanted to work again, but wasn't sure she'd have the endurance, since the play was scheduled to run for a few weeks. She told her agent that she'd check with her doctor first, and would try to give him an answer the following day. He understood, and said he'd wait for her call before contacting the client who wanted her for the show.

Stan Scottland knew she'd been hospitalized and was recuperating, but I don't think he knew how ill she really was. He might have wondered, though, because she used to call him, at least, once a week to see what was going on, and she'd hardly called in the last few months. Early on, she'd covered herself by saying she was just on sabbatical and enjoying a vacation from being on the road.

Joi called Dr. Wilson's office, told them the situation, and asked if the Doctor thought she was strong enough to go back to work. They said she should come by to have her blood tested before he could give her a definitive answer. It was usually a very busy office, but they told her to come in as soon as she could, and they'd be sure Dr. Wilson would see her.

Very excited at the possibility of working again, Joi was happy to know that people still wanted her. On those occasions when the phone stopped ringing, she'd begin to feel she'd been forgotten in the business and was getting too old for the parts she'd always played. It meant a lot that she still had options in her life and wasn't an aging sex symbol that nobody wanted. (How ironic that fate, by taking her at such a young age, would actually protect her from her greatest fear—growing old in show business and losing her desirability as an icon.)

That afternoon, we went to Dr. Wilson's office, and they ran the usual tests to check her blood count. The numbers were good, and he felt she should do what made her happy and what meant a lot to her. She was relieved to hear she was well enough to accept the offer, and the news seemed to ease her mind about her condition. It felt like a weight was lifted from her shoulders to know she was doing better than she secretly feared. She told me she really wanted to try this and asked if I was ready to do some packing. I, too, was relieved for her and couldn't have been happier. Of course, I answered, "Absolutely! Let's go!"

When Joi told Stan, he was initially concerned, but calmed down when he realized I'd be going, too, and wouldn't let anything happen to her. He knew I'd bring her home if there was a problem. Joi also called Stan Scottland and told him to send the contract for her to sign, reminding him that she needed the standard provision regarding a first-class round-trip ticket. As usual, she would turn the ticket in, and the refund would pay for both of our airfares, plus some nice extras. He agreed since they really wanted her for the show.

Our only worry was teaching Stan to take care of Mr. Pooper. A degree from MIT wasn't a prerequisite for taking care of a small bird, but this was Joi's little sweetheart, and she had to be absolutely certain Stan would take good care of him. He promised that nothing would happen to her little birdie, and she felt relieved after he demonstrated how he'd clean his cage and how he knew just the right amount of food and gravel needed in the bottom of the cage.

I think Stan really liked Mr. Pooper, but just hadn't had much of an opportunity to get to know him while Joi had him in "custody." The cute little bird was always on her shoulder from the first thing in the morning, when she uncovered his cage, to the last thing at night when she put his cozy cover back on while he slept. She also kissed his little beak goodnight, and laughed when Stan asked if he had to do that, too.

The rehearsals were due to start in about a week, so we decided to fly to Florida a few days early to get used to the time change and recover from jet lag.

We packed the way we always did, with the open suitcases on the bed, and Joi tossing clothing items from her closet. What landed in, went with us, and what didn't, stayed home. It always worked out that the clothing she especially liked managed to land dead-center, and the others seemed to bounce off the sides and land on the bed or floor.

It was a fun game we played, and we spent more time laughing and dancing around than anything. We were playmates, and it was my "job" to see that we had lots of fun, something easy to do because of Joi's playful nature.

The morning we were to fly out, Joi had her medicines with her and felt good enough to travel. Stan took us to the airport after she said her good-byes to Mr. Poose. (Sometimes, it was Mr. Poose, and, other times, it was just Poose or Pooper.) Joi, sad to leave the little guy, left a big lipstick mark that looked like a festive crown on his tiny head. (It reminded me of the lipstick mark she once left on me, but that was just a little bit different.)

Our flight went well, and there were no problems with turbulence. I was glad to see that the pilot wasn't a jet jockey, one who would take the plane down too fast, normally something that gave me an excruciating earache. He took off gently and landed just as nicely, making our flight much more pleasant than anticipated.

Exiting the plane, we saw there were people waiting for us at the gate. Joi was recognized immediately, since she always traveled as a movie star, in full makeup and apparel. Because the air conditioning on the plane always chilled her, she was wearing her tourmaline mink coat which exactly matched the color of her hair.

Joi signed a few autographs and took a couple of pictures with several of her fans, and then we were greeted by two gentlemen from the hotel who brought her a colorful bouquet of flowers. They had a nice large Lincoln, more than ample to carry us and our bags to the hotel.

The city was beautiful with lots of green foliage and big sprawling trees. The ride was pleasant and relaxing, and we arrived at the hotel in good time. It was lovely, and all we had to do was sign the register, and we were handed the keys.

We were helped to our room by a bellhop, who was so awestruck by Joi's beauty that he couldn't close his mouth. This wasn't a rare happening, actually.

Young men had an especially difficult time when around Joi. She was always kind, but sometimes I thought it was funny. This was one of those times, and it was made more so when Joi turned to give him a tip, but he'd already gone. All we could see was his cart careening down the hall. I couldn't stop laughing, but, truth be known, I kind of knew how he felt.

Joi had been offered the penthouse, but, since our terrible experience with the hotel fire in New York, we always made sure we weren't any higher than the second floor, and had it written into Joi's ontract. That fire had really left an impression on us and would forever dictate how we handled our accommodations. We had learned, almost the hard way, that fire always travels up.

We had a few days to rest before rehearsals began. Joi received an envelope with her script and the lines she needed to learn. I loved rehearsing with her and helping her get comfortable with her lines. We made a game of it, so it wouldn't become boring, goofing around with different dialects and changing gender with the accent. This, of course, made it more difficult, but was also more fun. When the actual part was read, it seemed like a piece of cake compared to how we'd rehearsed it.

We stayed in the room, just taking it easy and enjoying room service. Naturally, Joi had to call and talk to Poose and let him know she was still around. He'd sing her a song and tell her he loved her, which was all she wanted to hear.

Stan said he was doing well and teaching Mr. Pooper some new tricks. He wouldn't elaborate because it was to be a surprise for Joi when she came home. She was afraid Stan would try to "butch" him up, not appreciating the fact that he was Mama's little boy. Though Stan couldn't teach him to lift weights or play tennis, he could teach him to swear like a sailor. Still, Joi seemed happy that Stan was enjoying the little bird and was relieved to know Mr. Poose was safe and in good hands.

In a few days, it was time to go to the theater to meet with the Producer and Director, as well as the rest of the cast. Everyone was gracious to her and seemed very happy to have her on board. Joi was introduced to Lyle Waggoner, who was cast opposite her in the play, and was the epitome of tall, dark, and handsome. Towering over everyone at six foot four, he even made me look petite. At that time, he was a regular on *The Carol Burnett Show* and well-known for his work in films and television.

Everyone went right into rehearsal and was pleased at how well Joi knew her lines. They were also impressed at how she read them with so much expression, instead of the usual boring monotone that was common at the beginning of the rehearsal process. Joi was a pro and always ahead of the curve, instilling a sense of confidence in everyone she worked with.

Rehearsal ended, and we were invited to dine with the Producer and Director, as well as the Owner of the theater. Joi enthusiastically agreed, and we went with them to a lovely restaurant in a refurbished old mansion, the Southern charm just dripping off the walls as we walked in.

All the interior walls were painted a soft peachy color with pure white glossy trim on the cornices and crown molding. The glass-topped rattan tables were covered with the finest sterling silver, crystal glasses, and exquisite bone china plates, with a thin line of 24-karat gold adorning the rim of the accessory pieces. Charming cotton napkins and place mats repeated the soft peach color and white trim of the walls.

Floor-to-ceiling arched windows, spaced evenly every eight feet, were flanked on either side by beautiful, tall trees, while soft indirect lighting filled the room, accenting the trees and candles on each table and adding just the perfect amount of extra light. The plush carpeting, with a subtle floral pattern in various hues of green and peach, made the room interesting, but not gaudy.

A small waterfall in the center of the room completed the elegant décor. It sounded just like a brook in the middle of the forest. It was all exquisite, and, if the food was as good as the presentation, it would be like icing on a cake, and quite heavenly.

The Maître'd brought us our menus, assisted by a headwaiter and a few other attendants, and we found the selections delightfully imaginative without being too bizarre or unusual. Joi had taught me to appreciate a lot of different kinds of food, and, though I still couldn't choke down certain things, I was a lot more familiar now with foods that had once been foreign to me. My favorites were usually great steaks or Italian dishes (with no mention of internal organs), and I made sure to learn what the words were in French or Italian, so I wouldn't make an embarrassing mistake.

I ordered a Southern heart attack, which consisted of fried chicken, mashed potatoes and gravy, and a side of corn with butter melted on top. I hadn't eaten such delightful—and unhealthy—food since I'd been with Joi. Fried foods were not allowed, and neither were mashed potatoes and gravy. Our diet at home was mostly salads and lean meats, never anything that would leave a grease stain on a paper towel.

In fact, Joi was a true health aficionado, thanks to Bob Cummings and his mentoring. That was probably the reason she was doing as well as she was, instead of failing quickly as her doctors had expected. She'd been taking vitamins and Tiger's Milk for years, a health food product she'd been chosen to represent in the media ever since she'd been their TV and radio spokesperson. And she never ate junk food. I don't ever remember stopping with her at a fast food restaurant to grab a burger and fries.

When she heard what I'd ordered, her face almost fell to the floor. I knew I'd committed a mortal sin when it came to taking care of my body. Everyone was busy talking and laughing, so I spoke softly and told her I had been so good about eating the right food for so long that I just had to have some real Southern fried chicken from where it originated. One eyebrow went up, and then lowered, changing into a smile. She was right, and I knew it, but how often were we in the South?

She said quietly that she hoped I didn't get sick, since my body wasn't used to all that grease. I told her it was kind of like those occasional Pink's hot dogs we indulged in when we just couldn't fight the urge anymore. That little remark made her laugh, and she knew it was pointless to say anything more about it. I was going to eat a pound of grease and love every drop of it.

Joi had a beautiful salad and thin slices of rare roast beef with a side of asparagus, but my Kansas upbringing took over, and I lost my sensibilities. My dinner was lovely, especially the lightly browned and crispy chicken that I demolished as fast as it was served. I ate half of the potatoes and all of the corn. And soon—and suddenly—my belly felt like there was a war going on. I quickly excused myself.

Of course, Joi was right about the grease. My body wasn't used to it and objected strenuously when given this poison to my system. Embarrassed and feeling terrible, I lost my cookies.

Joi, knowing why I'd left the table so abruptly, came into the restroom to see if I was still among the living. Not once did she say, "I told you so," but the look on her face told the story. She took some paper towels, soaked them in cool water, and put them on my forehead. I know I must have looked a little rough by the expression in her eyes. In a few minutes, she asked if I was feeling any better, and I told her "a little," as I pulled myself together and we went back to join the other guests. I had learned an important lesson and knew my gastronomic pleasures would, for now at least, need to be much less adventurous.

The next day, still a little green, I helped Joi prepare for rehearsal. It all went well, and, when it was over, we went back to our hotel. I was feeling a lot better, but something seemed to be bothering Joi. I asked her what was wrong, if she was feeling ill, and she said she wasn't sure but felt kind of strange. I touched her forehead, and she was burning up.

Realizing she needed to see a doctor immediately, I called the Producer to see if he knew someone who could come to our room. He had a great personal friend who was one of the top doctors in town, and he promised to call him right away. In less than five minutes, he called back and said his friend would be right over to see her.

I tried to make Joi comfortable by putting extra blankets on her because she was now having chills along with the burning fever. I took wet washcloths and laid them across her forehead because she was perspiring as well. I was terribly worried. I hadn't seen her so ill since she was in the hospital, which brought me back to the grim reality I'd tried to avoid thinking about since we'd left Los Angeles.

Arriving within half an hour, the Doctor examined her carefully. When he asked me if she had any medical conditions, I had to be honest because it was important, and said she was on chemotherapy and was in remission. I didn't want to use the "C" word because it was not in our vocabulary. All we ever said was "growth" and "chemotherapy" and "remission," never that hideous word that conjured up such devastating nightmares.

The Doctor understood what I was saying and asked what chemotherapy drugs she was taking. When I told him Cytoxan and Oncovin, he said she might be having a reaction. She didn't appear to have a flu or any bacterial infection, but he couldn't tell without doing lab work and thought she should probably see her oncologist. He told Joi she was much too ill to continue with the play, and also offered to explain everything to his friend, the show's Producer.

I asked him to be discreet since her illness had not been publicized. He promised to respect her privacy and would only say she had an upper respiratory problem and would not be able to honor her contract. He did suggest, however, that it would be best to tell the Producer the truth, so there would be no repercussions as a result of her leaving the show.

In speaking with Joi, he assured her that her illness would remain a private matter, and added that they would make the flight arrangements for us to leave the following morning. He stressed that she see her doctor as soon as possible to get her medication adjusted, and then gave her something to bring down her fever and lessen the chills, as well as a shot to help her rest and sleep through the night.

I was so grateful for this fine Doctor's gentle approach and his respectfulness of Joi and the illness she was fighting. He assured Joi that she'd feel better when her medication was changed, suggesting she could then return to Jacksonville to star in another production; he said he looked forward to seeing her again soon. His encouraging and kind words touched me deeply, and made Joi feel a little better about leaving the show.

Joi had never left a production before it was finished, and this was the first time she'd not been able to honor a contract, a fact she found totally demoralizing. She'd always taken great pride in her work and never left anyone hanging out to dry. In fact, through the years, there were times when she was miserable in a production, but stuck it out because she was a consummate professional. Leaving before the curtain even went up saddened and embarrassed her.

The following morning, as we were getting ready to leave, Joi seemed to be feeling better than the night before, but said she still felt pretty shaky. I tried to tease her by saying that I was the one who ate the fried chicken, so I should be the one who was sick! She tried to laugh but felt so awful she could hardly smile.

I called Dr. Wilson's office before we left and told them she was possibly having a bad reaction to her drugs and was returning to Los Angeles that afternoon. They scheduled an appointment for her to see the Doctor at eleven the following morning. When I told Joi, she felt better knowing he'd be able to help her, and she then called Stan to give him our flight information.

The Producer and Director came to pick us up that morning to take us to the airport. They were very kind to Joi, reassuring her they would stay in touch with Stan Scottland and request her again when the part was right. As sick as she was, Joi was grateful to see that this bridge hadn't been burned.

On the plane, Joi slept peacefully. Her beautiful face was soft and creamy as always, and she did not look ill. I took her hand, careful not to wake her, and held it in mine.

The clock was ticking, and, this time, I could hear time passing…

Chapter 38

Lust for Life

Stan was waiting at the gate when we landed at LAX, along with the driver of an electric cart who would take us to pick up our luggage. Our Flight Attendant had allowed us to sit in first class when she realized that Joi wasn't feeling well, and then made sure we were the first ones off the plane.

In fact, she walked us up to where Stan and the cart were waiting. Joi had flown on TWA for most of her career, and many of the employees recognized her and treated her with great respect. Joi thanked her graciously and said she hoped to see her again soon.

The cart zipped along, getting us to our baggage in about ten minutes, so much better than the half hour it would have taken if we had to trek it. Besides, I knew Joi couldn't have made it, feeling as awful as she did. Once at the baggage claim area, she held on to Stan's arm and said weakly with a half smile, "The Birdie is a 'sickie' and couldn't do the show."

Stan cleared his throat gruffly and told her not to worry, that she'd be feeling better after she saw the Doctor the following day.

Our pink suitcases came down on one of the first carts, and the man who drove us picked them up right away and took us directly to our car in the parking structure. After Stan helped me get Joi in the backseat, I climbed in and held her head on my lap, gently massaging her temples on the way home.

I got her to bed as soon as we arrived at the apartment. She was weak but wanted to see little Pooper, so I brought him into the bedroom and sat him on her chest. He started kissing her and doing his little serenade.

"I love you, Joi baby," he kept repeating over and over. He even took his little foot to pry open her lower lip and kiss her, then made kissy noises demanding that Joi kiss him on his feathery head! As dreadful as she felt, the lovable little bird made her smile, and she was happy to be home.

Though very weak, Joi wanted to talk a little before she slept. First, I brought her a small bowl of chicken soup that Stan had gone out to get for her. After eating only a few spoonfuls, she asked me to sit next to her, saying that she couldn't understand why she was feeling so terrible now, when, only a week before, she had felt so good and full of energy.

I didn't know what to tell her. I reminded her that the Doctor at the theater said she might be having a reaction to the chemotherapy cocktail she'd been taking, and that perhaps Dr. Wilson could substitute a drug that would solve the problem. I assured her we'd know more in the morning, and hoped tomorrow would be a better day.

Joi slept fitfully that night, waking up once or twice, but seeing that I was there soothed her back to sleep. I slept with one eye open because I didn't want her to feel frightened or alone when she was in such misery.

The next morning, she actually seemed to feel a little better, although she didn't want breakfast and only drank a few sips of her coffee. After getting dressed, she played with Poose for a while before we left for Dr. Wilson's office. Stan had stayed home from work to help me take her to the appointment. It wasn't far from the Marina, so it didn't take long to get there, even in traffic. Joi was scheduled as the Doctor's last patient of the morning, so he could spend extra time with her if need be.

When we arrived at the office, Joi was ushered right in. Dr. Wilson took one look at her, said her color concerned him, and that he was glad she'd come home as quickly as she did. He wanted to run some blood tests to see what was happening, and, rather than send Joi to the lab, he asked the Lab Tech to come to his office to draw the blood. The Doctor then examined her, checking the lymph nodes under her arms, breasts, and groin. He said he didn't feel any that seemed enlarged, and this was a good sign.

Soon, the Lab Tech came back with the results of the tests, which showed that her red blood cells were very low. Dr. Wilson explained that the chemotherapy was apparently wiping them out along with the malignant cells; she'd need a transfusion, and he'd have to make changes in the drugs he was giving her.

The Doctor called St. John's and told them to expect her in a little while, that he wanted to keep her in the hospital, at least, overnight. He told Joi not to worry, that she was feeling this awful because her blood count was so low. The transfusion would solve that problem, and she'd be feeling like herself as soon as she had more blood to give her strength. Joi was relieved and grateful and wanted to get to the hospital as soon as possible, so the transfusion could stop this miserable feeling.

Since Dr. Wilson had pre-registered her, Joi could go directly to her room on the third floor, the same room she'd been in when she had her surgery. It was one of the VIP suites where I'd be able to stay with her after she was admitted. I recognized the charge nurse, Dolores (Dee) Halkovich, the main supervisor during the afternoon shift on the oncology floor. She had been so kind to us when Joi was in before.

Dolores recognized us immediately and came to our room to ask what was going on. When Joi explained the situation, she told her not to worry, that she'd make sure everything was taken care of. Sure enough, she checked, and the two units of blood were on their way up from the lab. She assured Joi she'd soon be feeling much better, and smiled when she said, "And that's a promise!"

Joi was comfortable in her bed when Dolores came back with the first unit of blood. She started the IV, and, much to Joi's relief, it didn't hurt her at all. Joi told her she was grateful since she'd had so much trouble the last time with bad veins that kept moving or collapsing.

The transfusion was started, and, within a half hour, Joi was sitting up in bed and talking with me enthusiastically! It was like there had been a time warp. My girl was back and feeling like the Birdie again. They wanted her to have the second unit since her hemoglobin was still low, but Joi said she was hungry and asked for something good to eat.

Dolores and I were both thrilled to see the difference in her demeanor. She asked Joi what she'd like, and she laughed when she said, "A cheeseburger!"

I couldn't believe my ears… Joi never ate hamburgers, especially cheeseburgers! She also wanted some fries and a chocolate milk shake. The kitchen was closed during a break between lunch and dinner, so Dolores sent someone to Sambo's next door to pick up her order. By the time Dolores came in with her food, Joi was absolutely ravenous! She devoured the cheeseburger, every French fry in the bag, and even said the chocolate milk shake was the best she'd ever had. She sat smiling for a bit, obviously happy to be feeling like herself again.

Stan had gone out for a while because he had trouble watching Joi hooked up to the IV tube. He couldn't handle anything that he perceived as negative, so he had to walk away.

When he got back and saw how much Joi had improved, he was ecstatic with all the wonderful changes he was seeing. (I could smell brandy on his breath, so he must have gone to get a small bottle of Christian Brothers, one that would fit in his shoulder bag.) She had been so ill and weak just a few hours ago, and now she was strong and full of energy. Joi told him what she'd eaten, and he couldn't believe that she would eat anything like the junk food she described. He looked at her, smiled, and then asked, "Who are you, and what have you done with the Birdie?"

She looked straight into his eyes and said, "The Birdie's back, and she's still hungry."

We all laughed.

"Well, okay," he said, then asked her what she might like, and she announced, "Some apple pie with vanilla ice cream."

Since Joi didn't normally eat these things, Stan decided they must be what the blood donor liked! Laughing, we thought it was extremely unlikely, but it was something we could all joke about. It made her giggle.

Joi had to wait for her pie because, a few minutes later, it was time for the second unit of blood. Looking queasy, Stan left the room when Dolores came in with it, mumbling that he'd be back when the transfusion was over. Dolores smiled sympathetically, understanding his discomfort.

I knew he would also have a nip or two when he left the room. Through the months ahead, this would become his way to deal with Joi's illness. I didn't judge him. "Whatever gets you through the night" made a lot of sense in those times.

Joi became stronger and stronger with each drop of blood, and she started talking about the things she wanted to do as soon as she was able to leave. She thought it might be fun to go to Disneyland, since she hadn't been there for many years and couldn't even remember the last time. She did remember the "E" rides and wanted to see *The Pirates of the Caribbean* attraction, which she'd heard about, but didn't think she'd ever been on.

She was chatting cheerfully with me, and I was incredibly relieved as I sat watching and listening to her. This was the Joi I hoped to see again, never knowing how long it might last, or if she'd ever come back to the way she was. The transfusions had done the trick this time, and now it was urgent that Dr. Wilson come up with some magical combination of drugs to keep her going. He mentioned that he'd come in to see her in the morning and would try some new drugs. She was anxious to try whatever medicine would keep her feeling as good as she did then.

It was almost dinner time before Stan came back and made the Birdie very happy when he brought Chinese food for all of us. He got Joi's favorite, moo goo gai pan, and brought me the barbecued pork fried rice, which he knew I loved. For himself, he got his usual choices of Chinese vegetables and an order of egg foo young. We ate until there was no more room, and then all three of us took a nap. I had my cot, which Dolores had set up for me, and Stan snagged the recliner on the other side of the room.

Stan settled into the recliner and was asleep the minute he released the lever and his legs went up. I lay comfortably on my cot—Dolores had brought me three extra pillows—and watched Joi breathing. She was sleeping peacefully and had a rosy-pink cast to her skin. She'd looked so ashen earlier, the sparkle had left her eyes, and it frightened me for her. I was deeply grateful to see how she was coming back to health … at least for now.

We slept through the night without anyone disturbing us, unheard of in a hospital. Sleep is something you do at home! In the hospital, they poke and prod and take blood during the night and tell you to get some rest! If they did come in on that particular night, they were so quiet that we had no idea.

When I woke up early, I went out to the nurses' station to see who was working. Mary Tomassini, the night supervisor, had been on the floor all night. Lovingly referred to as "Big Red," Mary was my other buddy who'd been so helpful, and that night she'd made sure no one would disturb our rest. I hugged and thanked her, and said I was so happy to see her. She and Dolores had a way of making you feel that someone really cared and that they were there if you needed them.

Joi and Stan woke up a little while after I did. Neither of them could believe we'd all slept through the night. Stan hadn't planned on staying at the hospital after dinner, but, once the "sleepies" took over, he was down for the count. I felt great, if a little stiff, and was again very pleased to hear Joi ask if breakfast was coming because she was hungry!

Big Red was almost finished with her shift, so she came in to say hello and see how Joi was feeling. Joi was so happy to see a familiar face and remembered how kind she'd been when she had her surgery.

Dr. Wilson came in a few minutes after Joi finished her French toast and eggs, with a side of bacon and two sausage links. He asked if her appetite was any better, and she laughed and said that, if it got any better, she'd have to hire Omar the Tentmaker to make all of her new costumes for the stage! He laughed, too, and was very pleased to see that she looked so much better that day than she had the day before. It was as if he were talking to a totally different person, one full of life and energy. He said it was great to see her back to herself.

He told her he had a few new drugs he wanted to give her, and that he'd seen great results with them in the past. It was a combination of three different drugs: 5-FU, Oncovin, and Methotrexate. He'd give them to her here with the IV, and, if she tolerated them well, she'd be able to take some of them in pill form. Then, she'd only need to come to his office on a monthly basis for a combo IV that would add to her cocktail. She was looking forward to feeling better, and wanted to do whatever it took to feel as good as she did that day.

Dr. Wilson started the IV and told her he wanted to see how she reacted to the drugs, so she'd need to stay, at least, one more night, just to be safe. She understood this and said, "No problem. As long as they feed me, I don't mind being at this hotel."

I loved that her humor was back. I felt like I could finally exhale, and then I realized…I was hungry, too!

Stan was up and ready to go home to shower and change clothes for work. Kissing Joi's cheek, he told her he'd see her after work, and, if she wanted something special to eat, all she had to do was call him at the office.

"Look out for the Birdie," he said to me, and also assured us he'd feed Mr. Pooper and clean his cage before he left for the day. It amused us to see that Stan was becoming as attached as we were to that little ball of fluff, even though he wasn't much on admitting he cared for a parakeet!

As the day passed, Joi seemed to be doing well with the new cocktail the Doctor had given her in the IV drip. She didn't appear to have any adverse reactions and was feeling good.

At lunch time, she asked if I would go back to Sambo's and get her another cheeseburger with a double order of fries and a chocolate shake. Aware of the size of her order, I told her I'd be happy to, but she'd better not bring up my episode with the fried chicken any time in the near future! She laughed and said, "I promise, but remember you're the one who was barfing in Jacksonville."

She loved to remind me when I did something she'd warned me against.

By that time we were "playing," and I told her I'd be right back and not to leave without me. Joi laughed and told me to hurry up, or she might just go outside and hitchhike home. When she said that, she lifted the sheet and flashed her leg like Claudette Colbert in the film, *It Happened One Night*, with Cary Grant.

I whistled and laughed. My Birdie hadn't lost her sense of humor. In fact, she was even more full of it than before!

I rushed over to Sambo's and ordered her lunch. The service was always fast, so I was out of there in about twenty minutes. While hurrying back to the third floor with our food, I saw Dr. Wilson walking into her room, and I sped up a little, so I wouldn't miss anything. He said he was pleased with the way her body was responding to the new chemo combination and asked Joi if she'd like to go home.

Bouncing, she laughed, "Would I ever!"

Smiling at her playfulness, he told her that he would discharge her later in the afternoon as soon as she had one more treatment. He wanted her to have a running start with the new drugs, and having her in the hospital was the best way to monitor her reactions, just in case she had a problem.

Joi was thrilled that she'd soon be well enough to go home to resume her life near the ocean. She told me how anxious she was to take walks again, particularly to the pier, where there were some cute shops and a great Mexican restaurant with terrific food. I told her she'd better watch this new and improved appetite, or I'd have to get a dolly to push her around.

She reminded me of my own family's genetics, and told me I'd been lucky so far.

"When you hit forty, there's a good chance you'll be pleasingly plump like your mother's side of the family."

She was only teasing me, but also suggesting that I'd better watch what I ate because no one looks good in bad genes. But the chips and salsa did sound good, as long as we didn't go over the top and eat like piglets.

Joi called Stan and told him she'd been released from her incarceration, and hoped he'd be able to pick us up after work. He was relieved, knowing she'd be coming home … at least this time … against all the odds.

Stan said that Mr. Pooper missed her and wouldn't sing a peep when she wasn't there. Hearing this about her little baby only made her want to go home more, as soon as they let her "fly the coop."

Joi had her last dose of chemotherapy, and it went as smooth as silk. She had no adverse reaction and could leave whenever she wanted. While we sat in the room waiting for Stan to bail us out, Dolores came in to wish Joi good luck. She was happy to see us go because she knew that the longer she had to stay, the worse her chances would be at ever getting out.

Stan showed up a while later to pick us up, looking exhausted, with wrinkled clothing like he'd slept in them again. Joi noticed his tired, rumpled appearance and asked, "Are you all right, Hubby?"

He said he was fine and would be even better when she was home.

I put Joi's few things together and freshened her up for the trip home, while Stan went to the office and took care of the bill. His insurance covered a lot of it, but certainly not a private suite. We had to do it this way, though, or they wouldn't let me stay with her, and she'd told them she wouldn't go to the hospital if I wasn't allowed to be there.

As we walked past the nurses' station, everyone stopped what they were doing and wished her well. She blew them a kiss and thanked them for all their wonderful care, adding that she hoped she wouldn't see them for a very, very long time. As the staff smiled and a few laughed and waved, we happily took the elevator to the car.

The Caddy was waiting for us, pretty as a picture. Stan had taken it to be washed and even had them put on a nice coat of wax. The tires were shiny like the day she first drove it off the lot. Joi loved this, since she was a bit of a stickler about having a clean car. She wanted to drive, but I convinced her to sit in the back with me and let Stan be our chauffeur. This was a good day now that my girl was coming home.

As we got closer to the Marina, the fog began to roll in, making visibility more and more difficult as we got closer to the water. Stan turned onto our street, just in the nick of time, before it became impossible to see brake lights in front of us. Our building was the very last one, and we were grateful when the car was finally in its parking spot. Joi was still feeling really good after her two transfusions. She got out and playfully bet me a dollar that I couldn't skip to the elevator as fast as she could. Not the least bit disturbed that we were both adults acting like kids, she did this kind of thing often enough that I was used to it and usually had fun.

I wasn't about to let her win this one, though, so I told her, "Double or nothing. Are you ready?"

She laughed, taking my challenge, "Two dollars, and you'd better pay up when I win."

"You're on!" I said, and we skipped (not easy when you're not a kid!) as fast as we could till we arrived at the elevator in a dead heat, both of us giggling. No one had won, but we had a few great, carefree moments.

Stan was used to our "silliness," as he called it, and had followed us very slowly, occasionally stopping to strike a match because his cigar kept going out. He saved his running for the tennis court, never using any physical energy unless it was to win a game of singles.

When we got to the apartment, Stan went right into his room and collapsed in his recliner. We understood because he hadn't rested well for two nights, and exhaustion was catching up with him. I passed by his room a few minutes later on my way to the kitchen and glanced in. He was out like a light. Fortunately, he'd put out his cigar, so this would be one night that Joi and I wouldn't have to worry that his burning cigar might torch the apartment.

After taking a couple of cups of tea back to our bedroom, I realized we were both relieved to finally have a little time and privacy to ourselves. Even in Florida, before her collapse, I knew something was sapping her energy, because she hadn't been interested in making love. Since that was one of our favorite things, I missed it and wondered if she did, too.

That night, though, I worried that being intimate might be too exhausting and, as she snuggled into me, I mentioned that perhaps we should wait a few days until she was stronger. She rubbed her head and hair across my breasts and whispered, "I'm feeling great. You worry too much, so how about a welcome home kiss?"

Well, the lady knew how she was feeling, and who was I to doubt her? We kissed and made love as passionately as that very first time we were together, that night in front of the fireplace at Fountainview West.

The transfusion had made a huge difference in Joi's physical stamina and desire. I thought I had a lot of energy, but I was a wimp compared to her. My body gave up on me in the middle of the night. Teasing, she asked if I'd lied about my age.

"I thought you said you were twenty-three; you're acting like an old poop," she whispered. I could hear the smile in her voice. Well, that was all it took, and I suddenly got my fourth wind.

A while later, snuggling, I asked if she still questioned my age. She was so relaxed; I barely heard her when she mumbled, "Noooo, my darling Rachel, I'll never doubt you again."

She then slowly turned and gave me the most delicious kiss ever. Simply put, I melted.

Soon, she fell asleep in my arms with her head on my chest, the way she always did. Usually, at some point, she would move during the night, and then we'd spoon until morning, but, this night, she stayed in exactly the same position. I couldn't sleep, wondering if our romp had been too much for her in her fragile condition, and I kept checking her breathing. It was shallow but steady.

Then, slowly, she sleepily looked up at me. Concerned, I asked if she was all right. She answered yes, and not to worry...that she just wanted to spend the rest of the night awake. She said, if she slept, she would miss how wonderful it felt to be wrapped in my arms as she listened to my heart beating.

I held her closer. And I understood. I had often done the same thing for the same reason. We both wanted to know the sheer wonder of these moments, never forgetting how beautiful they were...just basking in the warmth of our love.

Chapter 39

Calm before the Storm

Joi and I finally slept a few hours. Holding her in my arms through the night had been like having life breathed into my soul. If there is such a place as heaven, I knew it every time she told me she loved me. It was a feeling no words could express and evoked an emotion in me so strong and infinite, that I felt nothing could create an ending to such unparalleled joy. Even the inevitable.

Waking up first, I heard Stan filling the coffee pot. With any luck, he had finally slept a full night without waking up with nightmares. He'd told me recently that he was tormented by terrible dreams. The images eluded him after he woke up, but were frightening enough to make him bolt from a deep sleep in a cold sweat.

I asked if they were worse when he drank his brandy, and he said he didn't know, but he couldn't sleep without it. His mind would keep racing, and he would feel tremendously anxious. I suggested he talk to his daughter, Leslie, to see if she could get him a mild tranquilizer to take the edge off and help him sleep. She would know the best thing to help him with his stress, but I'm not sure if he ever said anything to her because he never brought it up again.

Stan never wanted to appear vulnerable, because, like so many men of that era, he felt it was a sign of weakness. He also had difficulty showing love or affection because, for him, that was the worst form of weakness.

By the time Joi opened her beautiful eyes, the coffee was ready, and I had put a cup on her bedside table. To start her day off right, I also brought her little birdie, Mr. Pooper, and sat him on her shoulder. He couldn't have been more adorable, and they played for, at least, an hour before Joi had to get up.

My girl was very happy to be home with Poose, who'd developed quite the vocabulary and even managed to put words together to make understandable sentences. "How about a kiss, Joi baby?" was one of her favorites, along with the kissing sounds that made her heart melt. When the three of us watched TV in the den, the little guy would take turns jumping onto each one of us. I felt honored when he would come to me, kiss my lip, and let me rub his little blue and white feathered head.

It was evident, though, that he spent more time with Joi, and his obvious love for her made her incredibly happy. She had originally bought him for me, but she was the one who needed him most, and he seemed to know he belonged to her.

As time passed, the weather at the Marina became more and more gloomy. A heavy white blanket of fog lingered all morning, only burning off later in the day. We couldn't go back to our Palm Springs home yet because Joi had to be near her doctor at this point. The trip back and forth, or worse, when there might be an emergency, was just not feasible.

Stan was the only one who ever seemed to go out. He'd bring food home every day or go to the market and buy enough groceries to last for a week or so. Joi never complained about being in pain, but her energy was low, and she seemed to be losing her enthusiasm.

It started gradually when we were still going out for a while each day, doing something, anything, to break the tedium of the weather, but, each day, she wanted to do less and less, and, eventually, it was just the two of us and Pooper staying inside. I didn't know if it was the depressing darkness that hovered over the Marina, or if it was the disease creeping back, one sad day at a time. I felt helpless.

One afternoon, Stan surprised us by suggesting we go on a day trip to Catalina Island the next day. I was thrilled and enthusiastically encouraged Joi to say yes. The thought of going some place fun, doing something different, seemed to lift her spirits, so Stan called and bought tickets for the ferry that left from San Pedro, just south of Los Angeles. I checked with the weather bureau, and it was predicted to be a glorious day, perfect for our sojourn. Our excitement started to build.

The next morning, Joi's mood seemed to have improved dramatically, similar to how she'd been after her transfusions. Stan noticed it, too. I couldn't wait to get her out of the apartment and into the fresh salt air. For a change, there was no fog hovering overhead, and the sun was shining brightly. We both hurried and got ready to go, while Stan was waiting for us in the lobby. As we walked out to the car, Joi's expression changed as the sunlight kissed her face. She began to smile, even had a little bounce to her step, and wanted to drive with the top down "to soak up as many rays" as she could.

Stan lowered the top, and we all climbed in. Joi had brought a pink silk scarf and a baby blue one for me "to keep our hair in place," she said, "when the wind whips through it at seventy miles an hour." She had it down to a science, showing me how to tie the scarf with one end twisted one way, and the other wrapped around her head the other way. She even had a special knot to keep it secure.

It seemed like geometry to me, which wasn't my strongest suit, so she repeated the demonstration a few times, and, when I still didn't get it, she did it for me and made sure the knot was nice and tight. She patted me on the head and told me I looked adorable. I smiled. I could tell she had a lot of pent-up energy and knew it would show up in how she drove. Yes, sir, it was going to be a lead foot kind of day.

Joi had been to Catalina before and remembered the best way to get to the Port of San Pedro. Here, big ocean liners, some as huge as skyscrapers, brought passengers from all over the world, while TransPacific freighters brought an assortment of cars, textiles, fish, and grain from the major ports on most continents. The closer we came to the pier where the Catalina ferry departed, the more exciting it became. Joi and I had fun trying to guess the registry of each gorgeous cruise ship.

That morning, Joi recalled exactly where to park the car, so it would be safe while we gallivanted around Santa Catalina. I hoped Joi would enjoy the trip on the ferry and have fun exploring the island. I knew some of the trivia about it, that it was owned by the Wrigley family and part of the island was private. The other part welcomed tourists who would sail their boats over for a day of relaxation and partying at night. There were a few restaurants and nightclubs where the revelers could party hearty.

All I really looked forward to was having a cup or two of coffee and a nice lunch overlooking the bay. The boat ride was fun, and I was grateful I didn't get seasick. Once docked, we walked around the shops for a little while, and then went into a cute, funky little place that smelled like it had wonderful food. Stan wasn't hungry just then, so he said he'd just wander around for a while and get back to us.

My stomach was growling, but Joi had been having a hard time eating, so I hoped this place would jump start her appetite. We decided to go in and have an appetizer or two while Stan wandered about.

We were ushered to a nice table where we could see the harbor, and a friendly young woman brought us menus. I started to tell her we would just have an appetizer for now, when suddenly Joi looked up from the menu, sniffed a couple of times, and asked the young woman what that "delicious smell" was. We were told it was their signature clam chowder.

"Great!" she pronounced, "I want the biggest bowl you have!"

"Me, too!" I said, and we both laughed.

"Ahh, the Birdie is finally hungry," Joi said with a sigh of relief (not realizing that I, too, had just exhaled).

As the garlic bread was served, she said she hadn't had an appetite for a few weeks and was frightened because she knew how important it was for her to eat. She explained she didn't want to upset me, so had tried to keep her worries to herself.

Reaching across the table, I took her hand and asked her to never do that again, to please tell me when things were bothering her. I explained that, if I didn't know, I couldn't do anything to help. We'd always shared our thoughts, dreams, and feelings, and to lose this intimacy would be a tragedy.

She said that if she hadn't started to feel better, she intended to eventually tell me about it. I reminded her that Dr. Wilson said this new chemotherapy combination might also have to be tweaked, and I thought we should see him in case he wanted to make an adjustment. She agreed and asked me to call in the morning to make an appointment.

As the Waitress put our chowder down, I felt better that we'd talked. It wasn't fair to her to be fighting the changes all alone, without my support. And now that I knew what was going on, she would never be alone with them again.

The chowder was divine, and I was hard pressed not to ask for another bowl, but I knew, when Stan got back, we'd be eating a big meal, so I settled on the last piece of garlic bread instead. While I was busy enjoying every morsel, Joi had been looking around for Stan and asked me, "Do you know where Stan is?"

"I don't have the foggiest…" I mumbled, as I tried to quickly swallow what was left of my bread.

"Well, let's go find him," Joi said. "We'll need a new table, anyway, and can always come back."

We paid our bill, giving our waitress a nice tip, as we usually did, and left, determined to find Stan. We decided to look first in all the little shops but, though we peeked in every one we passed, Hubby was nowhere to be found.

Finally, feet hurting and pooped, I told Joi that since I thought "he'd been kidnapped and taken to some tennis ranch in Bora Bora," we should give up and go back to the restaurant. She laughed, and, because our stomachs were starting to do flips again, we headed back to our now "fave" place to eat.

On our return, we asked the Hostess for a table for three and told her the name was Todd. Joi generally used Stan's name as she didn't want to draw any unnecessary attention by using her own. The Hostess asked if we were waiting for a gentleman by the name of Stan, and we gleefully said "yes," while she took us to his table. He'd become bored looking in shops and finally just wanted to have a cup of coffee, so there he sat for almost an hour, waiting for his two ladies to join him.

After the high-spirited, "Where were you?" from both sides, we were all happy we could now have an early dinner. We decided to split the seafood platter among the three of us, which came with shrimp, crab claws, clams, and gazpacho soup with chunks of lobster. I ate most of the shrimp and the soup, and Joi and Stan ate the rest of it. The entire meal was wonderful, and just enough to satisfy our hunger pangs without looking for a place to beach ourselves afterward.

The day passed quickly, and it was time to get onto the last ferry back to San Pedro, so we strolled to the pier and stood in line to get back on board. The sun was still strong, and I actually got a little color. Joi always protected her face, so she wouldn't have any sun damage. It worked, and her skin was perfect because of how she guarded her greatest asset.

On the ferry going back to port, we enjoyed walking around on the various decks. Joi and I relaxed for a time at the little snack shop downstairs, and then left Stan snoozing in the sun while we stood at the upstairs railing to watch the waves lick at the sides of the boat. The ocean was calm that afternoon with very few larger waves hitting the bow, and it was fun to watch the motion of the water... well, for most of the trip, anyway.

There were a few times when I felt a little nauseated, but managed to hold on. Stan joined us just as Joi began to look somewhat queasy, too, but he seemed to be managing the rocking of the boat quite well. If he had a problem, he'd never admit it. He boasted about his days in Connecticut when he went sailing every summer on the Atlantic, which was much rougher than the Pacific could ever be. It was obvious he saw himself as the consummate yachtsman, with sea legs of steel.

When we finally arrived back at port, we were very happy to be on a surface that didn't move. Being on land made all the difference to our tummies, but Joi still asked Stan to drive home and put the top back up, so she could lie down in the backseat. I'd been quietly observing her all day, and I knew things weren't right. She put her head on my lap, and I massaged her temples as we drove home. I planned on calling Dr. Wilson's office first thing the following morning.

Stan loved driving, so we breezed down the freeway like the Caddy had wings. He got us home even faster than when Joi had driven us earlier in the day. It was a good thing, too, because every little bump we hit seemed to bother her. She never complained, but the look in her eyes told me that my girl was in pain and just being stoic.

We went to bed that night without even watching the evening news on TV. Joi and I were creatures of habit, and keeping up on the news of the day was part of our usual routine. After Stan had fallen asleep in his chair in front of the TV, we headed to our room, grateful to end a fun but tiring day.

Though she hadn't yet said anything, Joi was obviously still not comfortable. I helped her into bed, turned on our bedroom TV, and put my arm around her. We halfheartedly watched until she fell asleep, when I turned the sound way down. I left it on, though, because the drone of the television soothed her and always helped her sleep. Since I could sleep through just about anything, I could tune out the noise or work it into a dream I might be having.

Breathing softly, she slept like always, on her side with her head on my chest and her leg draped warmly over mine. She woke for just a moment as I was pulling the sheets up around us, and sweetly kissed my cheek. Snuggling sleepily beside me, she softly told me to never forget how much she loved me. I pulled her closer, making sure she didn't see my tears. As she began to doze, I softly brushed the hair out of her eyes and whispered, "I promise, my darling, I won't forget…ever. I promise."

She heard my loving reassurance and cuddled into me to let me know.

The TV droned on, and, in a few minutes, her breathing became regular and smooth. I didn't sleep that night. I lay awake, holding her closer than ever before, counting her heartbeats, hanging on to her…even though I knew time would eventually take her from me.

Now, all I knew was that I didn't want to miss a minute of her…or us. I'd have way too much time to sleep…afterward.

Chapter 40

Gloomy Marina Days

We saw Dr. Wilson within a few hours after my call to his office the morning after our return from Catalina. As always, he was comforting, compassionate, and helpful. After evaluating Joi, he changed her chemotherapy cocktail, which, in the days to follow, seemed to help her without any major side effects.

She was still taking methadone every six hours and never complained about being in pain. Sadly, though, she wasn't the same Joi who'd been so playful and full of energy when she came home from her last hospital stay. There was something missing. I think now, looking back, that the reality of her disease had finally connected with her and had left an indelible mark on her spirit. At the time, it was a subtle change, but I knew her so well, felt the void, and deeply wished I could fill it.

A few weeks passed with still no apparent side effects to the new chemotherapy, but, as had happened when we got back from Florida, she wanted to stay in the apartment all the time. Again, we rarely went out except to go to dinner with Stan three or four nights a week. Usually, we stayed in the den, watching TV. I'd bring her tea and sometimes some cookies. When she felt up to it, she would try to read to me, but mostly she'd sit with her feet in my lap which I'd massage until she either moved or drifted off to sleep. Then, I'd quietly cover her with her favorite quilt and watch her rest until her beautiful eyes opened again. I always loved that moment.

It was still chilly at the Marina, normal for the winter months, but the morning fog stayed later and later each day, making her mood ever darker. To try to offset the clammy feel of the weather, I kept the fireplace going most of the time, giving a coziness and comforting warmth to our apartment.

Even Mr. Pooper seemed to enjoy the fireplace. At first, he was frightened and tried to fly away into Stan's room, but his little stubby wings wouldn't give him any loft, so he'd glide to the floor. Joi would put her finger in front of his little tummy and he'd jump right up onto his beautiful "elevator." If she was wearing slacks, he'd climb up her leg until he reached her chest, and there he'd stay.

During the past months, Joi's little bird had learned a lot, and one day she taught him a special tune he learned to whistle in less than a week. That little guy could not only whistle and talk, he made us both laugh when he'd try to nibble the food on Joi's fork. He was not usually successful, but sometimes she'd let him win, if it was food that wouldn't hurt him. (We were shocked to discover that parsley was toxic and could possibly do great harm. We only found out by chance, reading an article in Dr. Wilson's office.)

Poose seemed to be able to bring a sparkle back to Joi's eyes. I think he must have touched the part of her which yearned to fly away from the reality that was slowly becoming more evident. He was her wings, and, yet, neither could fly.

Through the weeks, Stan saw that fewer and fewer things were interesting to Joi. On one particularly miserable day, recalling how elated she'd been to go to Catalina Island, he suggested we spend the weekend in San Clemente, another colorful California location. Neither Joi nor I had ever been there, and it sounded like fun. Getting away from the fog and gloom was exhilarating to Joi and made me ecstatic as well. Joi smiled, did a few steps of her Birdie dance, and said, "I'm so happy! I can't wait to get away from this depressing place!"

We really wanted to go back to Palm Springs for the rest of the winter, but Dr. Wilson felt her health was too precarious to take a chance on being so far from the hospital for any length of time. Although we'd been told Palm Springs had a good hospital, Joi felt the doctors there wouldn't know the history of her condition, and she wouldn't feel comfortable with anyone but her own oncologists. She said they knew her body and seemed to be keeping her in remission.

The day before our sojourn, even though the idea of going someplace fun had lifted her spirits, Joi still didn't feel well at all. She came in the kitchen while I was fixing some tea for us and leaned against me, slipping her arm weakly around my waist.

"Please call Dr. Wilson for me, honey. I just don't feel like talking to anyone right now."

She asked me to tell him how she felt, that perhaps she needed another adjustment to her chemotherapy to feel like herself again. As we took our tea into the bedroom, I agreed to make the call.

After we'd rested a bit, she decided to take a warm bath, so while I ran the water, she got into her robe and pinned her hair up off her neck. (Thin as it was, there was enough to get wet if she didn't.) I made sure the water wasn't too hot and poured in her favorite bath oil and bubbles, so she could relax.

Pooper had been on her shoulder in the kitchen and now was in the bedroom on one of his many perches. It was kind of a birdie "playpen" with a wooden perch and swing attached. A four-inch ladder rested against the perch, which he could walk up and then swing to his heart's content. It was easily moved, so I placed it on the vanity next to the bathroom mirror. That way, my girl could enjoy watching her little bird friend while she rested in the warmth of her bath. Poose sang his special serenade while Joi, eyes half-closed, soaked in the tub.

I quietly left them and went in the den, knowing I could be candid with Dr. Wilson if I were alone. I called his office and asked the Secretary to tell him it was important. When he came to the phone within a couple of minutes, there was a concerned tone in his voice. I told him of the changes I was seeing in Joi and asked what he thought was going on.

"I'm not sure, Rachel, but I'm concerned that the chemotherapy is starting to lose its efficacy. There aren't that many other drugs to try, if these don't slow the disease. I'm afraid that her condition is changing, and that she's most likely no longer in remission."

He tried to say the words as gently as he could, but each one felt like a knife thrust in my heart.

"Are you sure, Doctor?" I asked, my voice beginning to shake. "What else can be done for her?"

I'd heard what he just said and already knew his answer, but I couldn't stop talking. His words hung in the air… *There aren't that many drugs… no longer in remission.* Grasping at straws, I pushed on, still hoping he'd say something to give me a rope to hang on to. I felt myself sinking and barely able to breathe.

Dr. Wilson became very quiet. Finally, he said softly, "Rachel, you know Joi's very ill, and, though her disease has been in remission much longer than any of us ever dreamed possible, I don't know how much longer the drugs will be able to help her. You know we're doing everything we can for her, and I only wish there were a magic drug that would save her life."

He had repeated what I already knew, but it would be so much easier if I could just pretend. I sat down, the phone heavy in my hand.

Knowing I had to tell her something, I haltingly asked if it would be okay to take her to Palm Springs for a week, since she was getting depressed at the Marina.

"We're going to San Clemente tomorrow, and we'll be staying there a few days, but do you think this will be too difficult for her?"

He told me to watch her carefully, and if she started to have more pain than usual, or began vomiting, to call him immediately.

"As for going to Palm Springs, let's see how she does on this short trip," he suggested. Gently, he said, "Take care of yourself, Rachel. You're going to have to be very strong to be there for her. It's not going to be easy, but I know how devoted you are to her. If there's anything within my power to help her, you can be sure I'll do it."

Feeling like my words were being said by someone else, I replied that I knew he would, and thanked him again. After our good-byes, I rushed to the other bathroom in our condo, where I broke down, sobbing like I never had before. I crumpled up a bath towel against my face to hide the wracking sound of my sobs. It was all coming home to me now, and the truth of losing her was more than I could bear. I felt like I was melting, and there was nothing I could do to stop it.

I don't know how much time passed, but I suddenly became aware that, as devastated as I was, I had to get it together, if not for me, then for Joi. She'd had her bathroom radio on when I left her and her birdie pal, so I didn't think she'd heard me, but I couldn't have red eyes when she got out of the tub.

Taking as deep a breath as I could, I splashed water into my eyes and patted them dry. They weren't as bad as before, but obvious enough to upset her. As I crossed the living room to the kitchen, I peeked in our bedroom and heard her talking to Poose in the bathroom. She hadn't heard, thank God. I went to the kitchen and made a salad for our lunch and decided to put lots of onions in it to provide an excuse for my bloodshot eyes. I covered the salad with plastic wrap, slid it into the refrigerator, and walked to the bedroom.

After being in the tub for over an hour, Joi finally got out while I was making lunch. When I came into the bedroom, I smiled enough to hide my emotions, and, to deflect attention from myself still further, I playfully asked, "Why in heaven's name does your skin look like a prune?"

Joi laughed and answered, "Well, it's one of those unexplainable mysteries of life … and why are your eyes so red?" She'd noticed them immediately.

I lightly said I'd sacrificed my mascara to make a wonderful salad with fresh-cut onion slices. She was sweet. "Your poor little eyes, honey. Check my purse; I think I have some Visine in it."

Joi believed my story, and I was so grateful she did. I'd been on the verge of falling apart, and, if she'd kept pursuing the question, I was afraid I would start crying again.

Checking her bag, I found a small bottle of eye drops "guaranteed to get the red out," and I was counting on their truth in advertising. It worked! My eyes looked as good as new, and there was still a little left in the bottle in case I had another meltdown.

Joi looked into my eyes when I returned, and said, "Those nasty onions made my honey's eyes tear. Maybe we shouldn't use onions, or, next time, use the bread trick I taught you." (She'd shown me a bizarre way to reduce the tears by dangling a slice of bread from her mouth while chopping an onion.)

Fortunately, I could feign memory loss to have an excuse for the redness.

"Ohhh, yes! Well, I obviously forgot, so please remind me again next time, okay?" I laughed, holding myself together with sheer force.

She said she would, but then, looking intently at me, asked if I'd spoken with Dr. Wilson.

I immediately felt tense and afraid that my expression would tell her something was wrong. I said I'd spoken to him and that he'd sent his best wishes for a fun trip to San Clemente, and had said to call his office immediately if she had any reaction to the new medications, that it was important to monitor the way her body reacted to these treatments. Joi seemed very satisfied with what I was telling her. She would now be watchful, but not overly guarded and concerned.

"What did he say about us going to the Springs for a week?" she asked.

"He didn't think it would be a problem," I explained, "but would know much more after our San Clemente trip. He gave me his personal phone number, and said it would be okay to use it if no one was in the office. How many doctors give you their home number?" I said with a smile.

"Well," she answered with a touch of anger, "I've had a lot of doctors give me their home number, and that's probably one of the main reasons I wasn't diagnosed properly! They were too busy trying to date me to even ask about the things I wrote on their stupid intake sheets. I told every one of them that I'd been having terrible abdominal pain and bled profusely during my periods. They obviously didn't think it was important enough to discuss with me. On the other hand," she continued, "they did have time to ask if I had plans for the evening, or if they could call me."

Joi became increasingly upset as she described her feelings that she was basically an "object," and that her medical needs were secondary to their libidos. I had watched this through the years and worried about it, but I was young and didn't know what to say to either her or the doctors she saw. How I wish I'd been wiser, but, as the saying goes, "If wishes were horses…" Sad but true.

Dr. Wilson, however, was different, and it pleased Joi to know he thought enough of her to give us his home number. It was a security blanket he'd graciously wrapped around her, a comfort to both of us.

Suddenly, Joi wrinkled her nose. "Rachel, I can smell those onions clear in the bedroom! Good grief, how much did you cut up to put in the salad?" she asked with amazement.

"Honey, I only cut up half of one of those beautiful, big onions you put in the fridge. I thought you liked onions…am I misinformed?" (I gave it right back to her.)

"I love onions," she responded, "sliced, sautéed, diced, fried, and especially fried onion rings, which are absolute poison to your body, but that doesn't change how much I love them and wish I could eat them. I do know better, however, and won't give in to my wanton desires." She laughed as she went through the litany. "I'd love to have some of the salad you made for us, especially since you sacrificed your makeup preparing it for me!" she said, touching the tip of my nose playfully.

We went into the kitchen, and Joi checked out the salad. I loved cooking and preparing food for her, and this salad had all the things she really enjoyed. I made sure to put in hearts of palm, which she'd introduced me to and which we both loved, as well as artichoke hearts, Chinese vegetables, baby spinach leaves, and fresh plum tomatoes. It was an amazing cornucopia of tastes and textures.

Joi was the expert at making the dressing, using extra virgin olive oil and red wine vinegar, as well as a blend of herbs she'd prepared and prepackaged. She stacked the individual packages in the spice drawer, ready to pull out as needed. When she finished putting together her delicious dressing, I piled our salads into two of our favorite bowls, and we headed to the den.

Using the coffee table as our dining area, we watched the fog roll in and hover in front of our windows. It was beautiful in a somber way, but Joi and I both were thrilled at the prospect of getting away to San Clemente. I'd always been on the go, from the time I got my driver's license at sixteen years of age, and I was starting to get more than a little stir-crazy, just sitting in the house all day.

But, truth be told, if being with Joi meant staying locked in for an eternity, I'd have gladly done so, no matter what the circumstance. She was my love, and nothing … not even what was to come … would change that … ever.

Chapter 41

San Clemente

The next morning, I woke up earlier than usual and felt excited about our trip. Joi was still sleeping, so I quietly went to the kitchen to make our coffee. Stan was up early, too, buttering his toast as I walked in, and I saw he'd already made our morning brew.

While pouring my coffee, I realized that I was nervous about telling Stan what Dr. Wilson had said because of how he always reacted to "bad" news. But I realized he needed to know. He had to be ready, as I was, for anything that might happen to Joi on our trip. Whether he wanted to or not, he had to know the clock was ticking.

I sat down with him at the table, which I never did, and he looked up at me inquisitively. Taking a breath, I told him what Dr. Wilson had said. Immediately, Stan's expression changed, and his eyes seemed to become empty. I explained that the Doctor had given us his home number in case Joi had a problem during the evening when the office was closed. My expression must have said the rest. He took another sip of his coffee, a bite of his toast, and, saying nothing, stood up and left the room.

Shaking off the feelings Stan had left me with, I fixed some toast for us and took it and Joi's coffee back to the bedroom. She was awake but still a little groggy.

"Wake up, honey," I said, smiling. "Enjoy your coffee while I take a quick shower. Stan is up and getting ready to go. I know it's tempting, but please don't go back to sleep, okay? We're going to have fun today and get some sun."

I kissed her forehead.

I set the tray on the bedside table and propped up the pillows on my side of the bed, so she could sit up to drink her coffee. Scooting over from her side, she sat up, ready for that magical first sip.

"Don't worry about me!" she said. "I'll be up and ready to go before you are!"

She was "up" that day, and I was grateful. I heard her laugh as I closed the shower door behind me. As I soaped up, I was surprised as that same door slowly opened, and, much to my pleasure, there she stood…dressed only in her smile.

"Want company?" she grinned. She was using that special throaty tone that always buckled my knees.

"Ohhh, do I ever!" I answered, as I slowly pulled her into the shower next to me. The steam and the warm water beating down took us away to where "we" were the only thing that mattered. In each other's arms was the one place we could both forget how sad our world was becoming.

With the sound of water hitting the glass doors and splashing on the tile around us, we barely heard Stan knocking on our bedroom door. The rapping was faint, but it broke the magic spell that we were under, bringing us back to reality. Joi opened the door to the shower and yelled out, "I'm almost ready, Hubby. I'll be out in a few minutes."

We looked at each other and realized we'd have to take a rain check and finish our wonderful interlude when we came back from our trip. One last lingering kiss under our imaginary waterfall, and we left our tropical island oasis to prepare for our oceanside adventure.

While I was still deciding what to wear, Joi had dried herself off, dressed, and was ready for her finishing touches. She wore soft yellow cotton hip huggers and a matching V-neck blouse with sleeves rolled up above her elbows. The color looked great on her, casting a glowing peach tone to her skin. In fact, if you saw her, you'd never imagine she was the slightest bit ill. That morning, she looked the picture of good health.

Even after our delicious morning, the idea of getting out of the condo and feeling the warmth of the sun would be an extra special treat. Stan showed up dressed like a ship's captain again in his blue and white. Just mentioning the sea seemed to trigger his wardrobe choice, and San Clemente was one of the most beautiful of seaside towns. He also smelled a little like brandy. I wasn't thrilled he'd be driving, but, since Joi couldn't, I'd have to live with it.

By the time Joi and I were ready to leave, we couldn't believe that the fog had dissipated and sunshine was everywhere! Now, we didn't really need to leave to get away from the depressing weather, but it would still be fun to go somewhere we'd never been before.

I was having problems with my hair that morning so was running a little later than Stan or Joi. It was getting longer than I usually wore it, reaching well below my shoulders. I was not thrilled with this because I have very wavy hair with a natural curl that gives it lots of body. Living at the Marina with the fresh ocean air made my hair look like I lived in a bayou! When I say my hair was big, that's not an exaggeration. There was nothing to keep it tamed and manageable, except possibly a ski mask!

When Joi saw me struggling, she told me how beautiful I looked, and said, "Don't worry about your hair. We'll put the top down, and the scarf will make it look just fine."

I had to laugh, knowing she'd meant to be reassuring, but it didn't quite sound that way. Especially when she followed her compliment with, "Let's go to the salon this week if we go to the Springs. You can get your hair cut and styled, and I can get rid of the dark streak down the center of mine."

During our time in the desert, we'd met a lovely woman who owned a beauty salon in Palm Springs. Joi and I had gone to her shop and were very pleased with her work. She knew just how to deal with my hair and had a way of straightening it with a reverse perm. She also was an expert colorist and did Joi's hair seamlessly. Her shop was in the center of Palm Springs, very close to the house. It would be a fun thing to do if we decided to go later in the week.

Stan knocked on the door again and asked if we were ready to go.

"We're ready, Hubby! We'll be right out," Joi called. We were both ready, except for lipstick. We made sure it was the last thing applied, so we could have another kiss before facing the world.

Joi didn't like to have her hair touched after she'd brushed it. She didn't like having it messed up, and I was always careful not to break the rule. I put my arms around her waist as I kissed her, so I wouldn't accidentally touch her face or hair. She was so used to being in the public eye that she thought of her hair and body as commodities that needed to be as perfect as possible whenever she was out of the house. She didn't want to disappoint her fans or have someone take a photo of her that wasn't complimentary.

We walked out of our room and saw Stan sitting in his recliner.

"What are you doing sitting in your chair, Hubby?" Joi asked in a playful, sweet voice. "I thought you were ready to go."

She knew very well that he was tired of waiting for us and had decided to sit down and nap until we finally came out of our room. Joi laughed as she grabbed him by the hand, pulling him out of his chair.

Joi went over to the birdcage and kissed little Pooper on top of his head. He chirped a bit and said, "I love you, Joi baby."

Stan had become attached to the little guy, too, and, though he'd never admit it, Joi and I had both noticed how well Stan took care of him. Once, we'd even caught a glimpse of Poose riding on his shoulder!

We walked to Joi's car and decided against putting the top down for the time being. It was a warm spring day, but the wind was whipping around strongly and would be chilly as we drove down the freeway. We could always put the top down when we got to San Clemente and were sightseeing along the coast.

Stan couldn't see us very well in his rearview mirror, which made cuddling in the backseat easy for Joi and me. But we were always affectionate toward each other, no matter who was around. Society doesn't judge affection between two women as being strange or unnatural, as they do with men. We didn't hide our love; we just didn't display any sexual innuendo. That was a very personal and private part of our lives that we shared with no one. There were only a few people who knew the depth of our relationship, but only because Joi had told them. Others may have assumed or had suspicions, but not because of any physical or verbal demonstration on our part.

The drive was long, but the scenery was exquisite. We drove along the Pacific Coast Highway through Laguna Beach, down the coast toward San Clemente. (President Nixon had a large home here that he called "La Casa Pacifica," but others called it the "Western White House.") Joi and I had read a little about this beautiful and charming town, so we'd know what we'd like to see when we arrived.

The Mission of San Juan Capistrano was just six miles north of San Clemente and was the first place we wanted to stop. We arrived around noon as the sound of church bells welcomed us to the old mission founded by Father Serra in 1776. We walked all around and through it, amazed at its aged beauty.

The main building had all the charm of the Spanish architecture that had such a great influence on subsequent architectural trends in California. Beautiful gardens filled with bougainvillea added vibrant color to the old stone church, Mexican tile walkway, and the smaller buildings of whitewashed adobe. We found the original building where Father Serra first said Mass almost two hundred years ago. Stan seemed particularly interested in the history of the mission, since American history was one of his favorite subjects.

We saw everything that the public was privy to, and wished we'd been there to see the swallows returning in the middle of March, as they did every year. We had missed it by just a few weeks, but hoped to go back again next year, if we were able. (It's strange how we take time so for granted, not even giving it a second thought … until it runs out.)

After walking all around the perimeter of the old mission, I noticed that Joi was starting to look a little tired. I found a lovely spot for us with a wooden bench where we could sit under the canopy of a magnificent old tree. I said to her, "Let's go, honey. Aren't you getting hungry?"

She sighed. "I am a little hungry, and I'm starting to get lightheaded," she said weakly.

I told Stan, and he left to bring the car around to where we were sitting. Joi didn't seem to be in a lot of discomfort, but I could see this was too much for her today. Her chemotherapy had been agreeing with her, without any real side effects, but her energy was a little less than usual, and, without realizing it, we must have walked a mile or so while investigating Father Serra's beautiful work. Since we were all fascinated with the mission's history, it had been easy to do.

Stan pulled up to about twenty feet from where we were sitting. Joi said the dizziness had passed, and she was starting to feel a little better, but I held her hands as she stood and put my arm around her to keep her steady on her feet. She was able to make it to the car without losing her balance.

We asked a friar, whom we had seen when we first arrived, if there was a really nice seafood restaurant overlooking the ocean, not too far from the mission. He told us about a charming place to eat on the San Clemente Pier and said it was only a few miles away.

We soon arrived at the San Clemente Pier which jutted out into the Pacific Ocean surf. I could see that Joi was not feeling great and knew that she needed to get some food as soon as possible. The medications she took in the morning were very rough on her digestive system, and all she'd had was coffee and a few slices of toast. The methadone alone was enough to make anyone nauseated, and the chemotherapy was certainly not soothing to her stomach.

Finding the restaurant, we asked for a window seat overlooking the water, and the Host took us to the nicest table in the house. The sun was bright, and the morning fog had lifted hours before we arrived. We could see Catalina Island in the distance, and sailboats were out for a lovely afternoon on the ocean. It was all picture perfect. It would have been the ideal setting for one of Bob Hope and Dorothy Lamour's *Road to...* movies. I could just visualize them in a small skiff approaching land after being shipwrecked on the way to Avalon Bay!

I told Joi what I was thinking, and she smiled and agreed. She thought that Dorothy should be wearing a sarong with a perfect white gardenia in her hair, as she often had. I laughed. It was good to think of anything fun or whimsical to keep from dwelling on what was really happening. Though she tried to relax and play a bit, I saw that Joi was really not feeling well, and now I wasn't sure that food alone would solve the problem. The signs of her change had been in front of my eyes for the last few weeks, but I guess I just hadn't wanted to see it.

"Are you okay, honey?" I asked.

Joi responded with a worried expression on her face. "I don't know what's happening to me, but I feel really strange."

I asked if she was in pain, and she said that she wasn't really hurting, but had a weird feeling in her belly. Thinking it might be hunger, I saw the Waiter and asked him to bring some warm sourdough bread while we were waiting to order. Stan had gone to the restroom and to look for a paper, but I knew she needed to eat now.

Our server rushed back with a wicker basket filled with steaming hot bread wrapped in a large white linen napkin. He had barely placed it on the table when Joi grabbed a piece like a hungry child, spread, at least, two pats of butter on it, and almost desperately began to eat. She ate as if she hadn't had any food for weeks!

"Honey," I said, "slow down. You're going to choke!"

She didn't listen to me but reached for another piece, ate that in two bites, and was reaching for another. I watched her with my mouth open in shock when a strange look came into her eyes and she doubled over in pain.

Quickly, I stood up and moved around to her on the other side of the table.

"Joi, Joi, are you okay? Are you okay, honey?" I asked.

She couldn't speak. I sat down next to her and put my arm around her as she gasped in excruciating pain.

Just as I was ready to call 911, Stan walked up to the table and saw what was happening. He looked panicked, and asked what we should do. I told him to sit down next to her and hold her while I made a call to Dr. Wilson. Then, I gently lifted her while Stan moved in beside her. As she rested her head on his chest, she whispered that the pain seemed to be getting a little better, although her face still showed signs of discomfort. I told her I was going to call Dr. Wilson, and we would do whatever he said to help her.

I quickly found the pay phone in the back of the restaurant next to the restrooms. It was in one of those old-fashioned private glass and wooden booths with a door that folded in the middle and a wooden seat where I could sit down.

Feeling faint, I was grateful I would have something to support me in case my legs became even weaker. In those old booths, the light automatically went on the minute you snapped the door closed. I didn't want people to see my face when I spoke with the Dr. Wilson, so I kept the door slightly ajar, and it stayed dark inside.

Stan had handed me a pocketful of change as I got up to make the call. It was long distance, and I remember wondering if Dr. Wilson would actually answer. He did, and he recognized my voice immediately.

"Rachel, is that you? What's going on? Is Joi all right? Rachel, what's happening?" he asked.

I told him that Joi had an attack of severe pain that lasted for what seemed like an eternity.

"It must have lasted, at least, five minutes, and she was doubled over in excruciating pain!" I told him frantically.

"Try to compose yourself, Rachel. Tell me exactly what happened before she had the pain," he said calmly.

I explained everything that had occurred when she first started to feel like something was wrong. I told him about the discomfort in her stomach and how she frantically ate the bread. Then, I listened to his words as endless thoughts were spinning around in my head.

"She needs to come home, Rachel. I want her to go directly to St. John's as soon as you can get her there. Do you understand, Rachel?" he asked quietly.

I spoke, but it sounded like someone else talking from far away.

"I do understand, Doctor, and can you please arrange for a room, so she doesn't have to go through the emergency department? She's in too much pain to have to go through that … please!"

He told me that, of course, he'd make all the arrangements and that they would call him the moment we arrived. He'd make sure her suite was available, so I could stay with her. This helped me catch my breath. I was starting to hyperventilate, knowing the nightmare was just beginning. I begged him to help her, and he said he'd do everything that he possibly could.

His voice was calm, deep, and kind. I held on to every word to keep from passing out.

"You have to be strong for her, Rachel. She's going to need you to be with her. I know how hard this is, but now is not the time for tears. There will be enough time later on, but be brave for her now."

He said what I needed to hear. I knew I couldn't fall apart on her now. I thanked him for his kindness and told him we'd be there within a few hours. I sat in the wooden phone booth surrounded by darkness.

Chapter 42

St. John's Revisited

I composed myself and walked back to the table, where I found Joi sitting up.

"You look like you're feeling a little better, honey. Are you?" I asked.

She nodded and said the pain had eased up, and she could finally sit up straight. I asked if she'd ever had this kind of pain before, and she said she hadn't.

When I told Joi and Stan what Dr. Wilson wanted us to do, I tempered it by saying he wanted to make sure the chemotherapy wasn't causing this kind of reaction. Joi felt better knowing he was going to meet us at the hospital and "get to the bottom of things." She said she didn't want to ever experience that kind of pain again.

While I was on the phone, Joi had eaten a cup of clam chowder with some oyster crackers, which was warm and soothing and made her stomach feel better. The soup—along with the half a loaf of warm bread she'd devoured earlier—had been enough for her, and she was no longer hungry. Stan had also ordered some soup for himself and polished off more of the bread. Although I didn't feel hungry, my stomach hurt and was in knots, so I had a piece of bread with a little butter to calm it down. (That bread was certainly the saving grace of our day!)

I was nervous about getting started because I realized how important it was to get Joi to the hospital. Although I didn't want to alarm her or Stan, I knew we had to leave very soon, so we'd be at St. John's before the rush hour traffic.

It didn't matter what day it was on the Pacific Coast Highway—every visitor to Los Angeles wanted to see the ocean. Early in the morning, it was swamped with tourists headed to the beach for the day, and, by late afternoon, it was the same exact thing, but in the opposite direction. Everyone left before sunset. It was now midafternoon, and we'd be able to get a head start before the insanity began on the highway.

In my conversation with Dr. Wilson, he'd recommended that Joi take an extra dose of methadone right away. That had finally kicked in, and Joi was ready for the trip. I'd breathe easier once Joi was at St. John's, where she could get stronger pain medication, just in case it happened again.

Leaving the table, Stan and I walked on either side of her, each of us holding one arm to keep her balanced, so she wouldn't fall. She said she felt a little better and that we shouldn't worry about her.

"What makes you think we're worried?" I teased. "We're not worried, are we, Hubby?"

Stan replied that she'd be playing tennis in a few days, but that she had to get the right chemotherapy formula to get her back on track. Stan was referring to a recent phone call Joi had received from Jack Rawley, our former penthouse manager. Jack had called about a women's tennis tournament at the Marina City Club, and asked Joi if she'd like to participate. Although Joi hadn't played tennis in quite a while, she said she'd really like to do it.

Hearing her talk like this had made Stan and I take a deep breath. Joi was a fighter, and she wouldn't give up easily. She'd managed to survive all the land mines in Hollywood, and was able to keep the scars hidden from most of the world. All we could do now was hope she'd rally again like she'd done so many times before.

During the heyday of her career, Joi had a good friend who was a boxer. He taught her all about fighting and said, "Never let them see your glass jaw." She learned from him that, if they knock you down, you'd better get up, or you're done for.

On several occasions, Joi had said she just wasn't going to let this "thing" destroy her, especially since she'd conquered her demons, alcohol and drugs, and was finally happy in her life. She told me once that, with me at her side, there was way too much to look forward to, and nothing was going to rob her of the life with me she deserved. But many months had passed since then, and time, as we knew, was not really on her side. Not now.

We arrived at the hospital in a little under two hours, just beating the traffic most of the way. Stan pulled up right in front, next to the wheelchair ramp, and we both helped Joi into a chair. After he parked, Stan would met us on the third floor in the VIP suites, where she was to be admitted.

I pushed Joi through the lobby and onto the elevator which was empty, except for us. Though she was obviously weak, her spirits were good as she turned to look up at me. She asked me to lean in closer, so she could tell me something important. I bent down, and she whispered, "The Birdie's going to beat this, honey. You don't have to worry, I promise. I love you, and nothing is going to take me away from you."

She reached up and petted my cheek and made me promise to remember what she'd just told me.

Just then, the elevator stopped and a rather portly man who smelled like too much aftershave got in. He pushed his button and then ignored us. I looked down at her, into her eyes.

"I know you'll be okay, baby, and out of here in a few days," I whispered. "Besides, I've got to be your ball boy—or girl—at the tennis tournament, don't I?"

I winked, and she smiled as the door opened and "stinky" got out.

Alone again, she looked up at me and said, "You'd better be there because I can't win without you."

The elevator stopped again, and this time on our floor. As I pushed her out into the hall, knowing that what I was about to say wouldn't compromise us, I spoke in my regular voice and said that nothing could stop me from being there to watch as she "whipped the fluffy little skirt off her competition!"

That made us both laugh, but she coughed too hard for us to continue. We stopped the banter for a minute, so she could catch her breath. She seemed so very frail, and, at that moment, I don't think I'd ever felt closer to her. I wanted every bit of strength I had to fill her with health. Taking a deep breath, I rolled her toward the nurses' station, only a few feet away from the room where we'd stayed the last two times.

One of our favorite nurses, Dolores (Dee) Halkovich, came out from behind the counter and gave us each a hug.

"Gee, I'm happy to see you both," she said with a warm smile, "but I wish it were socially."

We nodded in agreement as Joi said softly, "That would be nice."

Steering us past the nurses' station, Dee said that, this time, a lovely corner suite had been reserved, and she hoped it would be to our liking.

"Well, but are there fine linens and lovely cut flowers ordered for our stay at your establishment?" Joi asked pompously with an impish grin.

Dee laughed. Joi had a wonderful wit, and it was obvious that Dee really liked her and wasn't just starstruck like so many people Joi had known in her life.

The third floor was for celebrities or the very wealthy (quite often the same thing). The suite was beautiful and, at least, triple what was customary. Stan would be paying a very large percentage of the bill, but he knew Joi wouldn't stay without me. Unfortunately, hospital policy would not let me camp out in a room where someone else was a patient. It was the choice of a suite or a suite. There was no other option.

Dee rolled her into our suite and next to her bed. She folded back the sheets and duvet, demonstrating their quality and extolling the virtues of the room in general. Smiling, she pointed to the large color TV hanging directly across the room from the bed, the large picture windows, and window coverings to shut out the light, so she'd sleep better in the morning. That is, until they woke her, every hour on the hour, to take blood or check her temperature and blood pressure. There's no such thing as rest in a hospital, suite or no suite. We were just lucky to be in such a great place and one that would allow me to be with her.

The nurses were the best, and I hoped that Big Red Tomassini would be working the next shift. I asked Dee if Red was on the schedule, and she said she was. What a relief! There's nothing better in a hospital than to have a comfort level with the nurses in charge of your care. They can make or break a hospital with their attitude and compassion, and these nurses were the best in their profession, knowing exactly what to do and say at the appropriate time. Dee helped Joi change into two hospital gowns, one tied in the front and the other fastened in the rear. It's always so embarrassing to have your bum hanging out any time you have to get out of bed.

Joi was modest, contrary to many people's belief, and privacy was very important to her. Yes, she was a performer and wore the costumes that her persona required, but her clothing, though revealing, was never trashy. Joi was always a lady, and kept her dignity in the public eye. She had refused innumerable times to do a nude pictorial, even though she could have named her price if she had wanted to. She said there were plenty of pretty girls with nice bodies who would be happy to take their clothes off for money, but she wasn't one of them. She preferred leaving something to the imagination.

She told me, "Once they've seen you naked and in compromising poses, there's nothing left for them to fantasize about, and that, my dear, kills the intrigue." She knew what she was talking about. Her fans respected, as well as admired her looks and sex appeal, but she was always seen as a nice girl, something she felt helped her to be taken more seriously as an actress.

The nurses were finally done, and, by the time they left, they had Joi modestly gowned and propped up comfortably in bed. Dee made sure she was the one to start the IV, which could be very painful if not done correctly. While she was drawing blood, she asked Joi why she was back so soon to "visit." Joi told her everything that had happened, including her deep feelings of depression and the severe stabbing pains she had experienced earlier in the day.

When Dee was done, she took Joi's hand and assured her that her doctors were some of the best, especially Dr. Wilson, and that they would figure things out. I could see a peacefulness come over Joi's face. She needed to hear this. It gave her a feeling of confidence in her doctors, a very important factor since so many of her experiences in the past had been so negative. This time, though, she was beginning to feel that the people who held her life in their hands actually gave a damn about her. Dee's reassurance just added to her faith in them.

I was putting some of her things away in the closet when Dr. Wilson knocked on the door and came in the room. Dee was still sitting with us when he walked in, so she greeted him and asked if he needed anything or wanted her to stay during the exam. He said he would appreciate her assistance, so she stayed. This helped Joi feel more comfortable, like she had an advocate in the ring with her.

When the Doctor pulled the sheet back, I noticed that Joi's belly was double the size it had been earlier. It had swelled since we'd left the restaurant. Dr. Wilson asked if this had ever happened before, and she told him "never." He checked her belly and the lymph nodes under her arms and below her breasts. He then felt the nodes in her groin and palpated her belly once again. She was obviously tender.

"Joi," he said gently, "you have fluid in your stomach which is why you feel so sick. It can be very painful because of the pressure it's putting on the organs in your abdomen. We have to draw it out, so you don't have another episode of that terrible pain. I'll order a paracentesis, which is a cannula that can be inserted like a drain into your tummy. I'll be doing this right here in your room."

Dr. Wilson knew Joi would feel less fearful if she understood what would be done, so he carefully explained the procedure. "I'll freeze the area with a local anesthetic, so you won't feel any pain when I insert the drain. I'll also look at the results of your blood work to see what's happening in your system."

He tried to put her at ease by answering all her questions and reassuring her it wouldn't be painful.

Joi wanted it done as soon as possible, so there would be no chance for the pain to come back.

"When will you do it, Doctor?" she asked. "Could we please do it today?" she asked sweetly, just like a little girl.

He smiled and explained he would do it first thing in the morning, but for now he would put her on a stronger pain medicine, so, if she did have another episode like the last one, it wouldn't hurt like it did before. She asked what he was giving her, and he said it was morphine, and, if she had any pain at all, she was to call the Nurse, who would give her another shot.

After Dr. Wilson left the room, Joi seemed more at ease, but still needed a bit more reassurance, so she asked Dee if the paracentesis would hurt. Dee said she'd make certain she was given enough pain medication that she wouldn't feel a thing. She told her not to worry, and she'd be back right away with an injection to ease her discomfort and let her rest.

"Thank you so much," Joi replied weakly, as Dee left the room.

We were finally alone for a few moments.

"How are you doing, honey?" I asked as I stroked her arm.

"Oh, Rachel…please hold me, please!" she pleaded like a frightened child.

I'd been sitting on the edge of the bed, but I quickly leaned down next to her and, while holding her in my arms, I rocked her gently.

"Shh…I'm here, honey. Shh…it's okay, baby. I'll make sure no one hurts you. I promise." Joi had started to cry. "Don't be afraid, honey. Dee said she'd make sure you wouldn't hurt, right? You trust her, don't you?"

"Yes," Joi sniffled through her tears.

"Well, then?"

I could feel her starting to relax. Dee would be back soon, so I moved into a sitting position while still holding her hand. When Dee returned, I got out of the way, so she could give Joi the injection. Afterward, Dee told her she'd be feeling "pretty darn good" in a few minutes, and it would be a good idea to just let go and sleep if she could.

Joi's eyes started to get a little glassy, and I knew she'd be sleeping soon. Dee said she'd be back in a little while to check up on her, as she pulled the sheet and blanket up to a little below her chin. She then asked if I needed anything, and, feeling exhausted, I told her I'd love a cup of coffee, if possible. She smiled kindly and said, "No problem, Rachel. I'll bring you some in a bit. I just have to catch up on Joi's chart."

A few minutes later, Joi drifted off. I stood watching her sleep, and, when I felt my throat tighten and the tears begin, I wiped them away, took a deep breath, and walked out to the nurses' station. Dee saw me standing there and came over to talk with me.

"Are you all right, Rachel?"

Her kindness crumbled me.

"No, I'm not…" and I started crying.

She put her arms around me while I sobbed. And there she was, as sweet and comforting with me as I'd been just a little while ago with my girl. She soothed me with the same kind words, and, after I calmed down, she said exactly what Dr. Wilson had told me on the phone that afternoon.

"This isn't going to be easy, Rachel. You're going to have to be very strong for her."

I took a deep breath.

"Is this it?" I asked, terrified of what I might hear.

"Well… I don't think so," Dee said. "If the Doctor can change the chemotherapy, and she responds, there's a chance she'll be able to go home for awhile. The paracentesis will help with the pain in her belly. Fluid in the abdomen can cause a lot of pain. She's also quite weak and will probably need a transfusion, which will help her feel a lot better. The chemotherapy is making her very anemic, and that's why she's been so lethargic," she finished.

It felt like déjà vu. I'd heard these exact words twice before, here in the same hospital, but this time I was thrilled. We'd have more time together! That was all I'd been praying for. More time.

"Oh, thank God!" I said aloud. I thought to myself, afraid to say too much, *I can't lose her now… it's too soon! I can't bear to be without her…* and I began to weep again.

Dee put her hand on my shoulder. "I've got your coffee, Rachel, and I'm here if you need to talk. Let's go back to the room. You don't want Joi to wake up and not be able to find you."

She took my arm and, while carrying my coffee, walked me back to the room. Joi was still sleeping comfortably. Her face looked peaceful, angelic, and pain-free. I was so relieved for her. I sat on my cot, next to Joi's bed, as Dee handed me the large cup and left. I sipped the coffee and sighed. As I watched Joi sleeping, I hoped I was in her dreams. I knew she would always be in mine. Always.

As the afternoon passed, Joi continued to slumber, and I found myself dozing in my armchair until I heard the dinner carts rolling by. Stan had left after bringing us to the hospital, knowing that Joi would be busy with tests and seeing Dr. Wilson. He went home to pick up some things for her and a few things for me, such as the electric coffee pot and a can of coffee, so I'd have my caffeine. I had no idea how long we'd be here, so I asked him to bring me a few things to wear, too. Joi would want her face creams and her overnight bag with the toiletries she liked.

Wanting to freshen up for Joi before she woke up, I was in the bathroom splashing water on my face when I heard Stan come into the room. He'd returned with a couple of grocery bags filled to the brim with clothing, as well as Joi's pink overnight bag.

I could smell brandy on his breath, so I knew he'd needed a little "help" to deal with the situation. His face was somewhat red, and, at the time, I thought it was probably from the brandy. Now, thinking back, I wonder if it was from crying. He would never want anyone to know, though, as "strong and silent" was in his DNA. Little did he know how alone this made me feel, but then, I'm not sure it would have made any difference. Stan was who he was and doing the best he could with what he had to work with. I realize this now, but, at the time, not having his support was almost unbearable.

He handed me my clothes and the coffee supplies and put Joi's bag on the floor near my cot. He saw that Joi was sleeping, so he signaled me to come outside in the hall. We stayed close enough in case Joi awakened and started calling for me.

"What did the Doctor say?" he asked quietly.

I gained my composure and told him what was happening, that they were giving her morphine for the pain and would do a procedure to drain her belly in the morning. I explained to him what Dee had told me, and that she'd probably need a transfusion because of the anemia caused by the chemotherapy.

I tried to comfort him, recognizing that he just didn't know how to handle the situation.

"Hubby," I told him, "Joi is very tough, and she's not going to give up so easily. Let's go back to the room, so she doesn't wonder where we are if she wakes up."

We walked in just as Joi's eyes started to open. "Look who I found wandering around in the hallway!" I told her, feigning happiness. "The hubby is here to see you, and he brought your little makeup bag and your creams!" Joi was pleased to see him, and asked him for a hug.

He bent down and hugged her and told her she looked lovely. "The hospital gown has got to go, though, so I'll give Rachel some money to buy you something pretty to wear from the gift shop." He handed me a $100 bill, and asked me to find a nice robe for her. "Use the rest of the money to buy some food from the cafeteria if you want to get something to eat."

One of the things Joi and I were both grateful for with Hubby was how generous he could be. That day, I think it was a comfortable way for him to handle his feelings.

While they were talking, I set up my coffee pot. Stan was sitting in a chair on the other side of Joi's bed, and telling her how Mr. Pooper was doing. Her face broke into a wide smile, just listening about her little boy bird. She seemed happy to be chatting, so I told her I'd be right back, that I was going to the gift shop.

"Come back soon," she smiled and waved a little as I walked out the door.

As I approached the nurses' station, I saw that Dee was still there, writing on someone's chart.

"Dee," I whispered.

She heard me and turned around, got up and walked over. I told her I was going downstairs, and that Joi and Stan were chatting.

"Have they gotten any results back from the lab?" I asked.

Dee picked up her chart. "Well, her blood count is very low, and she'll definitely need a transfusion. They'll be bringing up a few units from the lab, so if you want to be here while they do it, you should come back sooner rather than later. I don't see any other results, but I'll let you know as soon as I hear anything."

Thanking her, I headed downstairs. I wasn't surprised about the transfusion. Joi had the same pallor she'd had the last time she'd been brought to the hospital, and I knew it would help her feel better, at least for a while.

I rode down to the gift shop, which was on the first floor of the hospital. The selection was hardly Neiman Marcus. There were only five robes hanging near matching fluffy slippers and nightgowns. I sorted through the rack and finally decided on a tri-color pink one, with dusty rose and two lighter shades striped down the front. It zipped from the neck to the bottom, so it would be easy to get on and off, if needed. This would be perfect for her, since the fabric was very soft and light, and I knew she'd like the pink tones because it looked great with her skin and was one of her favorite colors. I bought it with the money Stan had given me, and had plenty of change to get Joi something special to eat if she wanted it later. At that point, I was getting a little peckish, but my stomach still wasn't up to a real meal.

After taking the elevator to the third floor, I walked briskly back to the room, hoping they hadn't started the transfusion. The door was open, and I walked in just as a lab tech was hanging the first unit of blood. I took the robe out of the bag and held it out, turning it like a model against my body.

"Ohhh, I love it, Rachel!" she cooed. "Let me put it on before they do anything to me."

The Lab Tech excused himself and left the room while she changed.

I didn't see Stan outside as I came in, so I asked Joi where he was. (I had a hunch he'd left when he saw the blood coming into the room.)

"Hubby went for a walk, and he'll be back in about an hour. I think he went to the restaurant to get something to eat and to smoke his cigar."

She had insisted on getting out of bed to put on her new robe, but she swayed a little as I was draping it over her shoulders and zipping it up. I took her arm to stabilize her and sat her on the edge of the bed.

"You look absolutely beautiful," I whispered, as she straightened the pink collar. I lifted her legs and put them up on the bed, covering them with the sheet and blanket. "Is the Birdie comfy in her pretty new robe?" I asked, smiling.

She said she loved the color, and especially the way it zipped. "I love it, Rachel, but come here before they come back." I moved closer. She was still sitting up, and, as I bent toward her, she put her arms around my neck, kissed me softly, and whispered, "I love you. Please stay here with me."

I stroked her hair and promised again that I wouldn't leave her. I remember the sweet way she smelled as I nuzzled her neck, but the moment was broken when we heard someone coming down the hall toward the door of her room. I gently but quickly lowered her back onto the bed.

"Are you ready for your lunch?" Dee asked teasingly as she bustled into the room. "Your liquid lunch, that is." Joi smiled, knowing exactly what was on the menu. "You'll feel a lot better once you get some new blood in your body. Remember last time... how good you felt? You're very anemic from the medications you've been taking, and this will make you feel a million percent better."

The Lab Tech came in, and Dee read the information on the bag to make sure the blood was the right kind and everything was correct. Then, she began the transfusion into her IV. She told Joi it would take a while, and that she should just relax and watch TV.

I knew the drill by then and, taking one of the bottles of skin cream, I positioned myself at the foot of her bed to massage her feet. I knew this would relax her. It was one of our favorite things to do on a gray day in front of the fireplace at the Marina condo.

Joi lay calmly in her pretty new robe and quietly closed her eyes as I rubbed her feet. The TV droned in the background, and the muffled sounds of the busy hallway almost made me sleepy, too. Slowly, without my even realizing it, an hour had passed. I glanced up at Joi as I reached for some more cream and was delighted to see a big smile. She slowly sat up, like nothing had ever been wrong, obviously feeling much better.

"Well," I said with a smile, "looks like the Birdie is back!"

We both laughed, and she said (and why wasn't I surprised?), "I'm hungry. When can I eat?"

Even her voice was stronger, and I could see that her eyes again had that unmistakable sparkle of life in them. Happily, I got up and wiped my hands on a towel. About that time, Dee came back. "Ready for some real food, Joi?"

"How did you know?" Joi laughed. Dee smiled and removed the empty bag. She said she'd order dinner for both of us. I thanked her, and she left, leaving us alone again.

Joi took my hand that was resting on the side rails of the bed. She gently pulled me toward her, and I leaned down, thinking she had something to tell me. She lifted her head and kissed me…really kissed me. I let it happen, forgetting temporarily how hidden our relationship had to be. Feeling her love at that moment and seeing her smile was like a spring rain sprinkling down on the part of me that was withering under a scorching sun.

As our kiss ended, I looked into her eyes. They were moist but smiling, and her face was soft and pink. Could she look this lovely and feel so much if she wasn't going to get better? Of course not! I was suddenly filled with hope. My girl was going to beat this ugly thing, after all. I just knew it!

Chapter 43

Long Day's Journey…

I noticed that Stan had returned from his walk when I heard his voice in the hallway. Joi didn't realize he was back yet, and, because I wanted to talk to him alone, I told her I was going to the visitors' lounge for a cup of coffee, so I could drink it with my dinner. She nodded and teased, "Just don't get lost."

I smiled and left the room.

Stan and Dee were deep in conversation when I joined them. We were all relieved to know the transfusion had helped Joi come back to normal. Dee was explaining to Stan that the chemotherapy, like last time, had made her dangerously anemic, and she had desperately needed blood to keep from getting worse.

When Stan asked if Joi could go home now, Dee answered softly, "Let's see how the procedure goes tomorrow, and then we'll know a little bit more about the big picture." She glanced at her watch and said she'd get Joi's tray from the kitchen, but it might take twenty minutes to a half hour for the special order.

"Don't worry about that," Stan said. "I'll get her something she'll really enjoy from the restaurant." Then, as he headed for the elevator, he called to me, "Hey, Rach, do you want something? I'll pick you up a BLT…okay?"

I gave him a thumbs up as he went on his way.

After thanking Dee for being so understanding and helpful, I went back to Joi's room where I found her sitting on the side of the bed. She looked like the cat who ate the canary, with a big grin on her beautiful face.

"The Birdie's feeling a lot better, and she wants to go home!" she said happily.

As I took her arm to steady her and lifted her legs back onto the bed, I told her that she could go home soon, but she had to stay long enough to have the procedure in the morning.

"Besides, Stan's going to get us something to eat, so we'll both feel like tigers."

"Tiger" was one of her nicknames, just like the Birdie. She only used it to refer to herself when she was feeling especially good and full of energy, probably because of all the years she'd spent as a spokeswoman for Tiger's Milk. Pouting a little, but understanding, she said, "Okay," and settled into her pillows to wait for Stan and his gift of her favorite foods.

Hearing her say how good she felt was wonderful, and this was the first time I thought she might actually be able to leave the hospital. I'd been so afraid that all hope was gone, and that she'd miss her forty-third birthday party. April sixth was only a few weeks away, and we had plans to go to San Diego to celebrate at Sea World. Stan had already purchased tickets for us. Neither of us had ever been there, and Joi and I were both fascinated with dolphins. I also wanted to see some of Timothy's penguin cousins because I'd heard they had a wonderful penguin display. We both looked forward to this outing, and now I was optimistic that it could still be a possibility.

Joi couldn't believe how much better she felt and mentioned how extremely anemic she'd been, which apparently she'd been told by Dee or one of the other nurses.

"I was a quart low, and didn't know it," she said with a laugh.

"Well, two quarts, actually," Dee said as she walked in the room with the second unit of blood. She smiled, "You look like you're ready to fly out of bed, Joi, but you still need the other half of your lunch."

"I promise I'll be good and finish all of it," Joi said with a grin. Dee hung the bag and left.

As the minutes passed, every drop of blood seemed to be giving Joi back to me. Her face began to glow with her usual rosy peach coloring. The TV droned on in the background as Joi closed her eyes and dozed, while I sat comfortably next to her watching her sleep.

About a half hour later, Stan came back with two to-go boxes filled to the brim with food. As he put the boxes on the coffee table to the right of Joi's bed, he avoided looking at the IV pole. She was still dozing and hadn't heard him come in. I saw he had brought her favorite sandwich, rare roast beef on sourdough bread with a little bleu cheese dressing, and sliced onions on the side. The sandwich was cut in quarters, so it would be easier for her to eat, even though it was stacked so high she'd have trouble even biting into it!

Just about then, Joi opened her eyes and was delighted to see Stan and her sandwich! It was exactly the way she liked it, and they even put a "new" pickle on the side.

I was pleased and rather surprised at Stan who, instead of bolting out of the room at the first possibility, managed to turn his chair so the intravenous bag of blood was out of his line of vision. He asked Joi if she liked what he'd brought her, and she replied, "Ohhh, yes! The Tiger will sleep well tonight!" and continued munching.

Stan smiled just as I had when he heard that word. It made us both feel hopeful that somehow Joi would keep fighting the good fight and beat this ugly thing.

A while later, Stan stood and said he had to go home to take care of Poose and make some business calls. As he leaned over to give Joi a kiss on the cheek, he assured her he'd see her in the morning. Joi said to be careful and get some rest, and I told him to enjoy his cigar! He laughed as he left the room.

The food was great, and I ate every morsel of my sandwich, too. Joi was feeling even better than before, and seemed anxious to get out of bed. Her second bag was down to the last drops, and she was now getting just fluids to keep her hydrated. I said I'd check with Dee to see if it was okay for her to walk down the hallway.

"Why don't I just push the button, so someone will come?" Joi said confidently.

"Well, go ahead then," I said in agreement.

Joi pushed the buzzer, and we didn't have long to wait before Dee practically ran into the room, obviously very concerned that something was happening to Joi.

"Are you okay?" Dee asked, her mouth tense and ready for anything.

Sorry that we'd startled her, Joi apologized and explained she just wanted to go for a little stroll down the hall. Dee sighed with relief, and said she'd first have to take her vitals before letting her get out of bed.

After checking her heart and blood pressure, and obviously pleased, Dee said everything was excellent.

"You can go for a little walk, but take it slow and easy. You're doing a lot better, but you still have to be careful, Joi. Let Rachel and me help you walk for a few minutes, and, if I see that you're doing well, I'll leave you two alone."

She lifted the bag from the stand, and Joi almost scrambled out of bed! I caught her in my arms, and Dee cautioned her again as she headed out the door with the empty bag.

As we began our walk, Joi started to pick up speed.

"Whoa, little lady," I said in my best John Wayne impression. "You'd better slow down or yer gonna git yerself in trouble."

She started to laugh…not because my impression was so good, but because it was so bad! She laughed so much that she actually began to slow down, just as I hoped she would. She loved my poor attempt at impressions, and they always gave her a good chuckle.

Dee had stopped for something at the nurses' station, and, when she saw we were doing fine, she waved to let me know we were on our own.

We were side by side, my arm around Joi's waist to steady her gait, as we walked slowly through the halls. Joi smiled and said hello to everyone we passed. Some recognized her, but most didn't. But even in her condition, her sweetness brought a little sunshine into a very sad part of the hospital.

The third floor was a place of desolation and despair. Most of the patients were desperately ill, and many were terminal. I had been here a couple of other times with Joi, and saw very few visitors coming to see the patients. I guess when things seem hopeless, some people, even family members, hide from their own mortality.

That evening, Joi was so happy to be feeling good that she didn't want to stop walking. I knew she shouldn't do too much, though, so I told her we had to get back to the room to rest.

"Tomorrow's a big day, and hopefully we'll find out when we can go home again."

She said she was feeling so well that she didn't want it to end. I assured her it wasn't going to end, that she'd feel the same when she woke up in the morning. Of course, I had no idea if this would be so, but I hoped I was telling her (and me) the truth, and I knew she needed to hear something positive.

We turned a corner, and there was her room right ahead.

"Ahhh, kismet!" I laughed.

The coincidence gods were on my side. She finally agreed to go back to the room and watch TV for awhile before we went to sleep for the night. Neither of us were hungry because of Stan's sandwiches, so, once we got to the room, I settled her in and turned on the TV.

Dee's shift had almost finished, and it was time for Mary (Big Red) to come on for the night shift. Dee came in before she went in to "report"... the changing of the nurses where they discuss each patient, and what happened on their shift. It was also time for Joi to have another injection of morphine, which they were giving her every four to six hours. Though the transfusion had increased her energy and lifted her spirits, the fluid in her belly was still causing some pain, so Joi was glad to see Dee come in to give her the shot. Dee was the best "shot-giver," according to Joi, since it hurt less when she did it. When she was finished, Dee warmly wished us a good night and said she'd see us the next day. As she left the room, she looked back at me and smiled softly.

Although Joi wouldn't admit it, the walk had done her in, and the morphine was beginning to make her sleepy, so it was no surprise when she suggested we take a nap. Of course, I agreed, and stood up to fluff her pillows. Since we were in the habit of taking naps at home, we both lay down for a little snooze, leaving the TV volume on low because it helped her sleep. I wished I could hold her, but for now it would have to be enough being at her side on my little hospital cot. As we drifted off to sleep, I remember feeling peaceful for the first time in what seemed like days, even though it had only been hours. For a little while, it felt just like home.

I didn't know how much time had passed, but I woke up suddenly when Joi sat up in bed and practically shouted, "Johnny!"

Heart pounding, I shot up from my cot, afraid something had happened to her. But then I saw she was looking at the TV, and I realized it was just Johnny Carson's show that had her so enthusiastic!

Laughing, she apologized when she realized she'd about given me a coronary, but explained she'd heard his voice and suddenly woke up to his show. I sighed. It was after eleven o'clock and "just like home," where we watched *The Tonight Show* faithfully every night.

Joi was a favorite of Johnny's, and she'd been on his show quite a few times in her career. Though Johnny was known in the biz as quite a ladies' man, Joi said she really liked him, and he'd always been a gentleman to her.

Buddy Hackett was on that night, too, and she told me about the fun times they'd shared in Las Vegas and Puerto Rico. Joi appeared in her nightclub act at the same time Eddie Fisher, Judy Garland, and Buddy Hackett were in town doing their shows. Joi said they all knew each other, and it was great fun going from show to show to cheer one another on.

Joi's closest friend was Marjorie Meade and, in fact, she and Stan had their marriage ceremony at Marjorie and Fred Meade's home in Beverly Hills. When Joi and I first met in 1969, she and Marjorie were still best friends, but, in general, women were too jealous of Joi to become close, and men wanted to be close, but to be anything BUT friends!

It didn't seem to bother her, though. To Joi, her career was everything. In the 1950s and 1960s, because of her flair for comedy, Joi became popular on some of the top sitcoms of the day, including *The Adventures of Ozzie & Harriet*, *The Bob Cummings Show*, *I Love Lucy*, *The Beverly Hillbillies*, *December Bride*, *The Gale Storm Show*, and *The People's Choice*. She was also Superman's wife in *The Adventures of Superman*.

Joi also became a favorite guest (as herself) on not only Johnny Carson's show, but also the Jack Paar, Joey Bishop, and Merv Griffin shows. This brought her to the attention of a new public and created even more fans for the beautiful blonde with the perfect comic touch. She also began to be better known and admired by her fellow show business peers, and, behind the scenes, unlike the women who were jealous of her beauty, some very well-known actresses of the day found the idea of being "close" to Joi Lansing more than a little interesting.

In the 1950s, she knew Marilyn Monroe and told me she found her "sweet, but a little sad." She said the friendship ended when Marilyn asked Joi to go to Palm Springs with her for some "personal time." Joi said she'd had similar offers from women more than a few times in her career, but since she didn't "bend" that way, she'd never "tumbled." She told me she'd had no interest and didn't want complications in her life that meant nothing.

It had been a long and difficult day, and we were both very tired, but we realized we were finally alone in her hospital room. Joi was energized by the transfusion, and the morphine had blotted out the pain from her swollen belly. She felt like talking, and she playfully shared her "almost intimate adventures" with several of the most sought-after movie beauties of the day.

I had to marvel at that. What amazing women Joi had known through the years, and what fun it was for me to hear of their attraction to her! I think, in those days, the female stars were so sick of having to deal with the games of the powerful men in the industry that they took a kind of refuge—and pleasure— in the arms and passions of other women. I know I did, and I wasn't anyone compared to the women who no longer had stars in their eyes but were now successful actresses.

We both giggled like little girls at the fun of it, and then finally settled back, her hand in mine, while I snuggled up to her as best I could from the chair next to her bed. I looked over at her, thinking how beautiful she still was, even as sick as I knew her to be. She must have felt my gaze because she slowly turned her head and looked directly into my eyes. Tenderly, she put her hand on my cheek and said softly, "Rachel…you're the only woman I've ever loved. I want you to know that from the bottom of my heart."

Completely thrown by the intensity of her words and expression, I couldn't believe how fast my heart was suddenly pounding. I swallowed and, in spite of my dry mouth, responded that she'd never let me doubt it.

Then, I added lightly, mostly to keep myself from crying, "And you sure know how to make a girl feel special, letting me know you preferred me to Marilyn Monroe!" I exhaled as we both laughed. The moment was broken but, for me, one that would never be forgotten.

Johnny's show was finally over, and Joi was still feeling the morphine she'd been given earlier. She was drowsy and said she thought she'd better go to sleep. I agreed.

I got up and went over to the door and looked down at the nurses' station. There were only two nurses at the desk that night—one was Big Red. They were busy, so I figured the odds of them not coming in to check on Joi were pretty good. Feeling that our secret would be safe, I climbed onto the outer sheets and light blanket and lay down next to her. This always made her happy, and she snuggled her head against my chest as she began to drift off.

Holding her that way, I stroked her hair gently until she fell asleep. I kept thinking about what she'd said, and I swallowed as I felt the tension of tears in my throat.

At that moment, my joy and sorrow were tangled up in a way I had never known. Being loved by the one woman in my life to whom I had given my whole heart—while knowing that, unless we were granted a miracle, I was going to have to let her go—was just too much for me to hold inside.

With Joi in my arms, I could feel her, I could hear her breathing, and I could smell her sweet scent. Yet, that night, my tears fell silently, and I had never felt more alone in my life.

Chapter 44

Grasping at Straws

As the night passed, I could hear that Joi was still sleeping deeply. I'd stopped crying hours ago, but the ache just wouldn't pass, and I knew I had to get it together, so I decided to get up. I slid my arm from under her, being sure her head was comfortable on the pillow. Then, I slipped onto my cot.

I lay there for a long while, unable to sleep, and then I heard someone walk into the room. I hoped it was Mary, and I whispered, "Is that you, Red?"

In the soft glow of her flashlight, she saw I was awake and whispered back, "Let's go!" I got up and checked Joi, who was still out, so I knew I could slip away for a while. Frankly, I needed to get away from my emotions and hoped that Red would make me laugh, one of her many talents.

We left the room quietly and, as we walked over to the nurses' station, she looked at me and smiled gently, "How ya' doing, kid? Never mind. You don't need to tell me…I saw Joi's chart." She saw that my eyes were red and asked if I'd like a cup of coffee.

"You know me, Mary. I'd never turn one down. Thanks for asking."

Mary and a few other nurses were on a short break in a little room in back of the nurses' station. She brought my coffee, and we sat down. After a minute, knowing she'd be honest with me, I asked if she thought Joi would be going home. She paused, then replied, "If things go well in the morning, and they can drain most of that fluid from her belly, and if the Doctor can come up with a different mix of drugs to keep the cancer from spreading into her vital organs, she should be okay for a while."

I thanked her for being straight with me. At least, now I had a little hope.

As we sat and drank the coffee Red had made, one of the other nurses asked her to repeat a joke she'd told earlier. She wanted to tell it to her husband

and couldn't recall the punch line, so Red began to tell her jokes. A couple of other nurses were still there and joined in our laughter. Each joke seemed funnier than the last, or maybe I just needed a release. I needed to laugh, and Mary knew it, too. By the time we were done with our visit, she had helped me so much that I thought I could go back and try to get some sleep, which a while ago was impossible.

I'd been gone for over half an hour, and I knew I'd better get back to the room. I thanked Red, and she gave me a hug, saying to call her if Joi needed anything. I tiptoed back into the room, so Joi wouldn't wake up and walked up to the side of her bed to see how she was doing. She was still sleeping soundly, beautiful as always.

I freshened up and splashed some cool water on my face. I felt stronger now. Not happy, but stronger. I got back onto my cot, hoping to sleep, so I wouldn't fall apart if Joi needed me. Closing my eyes, I started thinking about San Diego and how much fun we'd have on her birthday. Finally, I fell asleep and didn't wake up until I heard a nurse from the morning shift come in to take Joi's vitals.

Instantly alert, I opened my eyes and was suddenly looking up into the face of an angel. Joi was peeking over the edge of the bed.

"Good morning, sunshine! Did you sleep well, honey?" Joi asked with her lovely smile.

"Well, I'm fine, but how did you sleep? How are you feeling today?" I asked, as I sat up and straightened my jammies. Joi said she felt great and had slept well all night. She wanted to eat, but remembered she couldn't have solid food until after the procedure, only a little something to drink.

Stan had gone home after we had our sandwiches the night before, but he'd left the percolator, so I made us a pot of coffee. We each had a cup or two and sat around watching *Good Morning America*, waiting for Dr. Wilson to come in to start the paracentesis. It was eight o'clock sharp when he walked through the door.

"Good morning," he said warmly. "I hear you're doing well, Joi, and I'm very happy with that good news." He continued, "This procedure might take a few hours, but it's necessary to get rid of what's causing the pain."

Joi acknowledged what he said and agreed.

"Then, can I go home, Doctor?" she asked hopefully.

"Well, if the new drugs I'll give you later today work the way I hope, you can go home tomorrow," he said reassuringly.

A nurse I didn't recognize stepped into the room to join him. She smiled at both Joi and me. She obviously worked with the Doctor because she knew just what to hand him. As she wiped Joi's belly with gauze, then sprayed a pinkish fluid on it, Dr. Wilson said, "It's just an antiseptic, Joi." The Nurse then handed him a small needle. "This won't hurt," he said, "but I want to numb your stomach skin, okay?"

Joi answered, "Yes, anything to stop the pain."

"It's going to be okay, Joi, I promise," I said, taking her hand and smiling a smile I didn't feel.

I hoped she wouldn't know I was as frightened as she was. As soon as Dr. Wilson had finished numbing her, he suggested we both look away. Joi turned her head toward me and closed her eyes. I could see how scared she was and continued holding her hand and petting her arm.

I was queasy just thinking about the procedure and squeezed her hand just a little tighter, not wanting her to be any more nervous than she already was. I hoped she hadn't seen the size of the cannula lying on the tray, which was, at least, a foot long and the diameter of a large straw. I couldn't think about what he was going to do with that thing, and prayed that it wouldn't hurt her, as he promised.

In a few minutes, he said the cannula was in place and asked Joi if it had hurt. She gave him a big smile and answered, "Not a bit!"

I sighed with relief as they covered her stomach, and I saw the fluid already start to drain into the sack above her bed. They had thoughtfully placed the stand behind Joi, so she wouldn't see it.

At that point, Dr. Wilson said, "You're doing fine, Joi. I'll see you in a little while."

As he got up to leave, he smiled at me and nodded. The bag was slowly filling, and I kept telling her it was going great, that the sooner it was done, the sooner she could have breakfast, and, more importantly, the sooner she could go home.

To pass the time, I turned on the TV and found a soap that we both loved but hadn't seen in a while. It kept her distracted. Apparently, she didn't hurt because she got quite caught up in the silly story, asking me every few minutes a question about the plot or characters.

The same Nurse came back again to cover the first bag and connect a second one. She assured us the Doctor would be back soon, and, not long after that, Dr. Wilson returned with the Nurse close behind him. He lifted the sheet a little (not so much that either of us could see anything) and commented that Joi's abdomen was considerably smaller than it was before.

Dr. Wilson told us to look away again while he removed the cannula. Joi looked at me, and my eyes were fixed on hers, so I wouldn't accidentally see what was going on a few feet away from my face.

"It's out, Joi," Dr. Wilson said. "You can look now."

We both sighed with relief. "See? I told you it would be okay!" She gave me a cautious smile.

Although the procedure seemed to go on forever, it actually took only two hours from start to finish. The Nurse efficiently removed the tray and the second bag... again all under a towel, so Joi wouldn't see anything to upset her.

Dr. Wilson said he'd ordered a blood test to see how her count was, and, after that, she could eat as much as she wanted. He promised to come back as soon as the test results came in. Shortly afterward, the tech came into the room and, as had been done a dozen times since she'd arrived, he quickly drew the necessary amount.

Joi watched and said, "Well, it looks just fine to me!"

The tech grinned and thanked her and headed into the hallway with a blush on his young cheeks. I think he recognized her. As sick as she was, there was no mistaking she was a beauty.

Back to the TV and more coffee. Now we had to wait until the Nurse told Joi the results were in, so she could eat. Curious, I asked her if it had hurt, and she said she didn't feel a thing. All she felt was a little pressure, and, though she wasn't anxious to do it again any time soon, at least, it wasn't painful like she'd been anticipating. She again made it clear that all she cared about at that moment was getting some food in her stomach!

Her angels must have been listening because, a few minutes later, we were pleasantly surprised when her tray was carried in by a perky little candy-striper. She cheerfully placed it in front of Joi and removed the metal lid from the plate with a flourish. Joi was delighted when she saw it was French toast and eggs, cooked exactly the way she liked them. She thanked the friendly young woman who smiled and left as Joi began to eat.

"Mmmmmm…good grief, am I hungry!" she said between mouthfuls.

I was eating an extra English muffin that had been on her tray, which I hadn't ordered but was thoroughly enjoying. I asked if she thought she'd want more to eat after she finished what was on her plate. "I don't know, but ask me again when I'm done," she said with a grin.

A few minutes later, after practically inhaling her breakfast, Joi sat back and impishly announced that she could not wait for lunch! We both laughed.

Satisfied for the moment, she said she was very happy to be rid of the fluid in her belly, and felt so much better without all that pressure.

"That's what was giving me all the pain," she said, not remembering that the Doctor had already told me. "Who knew that a little liquid could hurt so much? I hope Dr. Wilson will let us go home tomorrow at the latest."

I asked if she was hurting, and she said the only pain she was still having were hunger pangs, but she'd get over it after I brought her something good from Sambo's. I joked about it, but was actually a little concerned as to what her almost voracious appetite was all about. I said we should really discuss this issue with the Doctor since she wasn't quite ready to start modeling for "chubby lovers" at this point in her life.

As an orderly dropped by to take Joi's breakfast tray, Dr. Wilson came back in the room with a tray filled with vials and syringes which, he explained, were the chemotherapy drugs he wanted to try on her. He told us what was in each vial and said he'd done further research since he'd heard from us in San Clemente.

"There's been a lot of success with the combination of these three drugs, Joi, and I'm hopeful they'll help you, too. I want to make sure you have no allergic reaction to them, so I'd really like you to spend one more night here."

Joi said she understood and appreciated his concern.

He needed to use the IV port since her veins had become so fragile. Then, very slowly and carefully, he injected the chemicals that might save her life… at least for a while. As Joi and I watched, he explained that these particular medications needed to go in at a snail's pace, so she wouldn't have an adverse reaction to them. Joi nodded and then lay back onto her pillows, eyes half closed. Even then, as frail as she was, she was beautiful.

As time passed, Joi didn't appear to have any reaction to the new medications and seemed to tolerate everything very well.

"How are you feeling, Joi?" Dr. Wilson asked.

She responded that she was feeling fine, but was really, really hungry. Then she added, "Dr. Wilson, I can't seem to stop eating, and it all started with the transfusion! It happened the last time I was here, too. Remember, Rachel?"

I nodded.

He explained, "Joi, your increased appetite is from having healthy blood in your body. It's what's giving you an intense desire for food. Everything will level off, though, as your body catches up. Right now, it needs nourishment to give it the strength to fight, so don't worry too much about gaining weight. I sincerely doubt that will happen, and, if it does, we'll talk about it later."

He smiled as he told her to continue eating like "a heifer grazing in a meadow." We both laughed, and he continued with the chemo infusion.

The minute he stopped talking, Joi looked at me with a twinkle in her eye. "Rachel, would you please go to Sambo's and pick me up a rare roast beef sandwich? You know the way I like it!"

I told her I'd wait until she was finished with her chemotherapy, and then I'd head over to the restaurant.

Dr. Wilson looked up. "Rachel, I'll be staying here with Joi until you return, so don't worry. She's doing just fine, and, if there's any kind of problem, I'll be here."

I stood up and looked at Joi to see what she wanted me to do. She nodded, and I knew she didn't mind.

"You will get something for yourself, right?"

I told her I'd order two of the same sandwiches, and I'd go if she was sure it was okay. She promised she'd be fine, but to come back as soon as I could. Since Joi didn't seem to be in any distress or pain, I was comfortable leaving for a bit, secure in the knowledge that the Doctor was there in case of a problem.

It only took a few minutes to get to the restaurant, and, as I walked in, they knew what I wanted. Times two, this time. They recognized me by now and asked how my sister was doing. I told them she was doing well, and that either Stan or I would be back again later for the second round.

I hurried back to our room and was relieved to see Dr. Wilson still seated next to Joi, checking her heart with his stethoscope. He said he was very pleased with her response. I knew this round was much stronger than the last chemotherapy she'd taken, and that there weren't many more options, if any, to fight this hideous disease. All we could do was hope that these would work. I knew there were no guarantees, but I couldn't give up.

Thinking back, I realize I didn't actually have much faith in anything at that point. I could only hope she'd be able to celebrate her forty-third birthday at Sea World in San Diego, where she could see the dolphins and penguins, creatures we both loved. It was something she really wanted to do, and I wanted her to enjoy every single moment she could while on this Earth.

Dr. Wilson stood and seemed quite pleased she was tolerating the medications. He explained that most people initially have some sort of adverse reaction, but she was doing amazingly well.

"As I've said, I'll feel much better knowing you're here in the hospital just in case there is some sort of problem, although I honestly don't believe anything will go wrong." Joi told him that she understood and, again, thanked him for his concern. He continued, "If everything is good when I see you, I'll let you go home tomorrow afternoon."

Joi and I both thanked him as he closed the door behind him.

I took her hand. "Honey, I'll call Stan and tell him the show's been held over for another night, and hopefully he'll bring Chinese food if you'd like."

She told me she'd love some moo goo gai pan and, of course, some pork fried rice and whatever else he'd like to bring.

When I called Stan, he promised to pick up enough food for an army, and would see us after work. He wanted to go home first to check on Mr. Pooper and take a quick shower.

I was on the phone no more than two to three minutes, and, when I walked back to my chair to have my lunch, I noticed that Joi had already eaten her complete sandwich! Oh, well.

"Would you like half of mine, honey?" I asked her. "I'm not that hungry, and want to save room for my pork fried rice, anyway," I lied. "Please take half…okay?"

Joi looked at me and then looked at the sandwich.

"Well, if you insist!" she said.

"Oh, I insist!" I answered, and we both laughed.

After lunch, Joi decided to call her mother to tell her she was in the hospital and ask her to visit when she returned home. Virginia was aware that Joi was ill, but I don't think she knew how seriously. I never told her, and I know Stan didn't. They had a mutual disrespect for each other, and were only pleasantly civil when in the same room. I wasn't around at the beginning of their "relationship," but I knew there was some serious bad blood between the two of them.

Virginia always had a slight scowl on her face, which I noticed the first time I met her at our apartment. She never smiled, and, though she was passably pleasant to me, she would not look me in the eye. Her eyes were usually downcast, and I couldn't tell whether she was angry or just depressed. Something was wrong, but I never knew what. At first, I thought she might be suspicious about us, but Joi said she'd always been that way, and she didn't know why.

Joi was the polar opposite of her mother…sweet and kind and with a smile on her face, no matter how troubled she was. I never heard her say anything purposely unkind about anyone. She didn't even talk badly about the people who had used or injured her. When she spoke of them, it was only with sadness that they would knowingly hurt her. How Joi managed to be so different from her mother was amazing to me. Her mother was darkness, while Joi was light, somehow able to transcend her upbringing and let her inner beauty shine through.

I know that her grandfather, Ray, had a tremendous influence on her life and character. Maybe he was why she was so different from Virginia, since she always said he was responsible for raising her during her formative years. She loved her "Grampy" very much.

On that day, however, as unpleasant and selfish as her mother had been, Joi called and made the effort to reach out to her. She told her mother she'd probably be going home the following day and would love to see her.

Virginia wanted to know how Joi was doing, and offered to have the Christian Science practitioners pray for her. She explained they were people whose job it was to pray for individuals who were ill. Joi agreed, even though she wasn't religiously inclined, but thought it couldn't hurt to have people put in a good word for her.

Actually, Joi had no religious affiliation, contrary to all the studio publicity around that issue. She was born in Salt Lake City and into a Mormon family, but her mother drifted away from the LDS Church soon after she was born, and eventually gravitated to Christian Science.

Though Joi didn't personally belong to any church, she was spiritual in nature. She practiced what everyone else preached, and adhered to the most important tenet of religion—"to treat everyone as you would like to be treated."

Her mother said she would make arrangements for the practitioners to pray for her, and then asked if Joi's insurance would cover the cost! Joi was stunned. She was not quite ready to hear that her mother was worried about reimbursement for prayers said for her own child, yet she stopped herself from saying anything she'd regret. She told Virginia she'd check with Stan to see whether it was covered under their policy with Connecticut General. (Interestingly enough, we found out later that it *was*, in fact, covered by her policy.)

Stan had once remarked that as long as he'd had the misfortune of knowing Virginia, she'd never done anything for Joi that cost her a nickel. He said he couldn't believe how cold and insensitive she'd always been to her daughter.

I didn't say anything negative to Joi about Virginia, nor did I share the remarks that Stan had made. I knew it was important for her to have this connection with her mother, no matter how unkind she was.

Joi was close to her brother, Larry, who was eleven years her junior. (His birthday was on the exact same day as mine, only seven years earlier. Larry came into the world December 20, 1940, and I arrived on the same day in 1947.) Joi spoke with him quite often, and he came to visit us regularly.

Knowing it was my moral obligation to give him all the facts, no matter how difficult it would be, I had told Larry about how serious Joi's condition really was. She loved him very much, and he loved his big sister, too. After I told him, he did his best to keep an upbeat attitude whenever he came to visit, never slipping into melodrama or morbid conversation. He obviously agreed with the way Stan and I kept the promise of hope alive in Joi's mind. We all felt that destroying any possibility of her potential survival would only make her last days insufferable.

I don't know exactly how much of the truth Larry told his mother, but he was always respectful of our wishes. I guess family is family and, when the chips are down, it becomes more important. At least, it did for Joi. I only wish her mother had been as fine a woman as Joi was. Unfortunately, Joi would never receive from Virginia the kind of love that she readily gave to her mother. Then again, I thought of Joi as an angel, and sadly, without a miracle, in time it would be all too true.

Chapter 45

Home Is Where the Heart Is…

After lunch, Joi seemed to be feeling pretty good. They'd been taking blood samples every few hours after Dr. Wilson left, apparently just to make sure she was maintaining a normal hemoglobin level. There was some concern she could be bleeding internally.

Dee was back on shift, and it was great to see her smiling face as she walked into the room.

"How are you two doing?" she asked.

Joi smiled back at her, and said we were doing just fine.

"It seems as though we'll be able to get out of here tomorrow!" Joi told her happily. "If everything goes as planned, we'll be leaving after Dr. Wilson comes in on his morning rounds."

Dee seemed very pleased to hear this and asked how Joi's appetite had been. I said we were expecting Stan in a little while, and he'd be schlepping half of Chinatown with him.

"Her appetite is amazing," I told her, "and seems to be insatiable!"

Joi grinned.

We asked Dee what she knew about the test results on the blood. Dee had looked at Joi's chart and seen all the lab reports that had come in during the last twenty-four hours, but said she couldn't really discuss them with us before the Doctor read and interpreted them. However, she did hint that things were going as scheduled, and, except for some unforeseen change in her blood work, Joi would be able to leave tomorrow morning.

I trusted Dee, and so did Joi, and it was reassuring to have her on the team. Dee was about ready to leave when a lab tech came in. It was time for another blood draw, so Dee stayed while he filled a few vials.

Drawing blood from her IV did not hurt her at all, but the pain injections she received every four hours were a double-edged sword. It tore me apart any time she was in pain, but that hurt from the injections was good, in a way, because we knew she'd be feeling a lot better a few minutes later. The nurses would alternate injection sites so that she wouldn't bruise and to prevent her skin from breaking down and forming sores.

For years, I'd given her B12 shots every month, which Ted, the pharmacist, had provided. He also showed me how to inject her properly. Her doctors knew what I was doing, and had no problem with her receiving the B12. It's usually prescribed for anemia, and she was now the poster girl for that condition. But I didn't understand why the red fluid from the shot would seep out of her skin until Stan's daughter, Leslie, explained it to me.

Since Leslie was an RN, she'd given Joi shots many times before. She'd been around Joi a lot before I came into the picture and traveled with her when Stan wasn't available. She was only a few years older than I was, and she'd been initiated by fire, just as I'd been. Stan hadn't told Leslie that Joi had a serious problem, at times, with pills and alcohol, so, like me, she learned in the trenches without any forewarning or preparation.

Leslie told me that one time the studio was dissatisfied with Joi's "little boy's butt" and wanted her to have a more rounded, curvaceous look. She explained to me that the doctors pumped up her buttocks with silicone just like they'd done to her breasts. In those days, the doctors supposedly had no idea how dangerous free-floating silicone was to the human body, so they gave the shots with impunity, making big bucks on the bodies of all the stars and wannabes of the day.

In Joi's body, the silicone had congealed in the area where shots are usually given, and this made the injectable fluid seep back out again. Her skin and muscles would not allow the medications to absorb. Joi's nurses were confused by the way her body seemed to be rejecting the medications until I explained what Leslie had told me. They finally found a few places on her legs where the fluids would absorb into the muscles, and not bubble back like land that couldn't percolate.

No one ever said anything to Joi about the difficulty they were having, but I think she knew. Looking back, I actually think she knew much more about everything than she ever let me know. I now wonder, after all the time I spent protecting her from the truth…just who was protecting who?

Stan soon arrived with a tremendous amount of food, and we invited Dee and a few other nurses to come by and get something to eat when they were on break. The food from Paul's Kitchen was the best Chinese food I'd ever had in my life, even better than the Chinese restaurant at the Sands Hotel, which was reputed to be the finest in the country. The Sands' restaurant was great, but Paul's had them beat by a mile.

Before he came, Stan had gone home for a while and checked on little Poose. He was doing well because Stan gave him fresh water and food every day, but Stan said he looked depressed and didn't make a peep when he opened the cage. Joi really missed him, and it was obvious that he missed her just as much. It would be quite the homecoming when they got together again.

Joi seemed to savor every bite of the amazing food that night and, again, could not seem to stop eating. Stan had brought enough food for, at least, ten people, but Dee and her nursing associates didn't eat much, which left more for my ravenous beauty.

As if the Chinese feast wasn't enough, Joi said she wanted dessert, too, which she seldom ate. She asked Stan if he could run out for some ice cream. We all laughed, and I told her she was pushing her birthday!

"Of course," Stan said happily.

He hated being in the hospital and only did it because he knew how important it was to Joi. Any errand away from the hospital room, however, was greatly welcomed. One of his favorite expressions was, "Any action is good," and even though this wasn't the type of "action" he was referring to, it was still a pleasure, when very little in life at that time seemed to be pleasurable.

Dee came in just as Stan walked out. She walked over to Joi and said without her customary upbeat tone, "I just spoke with Dr. Wilson a few minutes ago, and he got the results from the last blood work. It seems as though your red count is starting to come down a little." (I caught my breath and hoped Joi hadn't heard me.) "He said you can go home tomorrow, but he wants you to have one more unit of blood tonight."

Joi seemed confused. "Why is my red count falling? Aren't the new drugs working, or are they causing the problem?"

"I don't know, Joi," Dee responded, "but it might be the new medications you're taking. They're very strong and could be causing the red cells to diminish, but, whatever it is, the transfusion will make you feel good, and you'll have the extra energy you'll need to go on your vacation. You did say you were going away for a few days? Did I hear you correctly?" Dee asked.

Joi replied that we were going to San Diego to celebrate her birthday. April sixth was only a little over a week away, and Joi would need all the energy she could muster.

"If the Doctor thinks I need the transfusion, I'd better do as he says. When will they do it?" Joi asked.

"As soon as they can get it ready in the lab," Dee answered. "It shouldn't take more than an hour or so, Joi. I'll give it to you as soon as it arrives. I know you're disappointed, but this will really help you feel better, I promise!"

Dee reached over and held Joi's hand for a moment. "I'll be spending most of the time with you as you're getting the transfusion. I can't stay here for the whole hour, but I'll be in and out making sure you're all right." She knew this new twist was bothering Joi and wanted to make her feel as comfortable as possible. "Rachel will be here with you, and she'll make sure that everything goes smoothly. If anything bothers you, she'll come and get me. I have every confidence that she'll watch you like a mother hen!"

Joi's face showed the first smile since Dee had come in with the bad news. "I know my Rachel will take good care of me. She always does! I'm okay; I just want to be well enough to go home, so, if I need a transfusion, I'll do it!"

Dee left the room, and Joi signaled me to come over to her.

"Please hold me, Rachel. I want to go home!" she whispered desperately. She was obviously terrified.

I pulled the side rail down and sat on the bed next to her. I kissed her cheek and rocked her and kept saying how it was all going to be okay. She was agitated and almost crying, so I held her closer.

"I love you, honey… it's going to be all right. You need to do this, so you'll be strong, so that we can go to see the dolphins and Timothy's cousins! You do want to see them, right?" I asked.

Her eyes opened wide as she answered my question. "Of course, I want to see them. You know I do! We're going to have fun at Sea World, and we'll celebrate my thirty-third birthday!"

I caught the dismissal of ten years and laughed. When we first met, she told me that women in show business always knocked off ten years from their actual age. I remember her saying, "It's easier if it's an even number, so you don't screw up when people ask what year you were born. Ten years is believable; fifteen or twenty no one will be able to get away with!"

"So this is going to be your thirty-third birthday?" I queried. "You look marvelous for your age, my sweet. I would have guessed you're no more than thirty at the most!" I said with a wink.

She loved it when I'd go along with a spoof. She knew full well that I was aware she'd be forty-three on April sixth, but she enjoyed playing these fun little games, and I loved them, too. It lightened things up and helped us both relax that day.

I heard Dee at the door and quickly got off the bed, with just enough time to bolt out of a questionable situation.

"Here we go, Joi. The magic elixir that's going to give you the strength to celebrate your birthday!"

Joi had wiped her tears away when I jumped up, and now she had to smile at the thought of a happy birthday and a magic potion.

Dee double-checked all the information printed on the bag against the information on Joi's wristband. Everything matched, so she was able to hang the blood bag and connect the tubing into Joi's IV.

"You'll be feeling great in just a little while, Joi. Do you have any questions about what's happening?"

Joi said she was fine, but was anxious to be feeling great, so she could get out of there the next morning.

"May I eat while I'm plugged in to this? Stan's coming back with something for me, and I'm starting to get hungry again. The Chinese food isn't working at all. I don't feel full any longer. I'm so hungry now—please tell me it's all right to eat!" Joi asked her.

Dee assured her she could eat to her heart's content, and not to worry about a thing.

Stan walked in with another large bag…AND the ice cream! Joi couldn't wait to get her hands on what was inside.

"Ohhhh, which one is mine, Hubby?" she asked.

"The Birdie's is the big one…because she needs her energy!" Stan answered with a smile.

She looked at both to-go boxes and determined which was hers, and handed mine to me. She opened hers, and started eating immediately.

The evening passed pleasantly enough. Joi finished her sandwich, the transfusion was uneventful, and we watched Johnny Carson again. With all that food plus the ice cream, we both seemed to sleep pretty well.

Dr. Wilson came in the following morning, just as Joi had begun her breakfast, and she stopped immediately to listen to him. He said he'd looked over the lab work that was done after her transfusion the night before and wanted to let her know how well the new chemotherapy combination was working. My heart jumped when he changed his normal poker face to a smile.

"You can go home, Joi, but…" he cautioned, "you're going to have to really take it easy. I don't think it's a good idea for you to go out of town now, at least not until we see how this chemo is affecting you." He continued, "I want you to come to my office twice a week to check your blood, and, while you're there, I'll be giving you your chemo IV every two weeks."

Dr. Wilson was obviously relieved to be able to tell her this. The last time I'd spoken with him privately, he didn't think she'd be leaving the hospital this time. I followed him into the hall and thanked him for being so kind to her.

He smiled softly. "She's a brave lady, Rachel, and so are you. I'm happy to help whenever I can. You two take care of one another, okay?"

He squeezed my shoulder gently before he walked away toward the nurse's station. At that moment, I knew if there was such a thing as a guardian angel, Joi and I were blessed with the one with a human heart filled with compassion and the kindest of souls.

When I walked back in the room, I found Joi had finished her eggs and was so excited to be going home that she called Stan to ask him to come and pick us up. Stan said he'd be there within the hour and to finish her breakfast while she waited. We both ate her toast, had some coffee, and got ready to go.

Stan arrived a few minutes before ten and stopped in to see us before he went to the business office to give them a check. Connecticut General paid a big chunk of the bill, but there was a lot left that was the patient's responsibility. I have no idea how much he paid, but, when he walked into the room after writing the check, he looked like he was three pints low. Still, this particular hospital, St. John's, had provided Joi with care that was beyond wonderful, and that was priceless.

We were out of there by eleven, and home within a half hour. As usual, I had been in the backseat with Joi's head on my lap. When we got home, since Joi was too weak to walk, Stan brought the wheelchair down to the car. Up we went, down the hall, and into our condo.

Both Joi and I were grateful to see the light spilling through our windows above the sea, dancing across our beautiful living room. What a relief! I put my hands on her shoulders, and she reached back to squeeze one of mine. Joi was home, and life would be good again…I hoped.

Chapter 46

Letting Go

After arriving home, Joi preferred to stay in the den and watch TV rather than go in the bedroom to rest. Stan helped me get her settled on the couch, directly across from the floor-to-ceiling windows overlooking the Pacific Ocean as it fed into the Marina. Joi had always found it peaceful to watch the large yachts as they lined up, moving gracefully back and forth in the water.

I made us both some tea and joined her on the sofa, where she rested her head on my lap, cushioned by her favorite down pillow. Little Poose toddled up to give her a kiss as Joi smiled and put him on her knee. It was a sweet homecoming.

Life was simple in those times. Joi was too weak to do much but rest, so this was how we lived, day to day, except for when she had appointments to see Dr. Wilson. I think Joi knew we had very little time left, even though neither of us dared to say those heartbreaking words.

We spent our time talking about the future and how lucky we were to have found each other. We daydreamed about the wonderful life we would have, about places we would go, and exciting adventures we would share. We relived all the times we'd already spent together… day by day and moment by moment. We spoke as if there would be no end to our life together, and we promised each other we'd stay in love, even if one of us was gone.

As the weeks passed, turning into months, I carefully etched every word she said in my mind. I was determined to never lose a second of our life together.

We always spoke as if there would be time to share growing old together, yet we refused to rush into the "growing old" part. Joi always reminded me, every night before we went to sleep, that if I didn't start taking care of my face, I'd look old before I was forty. Her advice was always with a sense of humor, but I took it seriously, nevertheless. Neither of us wanted to lose what beauty we had at that minute, even though we both knew how fleeting and transitory it could be.

Joi believed that every decade of a woman's life had its own beauty, and that the key to preserving it was to stay as healthy and happy as you could by surrounding yourself with the ones you loved the most. As time passed, however, I noticed her energy waning, and the light and sparkle of life behind her eyes were slowly fading. She still smiled, though weakly, when I came in the room or when little Poose kissed her and sat on her knee while preening his feathers. I knew she was in pain. It was an obvious effort for her to do anything more than lie on the couch and watch television.

Once in a while, on a good day, she'd feel like talking and tell me stories of her life, the experiences she'd had and the lessons she'd learned. I felt she was trying to guide me, preparing me somehow to live my life without her. I sat rapt, looking down at her beautiful face and into her deep green eyes as she lay on the pillow propped on my lap. I listened to every word. I knew, in the unspoken part of my feelings, I had to listen closely, that I'd never be able to hear those words again. Everything she said took root in my mind and heart, as if she planted tiny seeds that would nourish my young soul as I grew.

The summer days of June seemed too short. Each day that passed became more and more difficult for Joi to hold onto, and she seemed to be slipping away before my eyes.

Every Monday and Thursday was filled with blood tests and visits to the Doctor, but nothing was ever said about how she was doing on this new chemotherapy. Joi had stopped asking when she'd start to feel stronger; she knew by their faces she wouldn't want to hear the answer.

At home on the couch, I'd hold her in my arms hour after hour, wiping the perspiration from her brow while she tried to sleep. The combination of chemotherapy and methadone made her skin wet, and that turned into chills. I wrapped her in a blanket when she started to shiver and used my body heat to keep her warm.

During those miserable times, she never complained or shed one tear of self-pity. Actually, she seemed concerned for me. One time as she lay wrapped in a blanket in my arms, she whispered how grateful she was for "us." She spoke softly of all the happiness she'd had with me, and said she prayed every morning it would be another day with me in her life. At that moment, I held her tighter than ever before, refusing to ever let her go, even though I knew all too well how little power I had over what was to come.

Stan went to work every morning. He had to get away from the reality that the chemotherapy wasn't working. It was painfully difficult for him to see how her body was changing. She was still beautiful, but in more of an ethereal way. Since Stan had always worshiped at the shrine of her physical beauty, he couldn't bear to see his goddess crumbling before his eyes.

In his own way, though, Stan tried hard to take care of us. He brought food home every night, and made sure we had something nourishing to eat. Joi and I were both losing weight, but for different reasons. She could only eat things that were easy to digest, and soups seemed to agree with her the best. I could barely keep anything down and only nibbled when she ate, so she wouldn't notice.

With Stan eventually nodding off and sleeping in his recliner, Joi and I would lie on the couch most of the evening. We'd go to bed only if Joi felt like moving, and, if she didn't, we'd stay cuddled in front of the TV.

By the time June was almost over, Joi had become too weak to stand, and her belly was horribly distended. I called Dr. Wilson and told him how large she'd become, and he said she'd probably have to come back to the hospital if it didn't diminish in a day or two.

One evening, when Joi was dozing and Stan had gone into the kitchen, I gently slipped out from under Joi's head and followed him. He was fixing a drink, and I told him what Dr. Wilson had said. As usual, he seemed to have difficulty listening to what I was telling him. I knew there was nothing I could say that would make the truth easier for him to hear, so I left him alone to digest the bitter pill I'd just handed him.

In about an hour, Stan came into the den and sat down in his chair. It seemed obvious to me he'd had more to drink than usual. He kind of cleared his throat and then slowly looked over at Joi, who was still dozing and didn't know he was there. The expression on his face broke my heart, as I could tell he *really* saw her with the eyes of truth for the very first time. He now understood, as I had for so long, that no power on earth could keep this beautiful and so very special woman in our world with us.

The following morning, nothing had changed except that Joi's belly was even more distended than the night before. She was still terribly weak and now seemed unable to sit up. I called the Doctor, and he told me to bring her to St. John's right away.

Stan brought the wheelchair, and I covered her with a blanket. Again, we placed her in the back seat of the Cadillac where I sat holding her head in my lap, as Stan drove as fast as I'd ever seen him drive. Dr. Wilson had notified the hospital to admit her immediately, so, when we arrived at the emergency entrance, she was quickly taken to her third floor room.

Everything was ready on our arrival, and an IV was started as soon as she was in bed. They began to draw blood again for testing, and I noticed, this time, it wasn't a deep burgundy color as it usually had been before. It was considerably lighter in color, and I assumed the chemotherapy had wreaked havoc with her hemoglobin, and she would probably need another transfusion.

Soon, Dr. Wilson stepped into the room. I quickly looked at his face, hoping to see his usual warmth, but his expression was unreadable. Joi's eyes were closed as he walked toward her and, using his stethoscope, listened to her heart and lungs and then to the ominous sounds from deep within her abdomen.

He paused for a moment, a sad expression flickering across his face before he, once again, detached himself from emotion. He turned and looked at me. Stan stood away toward the door, slightly to my side. He told us that, like before, she would definitely need, at least, two units of blood, and this might bring her back to give us a little more time with her.

As I looked over at her, I started to cry. She was almost comatose and not aware of what was going on around her.

"Don't cry yet, Rachel. I'll try to keep her here as long as I can," Dr. Wilson whispered. I pulled myself together, as I had done so many times before. I couldn't fall apart now. It wasn't time yet. "I'll be back in a little while to check on her," he again whispered, as he walked quietly from the room.

Stan couldn't handle it and had to leave. Glad that Joi didn't see him, I watched him go. If she woke up and asked for him, I would say he was out having a cigar, and then step into the hall to get him back.

I sat by her bed as nurses changed her into a hospital gown and kept watch as they hung IV bottles of fluids. As soon as one was empty, a backup was ready to be plugged in. Within an hour, someone from the lab came up with two units of blood, which they started infusing right away. I watched as each drop of blood dripped into the plastic tubing and flowed into her arm at a much faster rate than the last time she'd needed blood. There was an urgency in the nurses' movements this time. I think they knew she was dying, and that she'd better "pink up," or she'd be gone.

Standing next to her, I nervously counted the minutes and stroked her arm while the life-giving blood pulsed into her frail, pale body. About a half hour had passed when I suddenly saw and felt a shift in her energy. I exhaled as I saw the miracle I'd been praying for begin yet one more time. I watched how her face almost imperceptibly changed from gray to light pink. Then, wonder of wonders, she slowly opened her eyes and smiled at me! I cannot begin to explain the feeling that washed over me.

"What happened, Rachel? Where was I? Where *am* I?" she asked sweetly. I leaned down and hugged her gently. I would explain everything in a minute, but at that moment all I knew was that my girl was back. In my arms. In my life. And "we" were going to live another day together.

Chapter 47

Be Strong for Her

The weeks in the hospital passed very slowly. In today's world, Joi would have been in hospice and kept comfortable until the end, but, in those days, hospice was unheard of, and the doctors tried to keep her going with transfusions and what seemed like dozens of new chemotherapy formulas. Some of their efforts worked, at least for a while, and, frankly, I didn't care what they did, as long as they kept my angel girl with me.

That first week, as had happened before, Joi was doing better after her transfusion. Every evening, when visiting hours were over, we would walk slowly through the halls for a while until she became winded. I had to believe that every hour would count toward regaining her strength, and the walks, though short, were important.

The halls were eerily quiet after nine o'clock. The only noises were the nurses' almost inaudible footsteps and the occasional rustle of a curtain being pulled back in a nearby room. Sometimes, I would hear quiet crying, and, at those times, I was glad if Joi was sleeping.

Joi had always been a night person, but here they wanted her to sleep as long as she could before the hospital noises began in the morning. They'd bring in her sleeping pills at about nine, much earlier than she usually took them at home.

I'd wait until she was sound asleep and then slip out to the nurses' station to visit with my saviors. The nurses always made it a point to try to cheer me up and take my mind off Joi's condition. Big Red was working almost every night, and, looking back, I realize she and Dee were the ones who kept me sane.

At that point, my feelings were a blur most of the time. I focused only on Joi's needs and didn't have time to think about my own, but, when it was quiet and she was at rest and I was alone in the night and its painful shadows, I'd realize it was really quite simple. I wanted to die along with her.

One night, I remembered that Joi had quite a few methadone tablets in her overnight bag, and, for a week or so, I found myself thinking they might be my way out. This brought me a sad kind of comfort, but then something made me tell Red about it... self-preservation, perhaps.

She went into Joi's room, got the pills, and then took me into the break room. No one was there, so she sat me down and, while holding my hand, quietly told me that Joi wouldn't want me to do anything to hurt myself. She said I needed to be Joi's strength... and then grow into the kind of woman Joi would be proud of.

Big Red, that dear, kind woman, said the words I needed to hear, words I would hold onto during the days ahead as Joi began to leave me. I knew then I had to have the courage to stay behind and be strong.

As the weeks passed, Dr. Wilson kept trying different combinations of chemotherapy drugs, but each one lasted only a few days and then would fail, leaving Joi even weaker than she'd been before.

One day, a nun came to our room, which didn't surprise me at first since St. John's is a Catholic hospital, and the nuns are in charge of management. Joi was lying half-asleep in bed, her face pale and her belly distended. Without reading Joi's chart, she walked over to her bedside and told her how happy she must be about her upcoming blessed event.

I gasped! I stood and looked at her with what could only have been a stunned expression and asked her to please leave the room immediately. I couldn't believe she hadn't bothered to look at the chart before she opened her ignorant mouth!

Joi had awakened when the nun approached her and heard what she said. She was visibly upset, her still beautiful eyes moist with tears. I sat on the bed and held her until she calmed down. Joi had always wanted to have a child, but, the one time she'd been pregnant, Stan had insisted she have an abortion. She was devastated, and I don't think she ever completely forgave him.

Finding a small towel, I moistened it with cool water and wiped her face gently, smoothed her brow, and tucked the sheet around her. I didn't care who saw us being loving with one another. Time was the enemy, and I would not be robbed of the few precious moments we had left. I kissed her softly before I left the room, telling her to rest and that I'd be right back. She gently responded and closed her eyes.

Without actually speaking about it, we both knew her abdomen was filling with fluid and the cancer was spreading throughout her body. The truth, however, had not yet been said to her, and, if I could prevent it, it never would be. I had to give her hope.

I stepped into the hall and saw Dee at the nurses' station, so I walked over to her. She was the Charge Nurse that day, and I could see how busy she was, but it was important to tell her what happened. When she saw the expression on my face, she stepped around the counter and said, "What is it, Rachel? Is Joi all right?"

I took a deep breath and told her about the incident with the Nun and how emotionally painful her comment had been for Joi. Dee was totally aghast and, placing her hand on my shoulder, assured me this type of incident would not happen again. When she asked about the Nun's identity, I could tell from her response that she knew who it was, so I felt confident she would protect Joi from any further intrusion.

Stan came by every evening and brought me pork fried rice from Paul's Kitchen. The hospital stays had, sadly, taken on a rhythm, and he knew the food from Paul's was the only thing I could keep down.

Except for when I slept, my insides were twisting and turning all the time and I wanted to scream. I needed something to calm me down, and, fortunately, Dee got me a doctor's prescription for Librium, which they kept for me at the nurses' station. The pills helped a lot, numbing my emotions enough, so i could function. I kept remembering the words that Big Red had said: "Be strong for her. Become the woman she would be proud of." I inwardly chanted them sometimes just to keep from breaking down in front of her. "Be strong for her. Be strong for her. Be strong for her."

Stan, too, was having serious problems watching Joi slip away. Every evening, he would leave a little sooner than the night before. Joi didn't seem to notice, or, at least, it didn't seem to bother her, as she was sleeping more as the days and weeks went by. She was growing increasingly weaker, and I could see she was tired of fighting for her life. All she wanted was for me to lie next to her in the hospital bed and hold her. Sometimes, it felt like my arms wrapped around her was the only thing that kept her from slipping away.

I knew the nuns would not approve. To be in bed with another woman, in those days, was unacceptable. Even on the top sheet, and even if the patient was dying. How very cruel and stupid it was, yet I still wanted to protect Joi's image, even as I was losing her. When I'd hear a nurse open the door, I'd sit up and just hold her hand.

At night, though, when the nuns were gone and the nursing staff was light, I would hold her whenever she wanted me to, and that was almost every night in those last couple of weeks.

Joi's brother, Larry, came as often as he could, and Joi loved seeing him. His beautiful, wide smile always made her feel better. He was kind and loving to me, as well, and made me feel accepted as Joi's partner. He understood our relationship and respected our love. Many times, he would take me out of the room, and we'd have lunch in the hospital cafeteria. His kindness was part of my support system; Leslie was the other part. She came to see Joi as often as her frantic schedule allowed. I understood, and so did Joi.

Virginia, Joi's mother, occasionally called to tell her the Christian Science practitioners were praying for her as much as "the insurance would allow." Though Joi didn't seem to mind, I was hurt and angry for her.

Her mother told Joi that she wasn't feeling well and made excuses for not coming from Santa Paula to see her. Joi tried to pretend it wasn't important, but I knew it hurt her.

As the days passed, one by one, her family and few friends began to keep their distance. Luckily, Joi was drifting in and out most of the time, so she wasn't aware of it. I was aware, of course, and was bothered by it, even though I understood.

On one of Dr. Wilson's visits, he noticed how extremely pale and weak Joi had become and ordered another transfusion. Within an hour, a nurse hung the first unit of blood, making sure everything was correct. I watched carefully, as I always did, and saw it flow, a drop at a time, until it reached her frail and bruised little arm. I anxiously awaited her returning color and smile, which, in the past, had always appeared whenever she received that life-giving substance.

This time, though, she suddenly opened her eyes wide and said with alarm, "Rachel, something is very wrong!"

She started to shiver, and her face turned beet red, so I ran to the door, yelling for a nurse. One came running, and, as she disconnected the needle, she explained that something might be wrong with the blood. She called the lab to come up and check, and then found Dee, who rushed in to take Joi's vitals. They weren't normal. Dee covered her with a warm blanket and said, "Rachel, hold this on her while I call Dr. Wilson," as she hurried from the room.

"It's going to be okay, Joi," I said. "The Doctor's coming. It's okay…it's okay," I whispered to her, not being at all sure that it was.

A lab tech showed up almost immediately, removed the blood bag from the pole, and then stood back while Dee checked to be sure it was the right blood type. (From the beginning of Joi's stay, I'd seen them comparing labels to be certain the blood was the right match.)

Because Joi's reaction was so severe, everyone was rushing. Soon, another tech came in with a second unit and handed it to Dee, who nodded her head, obviously satisfied it was correct. She hung it, started the flow, and we all watched closely, hoping it would all go well this time.

Almost instantly, the same thing happened! Joi cried out this time and shivered even more than before.

"What's happening? I feel awful! Please, what's happening?" she cried.

Dee quickly disconnected the needle, but continued to hold Joi's arm firmly.

"The Doctor's on his way. Joi," she said. "You may be allergic to the blood, but he'll know what to do. He'll figure it out, I promise!" She told us Dr. Wilson would be in as soon as he knew why this happened. Dee left with the Tech and blood in tow, indicating she'd be right back.

Another nurse brought two more warm blankets, and, as I comforted Joi, I pulled the blankets up to her neck. She finally stopped shivering and seemed less upset. When she closed her eyes, I stroked her arms to calm her while we waited. She began to doze and then seemed to slip into sleep, which I marveled at, considering how frantic she'd been just a short while ago.

When I heard someone step into the room, I turned, and it was Dr. Wilson. His face was gray as he looked at Joi and took her pulse, reading his watch carefully. Speaking quietly to me, he said, "Rachel, Joi's antibodies, from all the chemo, have made changes to her blood. Her own blood is attacking the blood that we're trying to transfuse." He took my arm gently and steered me into the hall.

When we were far enough away so Joi couldn't hear, he told me there wasn't anything else he could do except keep her comfortable.

"There's no more magic formula that I know of, Rachel, to help her win this fight." He knew my heart was breaking with every word, so he held me for a few moments, then said, "It won't be very long now. Maybe just a few days."

I could barely hear him as my blood was rushing in my ears, but I knew I had to listen, had to understand what to do now.

I took a deep breath. He continued in a soft voice, "Or she might surprise us all and last longer. Her heart is very strong, and so is her will to live. Rachel, when she stops fighting, that's when she'll go."

He squeezed my shoulder gently and left, walking slowly toward the elevator.

Holding my breath, I waited until I regained my composure. I was not about to fall apart now…especially not now. Now was when she would need me most. I took a few deep breaths and wiped my eyes before going back into the room.

Chapter 48

My Angel Girl

I found Joi starting to shiver again, so I pulled another blanket from the mahogany armoire that held the TV and laid it over the others. It was later in the day, and the staff was changing shifts, so they probably wouldn't check on Joi. At that point though, I almost didn't care what anyone would think as I wrapped us both up together. It took a while, but she slowly began to recover as my own body heat and the several blankets did the trick. My girl had finally stopped shivering and was peacefully dozing again.

As I slowly unwrapped myself and stood up, Joi took my hand and, looking into my eyes, said, "What's happening to me, Rachel? Why didn't the transfusion work?" She spoke quietly.

I lied. I told her I didn't know for sure, but would ask the Doctor when he came in again. She suddenly became agitated. "Please don't leave me, Rachel," she begged. "Please…"

As I smoothed her hair and kissed her cheek, I told her I'd never leave her, that I'd be with her forever. My heart was breaking, but Red's words, "Be strong for her, Rachel," pulsed in my head. I continued to reassure her that I would always be with her. Always.

Comforted, Joi closed her eyes. By then, she wasn't shivering at all. Again I lay next to her, this time staying on top of the sheets, so I could stand up quickly if I had to. I slowly and gently began rocking her. In a few minutes, her breathing was slow and steady, and I knew she was out. Carefully, I moved the blankets, hoping she wouldn't wake with my leaving.

Stepping into the hall where she couldn't hear me, I called Stan and told him the horrible news. There was silence at the other end of the phone.

"Will you come by tonight?" I asked. "I know she'd really love to see you."

Stan said he'd come by and bring me some food, but didn't know if he'd be able to go into the room. He added that it would be "too difficult to see her like that." I knew better than to say anything, even though I was sickened and disgusted.

I was so angry that he, like everyone else, was backing away from her. I knew how awful it was to watch someone dying, but it wasn't about us or our frailties; it was about her. About Joi. She needed to be with the people she loved, and she deserved much better than he was willing to give her. Though Stan had always been good to me, at that moment, I think I actually hated him.

That evening, Stan came by and stuck his head in the room, whistling a tune that Pooper always sang to Joi. I watched her face to see if she was aware of the playful sounds, but she was in a deep sleep and didn't stir. I got up from my makeshift combination chair/bed, and went to the door. Stan had been drinking more than usual and smelled of brandy. He handed me a bag with clean clothes for me to wear and my daily sustenance of fried rice.

"I hope you understand, Rachel," he said. "I just can't go in and see her like this. I wish I could be there for you and her, but I just can't do it!"

He looked disheveled and broken, and now I understood. Stan could only do what he was capable of doing, nothing more, nothing less. In his own way, he was suffering, too, but he couldn't take any more pain, not even for Joi.

It was August third. Joi was growing weaker every day, but she'd already lived longer than Dr. Wilson predicted. She was now on day six. Though she slept most of the time, she occasionally opened her eyes and smiled at me. I would massage her feet, once again, not knowing what else to do to bring her a little comfort.

One afternoon, as I sat on my bed drinking a cup of coffee, another nun walked in and asked to speak with me outside the room. I didn't know what she wanted, but went out of courtesy. (She had a grim expression on her face but, having grown up in a Catholic school, I thought it didn't seem out of character.)

Once out of the room, she turned and, in an officious voice, informed me they were concerned about my continued living arrangements in Joi's room. I gasped, not understanding.

"Why?" I asked quietly.

She ignored my question, having her cold speech mentally prepared and not willing to let my feelings affect it. She said it wasn't healthy for me to stay in the room with her, day after day, that I should go home and visit periodically and not continue my deathbed vigil. I panicked and felt everything in my stomach start to rise, gagging as she declared what was "good and healthy" for me.

I was so afraid she could have me physically removed that I didn't want to say what was on my mind. I merely stated I would discuss this with Dr. Wilson, and she shouldn't worry about my health.

As I hurried to the nurses' station, I asked for Dee, and was told she was in with a patient and should be right back. I paced up and down the hall until I saw her walking toward me. When I caught her attention, she started to run toward me, and I realized she thought Joi might be gone.

"Is Joi okay?" she asked.

I explained to her that Joi was the same. "But they want to kick me out of here!" I wailed. "A nun came in and said that I should leave Joi, and I won't do it! They'll have to shoot me if they want me out of here."

By that time, I was crying and told her that I'd promised Joi I would never leave her, and I just wouldn't.

Dee calmed me down, saying that she'd speak with Dr. Wilson. "He won't let them force you to leave Joi. He knows how important it is to her to have you with her."

I was shaking from fear, but, after listening to Dee's soothing words, I stopped trembling and went back to the room where Joi was sleeping. I took comfort in the quiet room and gratefully petted Joi's sweet cheek before I went into the bathroom to freshen my own. I looked in the mirror. I looked tired, but strong. There was no question I'd be with my girl to the end.

I spoke with Stan two or three times a day since a phone was right next to my little corner of the world. He called to ask how Joi was doing, and one day told me how upset he was after speaking with Virginia, her mother. Apparently, she was planning Joi's funeral without even allowing me to tell them what she wanted. Virginia assumed that Joi wanted to be buried in the family plot in Santa Paula, and Stan thought she should be with the other famous stars in Hollywood. I knew Joi didn't want any part of being buried anywhere—she wanted to be in a crypt or mausoleum, above ground.

I explained to them what she wanted, but I was completely ignored. In those days and with those people, the fact that Joi and I were deeply important to one another did not matter one iota to them. I was invisible. I didn't count, even though I was the only one who knew what Joi wanted.

Stan and Virginia had become enemies many years ago, and I don't know who held more contempt for whom. They bickered about who would pay for the funeral, and Virginia finally agreed to do it, provided Joi was buried in Santa Paula. And though it upset me, Stan agreed. He commented that it was "about time the witch finally did something right for her daughter." Again, I tried to tell someone about what Joi had said she wanted, but nothing I said mattered. No one listened. It was as if I didn't exist.

It absolutely tore me up that I didn't have the money to take care of Joi and wasn't able to carry out her wishes. This was the same arrogant selfishness that had surrounded her throughout her life. The power brokers of showbiz didn't care what she wanted, either, and tossed her around like a side of beef.

Every morning I could tell Joi was becoming weaker and fading in and out of a coma-like state. I stayed in her bed until I heard footsteps, and then I'd slide down into the chair next to her bedside. The only miracle keeping her on this mortal plane was the strength of her heart and her fighting spirit to stay alive. She had beaten all the odds and survived over two years longer than the medical profession had predicted.

As time passed, Joi was my only focus. I'd sit looking at her face for hours memorizing every expression. Her breathing was quiet and shallow, and there were very few changes I could see. She was almost motionless, but, occasionally, her eyes would flutter and open a little, and I could see their beautiful green shine as they tried to focus. The morphine that was sparing her from pain was also stealing her away, slowly.

Day became night, and late in the evening, I'd walk out of the room. There was a tightness in my chest as if my heart was being crushed each time it took a beat. I'd walk up to the nurses' station just to chat with anyone willing to listen.

One night, I saw a pile of papers stacked on the corner of the counter which separated me from my guardian angels in white. I casually glanced at them, but then gasped for air. My eyes had fallen on an official paper on top. It was Joi's death certificate. Of course, I knew there had to be one, but coming on it that way shocked me.

The nurses could see I was on the brink of falling apart, and, as had happened too many times before, they ushered me into their break room and tried to calm me down. Red came in, saw I was sobbing, and asked everyone else to leave. She gently explained it was wrong that the papers were not put away, and I should never have had to see them. Red knew how upset I was and did her best to keep me from imploding. Before returning to work, she brought me some tissues and a cup of coffee and said I could stay there as long as I wanted.

Sipping my coffee, I sat and thought. Seeing the words "death certificate" shouted the reality of her life coming to an end. There was no more deluding myself that some miraculous event would save her. Deep down in my heart, I'd been ignoring the facts and hoped they were wrong about her, and she'd win this fight. It seemed so unfair. She was too young and too beautiful to die so soon. Life couldn't be this unfair to her and to us, but there it was in black and white, waiting for pen and ink to finalize a life that had so much more love to give. I went back to the room to be with her as long as the fates would allow, staring at the large black and white clock and wondering how many times the little hand would go around and around before our world would come to an end. How many more hours did she have…did we have? I heard the clock relentlessly tick away the minutes and hours of my dear love's life.

Eventually, I watched the sun come up through the separations in the blinds, and saw the morning light fall softly on Joi's thin, but still beautiful sleeping face. The day passed as Joi's condition worsened. She hardly moved, was now in a coma, and the nurses came in less and less, giving me time to be alone with her. They were told I was her sister, but, at least, some must have known our relationship was more than we were telling.

Maybe it was selfish, but I was desperately in love and could not bear to be left without her. I held her frail little body as close to mine as I could. I begged her to stay, whispering to her, hoping she could still hear me, "I love you, baby girl. Please don't leave me. I don't think I can make it without you. I don't want to live without you."

I think she heard me. Her eyes moved, and her lips seemed to be trying to make words, but no sounds were audible. I knew she wanted to say something to me, but couldn't. All I could do was hold her gently in my arms, dreading the time she'd be taken away from me.

The nurses came in periodically, making sure she wasn't in any distress. She was peaceful. The morphine cocooned her, keeping the excruciating pain from torturing her last hours. There was nothing more to do but wait.

That night was long. I was afraid to fall asleep because I didn't want to lose any time that might be left. Red came by at seven in the morning before she left for the day, checked Joi's vitals, and noted that her heart seemed to be slowing down and weakening. It wouldn't be much longer, she said, as she put her arm around my shoulder.

"I don't know if I'll see you tonight, but, if I don't, I'll keep in touch with you, Rachel," she said softly.

Nurses try not to get too involved with patients, or they'd never be able to take the sadness of this part of the job, but I knew that Red and Dee really cared about Joi. It was obvious in the way they treated her. Joi thought the world of them, and they could sense her sincerity.

Before she left, Red said it might be a good idea to take one of the pills the Doctor had prescribed for me, that it would help keep me strong through the hardest part of this nightmare.

"Yes, I need all the help I can get," I replied.

The tranquilizer kicked in pretty fast, and I could feel my body start to calm down. It didn't dull my senses, but it helped numb my emotional reactions. I could still feel everything going through my mind and heart, but it seemed I was able to postpone my true reactions, perhaps until a more appropriate time and place. Now was not the time to be weak and useless to Joi. I'd promised to be with her forever and to be her strength when she needed me. It didn't matter what was happening to me; she was the one whom I would not fail.

Stan had brought me some clean clothes earlier, and I decided to take a shower. When I checked on Joi, her breathing was stable, and she appeared to be comfortable. I could shower and wash my hair in fifteen minutes or less and didn't think anything would happen while I washed away the remainder of the tears I'd shed the night before.

The warm water was healing and made me feel grounded, while the steam cleared my head. I began to feel more like me, like the woman Joi had always loved and respected, renewed and infused with the strength I would need. What wonders something familiar can bring … so simple, yet so important.

Leslie came by as often as possible and watched Joi, so I could take a short walk to clear my head. No one else came until the early afternoon of the seventh of August.

Joi had been friendly with a well-known Beverly Hills attorney and his wife, Jan, who learned from Marjorie Meade that Joi was in the hospital. That day, not knowing how terribly ill Joi actually was or how inappropriate her timing would be, Jan decided to visit.

I'd only met Jan once or twice, but I liked her and so did Joi. Not wanting to be rude, and because I knew Joi wouldn't even be aware of the visit, I let her come to the room. When Jan stepped in, she immediately realized the situation, but, unlike so many people who panic in the face of death, Jan gently stroked Joi's arm and said good-bye to her.

Then, apparently seeing how gaunt I looked, she quietly suggested I join her for lunch in the hospital cafeteria. Though I really didn't want to leave Joi, not even for a moment, I felt weak and thought I needed something to eat. I wouldn't be gone very long and would let the nurses know exactly where I was, so I kissed Joi on the forehead and whispered that I'd be right back.

We walked to the cafeteria, and I ate my standard BLT that always made me feel better. Then, suddenly, I began to feel anxious and told Jan I needed to get back to the room. She said she'd pay the bill and meet me there. I walked quickly toward the elevator. "Something's not right! Something's not right," kept pulsing in my head. The elevator seemed to be crawling, and, when the doors opened, I exploded into the hallway.

The moment I exited the elevator, one of the nurses ran up to me and told me to hurry into the room. Something was happening to Joi, and I'd better go quickly. I rushed in and couldn't believe my eyes! Joi was sitting straight up in bed, her eyes closed. I ran to her and put my arms around her.

She was shuddering.

"Joi? What is it? Joi?"

She sat in that position for what felt like minutes, and didn't seem to know I was there.

"Joi?" I whispered.

Slowly, she opened her eyes and her mouth and took a deep breath of air. As soon as she did that, she and I fell back onto the bed, and she went limp in my arms.

Everything went into slow motion. I didn't realize what happened, but the nurses surrounded me and told me she was gone.

"Rachel, your sister has passed," one of the nurses said quietly, as she slowly took my arms from around Joi and helped me sit down.

They closed her eyes.

I had never seen anyone die and hadn't known what to expect. *This was not the way it should be,* I thought. She should have just closed her eyes and drifted away peacefully. The woman lying in that bed was not my Joi. My angel had flown away like a butterfly, leaving her empty shell behind. I felt nothing. I was numb.

My Joi was gone, and I begged the nurses to take me away. I couldn't bear to see her like that ... it was not how I wanted to remember her. I knew she was finally free from all the sadness and disappointment in her life, but my deepest wish at that moment was to have flown away with her ... my dear, dear girl.

Dearest God—
Please protect your beautiful angel.
Blow gently on her wings,
so she may fly high above the pressures
and agonies of this world.
Allow her ears to hear only beautiful music and
silence the ringing of the bells that are calling her too soon.

And whisper when she sleeps,
tell her how much I care.

~ Rachel Lansing, 1972

Epilogue

Joi's life and death were the culmination of a perfect storm... her wish to never grow old... an unethical doctor who gave her a "lifetime" prescription for estrogen (when she was in her thirties and didn't need it)... another greedy group of doctors who pumped silicone into her body... and the Hollywood studios and lust-filled producers that lured her like the Sirens. All of these things helped feed a fragile self-image which clouded her judgment. They culminated in a deadly seduction... which drove her to a self-destructive, but oh, so alluring desire for stardom.

Though it all began with Joi, my life since then has had many twists and turns. I held lots of day jobs until I found my Art Soul with my paintings and jewelry design. Even now, I find most enjoyment in my art. I also find great solace in my prose. My art and my prose express my passions and emotions.

Loneliness is a raging thunderstorm...
It starts uneasiness in your mind...
Then it builds and consumes all your thoughts...
A few tears fall from eyes
which have no one to see...
Thunder shakes the earth...
and releases the tension of mind...
The few tears become a deluge of rain.
At the most forceful crescendo of the storm,
Lightning strikes... and rips your soul apart.

At last, the storm leaves the rubble
it has created.
All that is left… is silence..

~ Rachel Lansing, 1972

Index

CPSIA information can be obtained
at www.ICGtesting.com
Printed in the USA
LVHW012257010720
659519LV00019B/2165